Praise for Three Views on E
and Evangelic

barcode D0078002

The increasing importance of the dialogue between Eastern Orthodoxy and evangelicalism has raised many difficult questions for both sides. In this important and timely book, such issues are debated openly and honestly by leading representatives of each tradition. It will be essential reading for all involved in, or reflecting on, this dialogue.

> Alister McGrath, professor of historical theology,
> Oxford University, Oxford, England

Nearly five hundred years before the Reformation, the Orthodox Church also parted ways with Rome. Now the descendants of those two groups are talking with each other. This is one conversation you won't want to miss!

> Father Peter Gillquist, director of missions and evangelism
> for the Antiochian Orthodox Archdiocese of North America
> and publisher of Conciliar Press, Santa Barbara, CA

A timely and important subject—the theological compatibility of evangelicals and Eastern Orthodox believers, with some of the most capable commentators on the scene. It will introduce evangelicals to Orthodoxy and the Orthodox to evangelicals and show where the fault lines are between them, with no fudging, and where the Spirit is leading the church toward a more perfect embodiment of the union of believers in Christ.

> Tom Oden, Henry Anson Buttz professor of theology,
> Drew University, Madison, NJ

Fidelity to Scripture and commitment to doctrinal truth make for stimulating dialogue between evangelical and Orthodox theologians in an otherwise tired ecumenical world. The frank and sometimes sharp exchange of views expressed in these essays significantly define key theological and practical issues from which informed Orthodox and evangelical Christians will be strikingly challenged and enriched.

> Father Theodore Stylianopoulos, Archbishop Iakovos
> professor of Orthodox Theology and New Testament,
> Holy Cross Greek Orthodox School of Theology, Brookline, MA

Three Views on Eastern Orthodoxy and Evangelicalism clearly speaks to the current evangelical quest for identity. Those who ask "who are we?" will find the arguments for and against an evangelical association with Eastern Orthodoxy to be thorough and compelling. While an answer is not forthcoming, the questions raised will lead evangelicals into deeper and fruitful paths of discussion and action.

> Robert Webber, Myers professor of ministry
> and director of M.A. in worship and spirituality,
> Northern Baptist Theological Seminary, Lombard, IL

This is the best book I have read on the most important dialogue in the Christian world. I wish it much success.

Father Michael Harper, dean of the British Antiochian
Orthodox Deanery, Cambridge, England

Here is an assessment of relations between evangelicals and Eastern Orthodox that is fair-minded yet frank. While the difficult issues of belief and practice are not slighted, the treatment is accessible to members of both parties as well as those of neither.

William Dyrness, professor of theology and culture,
Fuller Theological Seminary, Pasadena, CA

An engaging and intriguing attempt to look critically at varying views within Eastern Orthodoxy and evangelicalism, which helps one better understand the bridges and barriers that exist between them. The dialogue is bluntly straightforward and polemic at times, yet refreshingly authentic and thus enlightening. The book itself offers another positive witness to the importance of ongoing, sincere dialogue among the Christian traditions.

Father Luke A. Veronis, Orthodox missionary and instructor of missiology,
Holy Cross Greek Orthodox School of Theology, Brookline, MA

Increasing numbers of evangelicals are being attracted to Orthodox spirituality, while Orthodox are being drawn by evangelicals' dynamic biblical witness to assured salvation. This openhearted and scholarly book will be a timely help for more scholarly readers to understand how far the two positions are compatible.

Martin Goldsmith, associate lecturer,
All Nations Christian College, Ware, England

Three Views on Eastern Orthodoxy and Evangelicalism is an important contribution to a long-overdue ecumenical dialogue. The book gives even more than the title promises. It offers three answers to the question, "Are Eastern Orthodoxy and evangelicalism compatible?" The three answers: yes, no, and maybe. In addition, the five authors offer us a genuine Eastern Orthodox–evangelical dialogue. My hope is that evangelical and Eastern Orthodox readers will not be paralyzed by the answers but will be given energy to continue and to deepen the dialogue. Christian witness in today's world requires no less of evangelical and Eastern Orthodox Christians.

Father Leonid Kishkovsky, ecumenical officer,
Orthodox Church in America, Syosset, New York

THREE VIEWS ON EASTERN ORTHODOXY AND EVANGELICALISM

Books in the Counterpoints Series

Church Life

Exploring Theology

THREE VIEWS ON EASTERN ORTHODOXY AND EVANGELICALISM

- **Bradley Nassif**
- **Michael Horton**
- **Vladimir Berzonsky**
- **George Hancock-Stefan**
- **Edward Rommen**

- **Stanley N. Gundry** *series editor*
- **James J. Stamoolis** *general editor*

GRAND RAPIDS, MICHIGAN 49530 USA

ZONDERVAN™

Three Views on Eastern Orthodoxy and Evangelicalism
Copyright © 2004 by James J. Stamoolis

Requests for information should be addressed to:

Zondervan, *Grand Rapids, Michigan 49530*

Library of Congress Cataloging-in-Publication Data

Three views on Eastern Orthodoxy and evangelicalism / James J. Stamoolis, general
  editor ; contributors, Bradley Nassif . . . [et al.].—1st ed.
      p. cm.— (Counterpoints)
  Includes bibliographical references and index.
    ISBN 0-310-23539-1
    1. Evangelicalism—Relations—Orthodox Eastern Church. 2. Orthodox East-
ern Church—Relations—Evangelicalism. I. Stamoolis, James J. II. Nassif,
Bradley. III. Counterpoints (Grand Rapids, Mich.)
    BX324.5.T48 2004
    280'.042—dc22   2004007130

Printed in the United States of America

---

05 06 07 08 09 10 /❖ DC/ 10 9 8 7 6 5 4 3 2

CONTENTS

FOREWORD

J. I. Packer

A venerable British ballad begins by declaring, "It's a long way to Tipperary, / It's a long way to go." Substitute for Tipperary the desired togetherness between, on the one hand, North America's evangelical church—as the great cluster of evangelical denominations, freestanding Bible churches, and evangelical networks within the subevangelical mainline are currently called—and the Western outposts of the Eastern Orthodox communion on the other hand, and the words of the song fit with ominous exactness: indeed, "it's a long way to go." But our common Lord Jesus Christ, who is the focus of all our worship and the mediator to us of all the divine life we share, has made it clear that he wants his people to be one in faith, love, and outreach to the world. Starting from where we are, convergence must be attempted and feelers put out to that end. In the audacity of obedience, therefore, we square up to this task.

What sort of convergence and what form of fellowship will best fulfill the Lord Christ's desire for our oneness? The top-down ecumenism of the mid-twentieth century envisioned full sacramental communion within full organizational union in all cases, anticipating that such restructuring would, as if by magic, revitalize local congregations for Samaritanship and evangelism. The era in which this was touted as the mandatory goal in planning has now ended, and a more modest, bottom-up, mission-focused ecumenism is replacing it, at least among cutting-edge thinkers. This ecumenism acknowledges that the path to full communion and structural integration is out of sight at present and may remain so, and that the way of wisdom for us is to

9

practice doing together the things required of all churches—at every point where conscientious conviction does not direct us to do them separately.

So the better answer to the question posed above begins with a vision of partnership in proclaiming Jesus Christ as the Savior whom everyone needs, in the work of catechesis and the discipling of converts, in providing pastoral resources at all levels for the needy, and in upholding Christian standards and values in today's pluralistic society, which is so distressingly adrift spiritually, morally, and institutionally. The path to such partnership must be prepared and the ground cleared by seeing if the beliefs of the two groupings can fit into each other's frame of understanding to the point where each recognizes adequacy in the other for the proposed cooperative tasks.

The Chinese proverb says that a journey of a thousand miles begins with a single step. Well, this book helps us take the first step and makes a welcome start on the theological explorations that must precede any further moves. In these groundbreaking pages, the reader will find a series of courteous yet forthright exchanges at a fairly deep theological level between men of real learning on themes of real importance. Starting from cold, as it were, these essays cover a lot of ground and are calculated to prompt much useful thought. Most aspects of the Orthodox-evangelical interface are reviewed, and from the to-and-fro that takes place the reader will learn much.

Yet I predict that every now and then it will be felt that, even with the best will in the world, the conversationalists are not quite on the same wavelength; and I see two reasons for this.

First, while the discussions are primarily about the gospel, the conversationalists exhibit two different ways of believing in the church.

That evangelicals are pietistic individualists who have no deep interest in the church and no clear doctrine regarding it is a widely disseminated untruth, reinforced whenever David Bebbington's familiar profile of evangelicalism as an eighteenth-century product centering on the Bible, the cross, conversion, and evangelism is treated as a lowest common denominator rather than a highest common factor. What is true, however, is that evangelicals typically see the principle of the church's existence as a personal response of faith to the God of Scripture and to the crucified and glorified Son of God as set forth in Scripture.

The church, then, is essentially a community of believers who meet to do what, according to Scripture, the church does in the way of worship and service. The two ordinances (sacraments) that Christ instituted are seen as the word of Christ made visible and visibly enacted for the stirring and strengthening of faith and the confirming to believers of their status and destiny in Christ. That is the ministry (so most evangelicals believe) that Christ by his Spirit is present actually to fulfill as the sacraments are administered in the context of praise and petition to the triune Lord. In this ecclesiology, personal discipleship to Jesus Christ is the paradigm on which all further disclosure of the supernaturalness of Christian life and church life is based. The claim made is that this is the consistent New Testament thought-pattern—and all its phraseology and imagery relating to the church should be understood in these terms.

Orthodoxy, by contrast, in a manner similar to Roman Catholicism, sees the church as first and foremost the extended form and reality of the incarnation, resurrection, and glorification of Christ himself. Ontologically and eschatologically—that is, both in itself as of now and as an anticipatory pointer to its own future—the church is the fullness of Christ, the realization of his presence and power. It is and always was intrinsically this, prior to anyone's personal response to Christ. Ever since our Lord returned to heaven, the church has been simply *there*; all who receive the sacraments, no matter how limited their understanding and devotion, are part of it, and eucharistic worship, which itself is heaven on earth, constantly channels to worshipers the divine life of which adoring faith and faithfulness are the proper acknowledgment. In this ecclesiology, union with Jesus Christ in his corporate fullness through the medium of the sacraments is the paradigm. Here the claim made is that this is the authentic and authoritative understanding of the New Testament witness to the church, a doctrine with which all concepts of conversion, nurture, and destiny should be brought into line.

The difference, then, between the two casts of mind this doctrinal divergence generates sometimes operates as a smudging factor in the discussions that follow—and this difference would need to be a primary agenda for future dialogue.

The second reason for wavelength wobble is that two versions of evangelical theology are speaking in these exchanges. How far apart they really are is open to question, but they certainly see themselves as different and sound different when they express themselves. Both have a North American pedigree of comparable distinction. Both are very much live options today. Both agree on the evangelical approach to ecclesiology I outlined a moment ago, and both cheerfully cooperate in a variety of ministries and in such ventures as this book. But they spar with each other constantly, and traces of that division surface in these chapters from time to time. The two versions may be labeled the *reformational-Reformed* and the *baptistic-Wesleyan*. Both are Bible centered and Christ focused, and both seek a canonical interpretation of the Scriptures according to the analogy of faith (that is, the principle of internal consistency). But the former finds in Scripture a rationally articulated God-centeredness with regard to the economy of grace and the church that the latter with its more narrowly pietistic orientation does not find. To avoid moments of puzzlement as one reads, this difference should be recognized at the outset.

The song I quoted in the first paragraph ends thus: "It's a long, long way to Tipperary, / But my heart's right there." The quest for closer theological rapport between Orthodoxy and evangelicalism is an important one for the future, and there surely is more to be said in pursuing it than has been said in this book. May this present pioneer venture in reconnaissance—for that is really what it is—move many hearts to join in walking the long, long way (as it is certain to be) toward that manifestly God-honoring goal.

J. I. Packer is professor of theology emeritus at Regent College in Vancouver, British Columbia. He also serves as a contributing editor to Christianity Today.

INTRODUCTION

James J. Stamoolis

There are many books on the Eastern Orthodox Church, covering all aspects of faith and life.[1] Evangelical churches have been analyzed, quantified, and described in numerous publications.[2] Evangelicals are rediscovering the value of patristics, which forms the basis of the Eastern Orthodox Tradition.[3] There are books that answer evangelical objections to the Eastern Orthodox Church[4] and others that chronicle the journeys of Protestants to Eastern Orthodoxy.[5] There are several published

---

[1]The major Orthodox publishers are Holy Cross Orthodox Press (www.hchc.edu/bookstore), St. Vladimir's Seminary Press (www.svots.edu/SVS-Press/index.html), Light & Life Publishing (www.light-n-life.com), and Conciliar Press (www.conciliarpress.com).

[2]A plea for common agreement among evangelicals is found in John Stott, *Evangelical Truth: A Personal Plea for Unity, Integrity and Faithfulness* (Downers Grove, Ill.: InterVarsity Press, 1999).

[3]See, for example, D. H. Williams, *Retrieving the Tradition and Renewing Evangelicalism: A Primer for Suspicious Protestants* (Grand Rapids: Eerdmans, 1999); Robert E. Webber, *Ancient-Future Faith: Rethinking Evangelicalism for a Postmodern World* (Grand Rapids: Baker, 1999); and Thomas C. Oden, *The Rebirth of Orthodoxy: Signs of New Life in Christianity* (San Francisco: HarperSanFrancisco, 2003). These three authors all call for a return to orthodoxy as defined in correct doctrine, not necessarily a return to the Eastern Orthodox Church. Oden is also the general editor of the thirteen-volume *Ancient Christian Commentary on Scripture* series (Downers Grove, Ill.: InterVarsity Press).

[4]See, for example, Paul O'Callaghan, *An Eastern Orthodox Response to Evangelical Claims* (Minneapolis: Light & Life, 1984).

[5]Many of these conversions are documented in various books. See, for example, Peter E. Gillquist, Becoming Orthodox: A Journey to the Ancient Christian Faith (Ben Lomond, Calif.: Conciliar Press, 1990), which describes the pilgrimage of a

dialogues between Eastern Orthodox and other Christian tradi-tions.[6] What has been lacking, however, is a volume that brings together advocates of each position for a mutual interaction. In this book, each author has written a chapter on his view of the compatibility of evangelicalism and Eastern Orthodoxy. Each chapter is followed by responses to that author's opinion from the other contributors and then the author's response to them. This exchange of viewpoints allows the discussion to proceed to a deeper theological level.

What makes this interaction especially interesting is that the authors also become personal in their writings. One of the contributors grew up in the Orthodox Church, was converted at a Billy Graham crusade, studied in evangelical and Orthodox seminaries, and is now an Orthodox deacon. Two of the authors have converted from the tradition of their parents. One, raised as an evangelical, has subsequently become an Orthodox priest. The other was born Orthodox and came to evangelical convic-tions while studying in a university.

But this is also a theological book because all the authors, as trained theologians, have given solid reasons for the beliefs they hold. If you are looking for the theological arguments for each position, you will not be disappointed.

WHO ARE THE ORTHODOX?

The Eastern Orthodox Church is best described as the com-munion of churches recognizing the patriarch of Constantino-ple and in turn recognized by the patriarch as belonging to the "family" of Eastern Orthodox churches. This mutual recognition is based on adherence to Orthodox faith and practice. While the highest-ranking prelate in the Orthodox Church is the ecumeni-cal patriarch of Constantinople, he does not have the same

---

group of Campus Crusade for Christ staff to the Orthodox Church. See also Franklin Billerbeck, ed., Anglican-Orthodox Pilgrimage (Ben Lomond, Calif.: Conciliar Press, 1993); Peter E. Gillquist, ed., Coming Home: Why Protestant Clergy Are Becoming Orthodox (Ben Lomond, Calif.: Conciliar Press, 1995). One of the most vocal con-verts to the Orthodox church is Frank Schaeffer, the son of the well-known evan-gelical apologist Francis Schaeffer. See Frank Schaeffer, Dancing Alone: The Quest for Orthodox Faith in the Age of False Religion (Boston: Holy Cross Orthodox Press, 1994), who finds Protestantism responsible for secular Western society and defends his conversion to the Orthodox Church.

[6]See the catalogs of Orthodox publishers and the World Council of Churches.

authority that the pope (or patriarch) of Rome exerts. The patriarch of Constantinople is the "First among Equals" of the ancient patriarchates: Jerusalem, Antioch, Alexandria, Rome, and Constantinople. All but Rome still regard Constantinople as having a primacy among equals. The ecumenical patriarch has no authority to speak *ex cathedra* in a manner that is binding over all Orthodox believers. There is no equivalent to the magisterium of the pope of Rome.

It is important to note that there are ancient churches in the East that are not considered Orthodox. These groups, sometimes referred to as Oriental Orthodox or Non-Chalcedonian churches, are not in communion with the ecumenical patriarch.[7] The Eastern Orthodox Church is, therefore, a communion of churches that accept the same theological, liturgical, and canonical norms.

While theology is important to the Orthodox, it is also true that the forms have deep meaning. The etymology of the word *orthodoxy* is "right *[ortho]* praise *[doxia]*." Thus, while Western churches have tended to use the term "orthodoxy" to mean "correct doctrine," the Orthodox Church is concerned with getting worship right. The Orthodox Church focuses more on God than on the individual. Timeless truths and practices become the vehicle to communion with the triune God.

This doesn't imply that evangelicals aren't concerned with the priority of worship and have no desire to get worship "right." The interest in worship and its renewal is very strong in Protestant churches these days.[8] Worship is increasingly seen as the key to knowing God and his will for humankind.[9]

The church of the West divided from the church of the East in 1054, according to the customary dating. In that year the papal legate put a bull, or edict, of excommunication on the altar of Hagia Sophia in Constantinople, hardening a division that had been growing since the two began to drift apart centuries earlier

---

[7]The schisms of the fifth and sixth centuries resulted in what is now called the Oriental Orthodox churches (see Timothy [Kallistos] Ware, *The Orthodox Church* [Baltimore, Md.: Penguin, 1997], 4). It is not the purpose of this study to engage with these other Eastern churches, but for a thorough overview see Aziz S. Atiya, *History of Eastern Christianity* (Notre Dame, Ind.: University of Notre Dame Press, 1968).

[8]See Robert E. Webber, *Signs of Wonder: The Phenomenon of Convergence in Modern Liturgical and Charismatic Churches* (Nashville: StarSong, 1992).

[9]"Missions is not the ultimate goal of the church. Worship is. Missions exists because worship doesn't" (John Piper, *Let the Nations Be Glad! The Supremacy of God in Missions,* 2d ed. [Grand Rapids: Baker, 2003]), 1.

over theological approaches.[10] Constantinople responded by excommunicating Rome. The separation was exacerbated when Constantinople was sacked during the Fourth Crusade and ruled by a crusader prince and a Latin patriarch for seventy years. Although the division between the Roman Catholic and Eastern Orthodox communions has been somewhat healed by the lifting of the respective anathemas, the issue of Uniate churches (former Eastern Orthodox churches using Eastern liturgical rites but under the authority of Rome) has reopened old wounds.[11]

WHO ARE THE EVANGELICALS?

The term "evangelical" has at least four distinct meanings. The most common meaning, and the way the word is most frequently used in this book, is to refer to churches and organizations that are part of the "evangelical movement" of the twentieth century. This movement arose from the heritage of men like B. B. Warfield, James Orr, and J. Gresham Machen who defended historic Christianity against theological liberalism.[12] These men and others published a series of pamphlets called *The Fundamentals* that defended core theological truths: the authority of the Bible, the virgin birth, substitutionary atonement, the bodily resurrection, and the deity of Jesus Christ.[13] The theologians and church leaders involved in early twentieth-century fundamentalism had

[10]See Ware, *The Orthodox Church,* 4.

[11]The existence of the Uniate churches remains a problematic area between the Eastern Orthodox churches and the Roman Catholic Church. The events of the late twentieth century, which saw the collapse of Communism, have produced more Uniate churches in the countries of Eastern Europe. These "converted" parishes were and still are allowed to keep the Eastern Orthodox liturgical rites, and their priests can be married. An older but still useful introduction to the Uniate churches is Adrian Fortescue, *The Uniate Eastern Churches* (London: Burns Oates and Washbourne, 1923). For more on some of the concerns raised because of these churches, see Maximos IV Sayegh, ed., *The Eastern Churches and Catholic Unity* (Edinburgh: Nelson, 1963).

[12]See, for example, J. Gresham Machen, *Christianity and Liberalism* (Grand Rapids: Eerdmans, 1923). Machen argues that liberalism is not Christianity at all but an entirely different religion.

[13]*The Fundamentals,* originally issued between 1910 and 1915 by the World's Christian Fundamentals Association, is available again. See R. A. Torrey, ed., *The Fundamentals* (Grand Rapids: Baker, 2003); R. A. Torrey, ed., *The Fundamentals: One-Volume Edition* (Grand Rapids: Kregel, 1958).

two goals: (1) the reorientation of Protestantism toward the cardinal doctrines of the Christian faith and (2) the reclamation of American culture. When the second goal was not realized, the fundamentalist churches retreated from public involvement to strengthen their own educational and missionary enterprises.

Evangelicalism emerged out of fundamentalism after the World War II era. It had the same theological convictions but with a social conscience. A landmark book (published in 1947) was Carl F. H. Henry's *The Uneasy Conscience of Modern Fundamentalism,* which called for engagement with society.[14] New institutions such as Fuller Theological Seminary and *Christianity Today* magazine became the standard-bearers for evangelicals' engagement with contemporary culture. Its patrons became the evangelist Billy Graham and key evangelical theologians such as Carl F. H. Henry and Kenneth Kantzer.[15] Twenty years later, the fundamentalists came back into the public arena with the founding of the Moral Majority and attempted again to influence the American landscape.

Those within both movements would see distinct differences, with the fundamentalists more often concerned with lifestyle issues (use of alcohol, attendance at "Hollywood" movies, and the like) and with scientific theories that appear to contradict the Bible (certain theories about the dating of the earth, evolution, and the like). From a theological perspective, however, the fundamental tenets of the Christian faith would be held in common (though some fundamentalists see a continuing weakening of the authority of Scripture on the part of some who claim to be evangelicals).

In part because of this theological concurrence, observers outside the evangelical camp often lump together evangelicalism and fundamentalism, much to the consternation of both groups. This confusion is understandable, since lines that, close

---

[14]This book has just been reissued (Carl F. H. Henry and Richard J. Mouw, *The Uneasy Conscience of Modern Fundamentalism* [Grand Rapids: Eerdmans, 2003]).

[15]I know of many other evangelicals, such as Harold Ockenga, who provided theological and organizational muscle to the movement. Mention should be made of John Stott and J. I. Packer, who are evangelical Anglicans. Henry and Kantzer organized a key conference on evangelicalism in 1989 that served to pass the torch to a younger generation. The proceedings of this conference were published in Kenneth S. Kantzer and Carl F. H. Henry, eds., *Evangelical Affirmations* (Grand Rapids: Zondervan, 1990).

up, appear very fixed, distinguishing one position from another, are more blurred when the positions are seen from a distance—much like the hiker who thinks he is looking at one mountain range but discovers (when cresting the first mountain) there is a wide valley between two distinct ranges. So to the (theologically distant) observer, distinct theological positions may appear closer to each other than they appear to those who hold them.[16] While evangelicals and fundamentalists may see themselves as having significant differences, especially regarding how to apply biblical teaching to their interaction with society, the distant theological observer, who shares few of these traditions' theological convictions, sees them as one phenomenon, not two.

A second definition of "evangelical" comes out of the evangelical revivals of the eighteenth century and the churches and organizations that sprang from the waves of revival and renewal. This historical usage is appropriate because the focus of the revivals was on conversion and on subsequent Christian behavior. The need for a personal application of the truth of the gospel by faith remains a hallmark of evangelicalism.[17]

A third, and classic, definition, much in use in Europe, refers to the churches of the sixteenth-century Protestant Reformation as "evangelical churches" because of the Reformers' emphasis on the evangel, or gospel. A fourth definition applies "evangelical" to the New Testament's proclamation of God's work in Jesus Christ, the "Good News" of the possibility of reconciliation with God. Any church or organization that proclaims this Good News, or evangel, qualifies as being "evangelical." This, of course, opens all of church history to reinterpretation, because evangelicals could then be found from the apostolic age to the present. Some developments in church history were distinctly "evangelical" in their origin. An example is the monastic movement that produced most of the missionaries who evangelized Europe.

While all the above are legitimate definitions of "evangelical," this book sets out to look at the contemporary evangelical church and analyze its compatibility with the Eastern Orthodox Church. It is difficult, if not impossible, to avoid referencing the

---

[16]I owe this illustration to the late Kenneth Kantzer, who was my theology professor and seminary dean.

[17]This is most often expressed as "having a personal relationship with Christ." The focus of this evangelical statement is that the relationship with Christ is "by faith," apart from any religious observances or works.

fourth definition, since all traditions that take the Bible seriously would want to be perceived as being in continuity with the Scriptures.

Certainly there are traditions among those who call themselves evangelical (using the first and third definitions) that are closer to specific Eastern Orthodox doctrinal positions than they are to the viewpoints of some other self-confessed evangelicals. I was at a conference where a speaker was describing the differences between Orthodox and evangelicals. Present were a strong contingent of Scandinavian Lutherans and a group of Plymouth Brethren. As the speaker contrasted the Orthodox view on Communion with his perception of the evangelical view, the Brethren agreed that the Orthodox were in error on this point. The Lutherans, however, felt that if the Orthodox believed thus on the Lord's Supper, they must be evangelical! The tables were turned when the doctrine of the perseverance of the saints was discussed. The Lutherans reversed their acceptance of the Orthodox, while the Brethren delegates thought that the doctrine described was similar, if not identical, to their view. The presenter, in my opinion, made several errors, not the least being his assumption that all evangelicals agreed with his interpretation of "true evangelicalism." Nevertheless, this anecdote illustrates the point that there is considerable breadth in what those who call themselves evangelical believe about certain theological issues. Is evangelicalism, by its very nature, a minimalist position? Is agreement on certain core doctrines all that is required to be in the camp? This issue will be discussed in the essays and in the responses that follow.

THEOLOGICAL PARADIGMS CONTRASTED

As the reader will discover, there is a high regard for the authority of Scripture in both Eastern Orthodoxy and evangelicalism. The questions that separate them are most often questions of interpretation and of the role of Tradition.[18] The reader

---

[18]When spelled with a capital *T,* Tradition refers to the universally accepted articles of faith that are not necessarily explicit in the Bible. The Orthodox would argue that some of the elements of Tradition are implicit, while others were handed down orally by the apostles through apostolic succession. In addition to Tradition, there are traditions that are local or national in nature and not binding on the entire Orthodox communion.

is advised to keep in mind the points of reference of each contributor because each author writes from within his own understanding.

The disagreements between evangelicals and Orthodox, in essence, center on the issue of theological paradigms. Because of the language shared by both the Bible and the early church fathers, much of our language is similar. But the understanding of these words often shows the differing theological framework from which each position starts.[19] What follows is an examination of the Eastern Orthodox paradigm. The evangelical paradigm, apart from certain core beliefs mentioned in the preceding section, is harder to define, for it encompasses both those who are Reformed and those who are Wesleyan. To avoid presenting a minimalist paradigm, I refer the reader to the essays that follow, which outline the evangelical position.

One way of looking at the differences in theological paradigms is to note that Western Christendom historically has been defined, for the most part, by legal concepts.[20] While Tertullian is credited with introducing this terminology, it is Augustine who shaped the Western theological framework. Even those who react against Augustinian theology do so in the categories of thought that are juridical in terminology. Augustine's doctrine of justification is considered by Eastern Orthodox theologians to be too individualistic. From the Orthodox viewpoint, the fuller meaning of salvation is lost. As is noted by the contributors, a fuller meaning of salvation doesn't necessarily preclude personal sin

---

[19]The difference in the framework is found to be between East and West rather than between Roman Catholic and Eastern Orthodox on one hand and Protestants on the other. This is not what one might expect from looking at the externals of the respective communions, but the different paradigm is well understood by the Orthodox. Alexis Khomiakov, a Russian lay theologian of the nineteenth century, wrote, "All Protestants are Crypto-Papists.... To use the concise language of algebra, all the West knows but one datum a; whether it be preceded by the positive sign +, as with the Romanists, or with the negative sign -, as with the Protestants, the a remains the same" (cited in Ware, *The Orthodox Church*, 9). Interestingly, Khomiakov is an example of another difference between the Western churches and the Orthodox Church in that the theologians of the East in the last few centuries were primarily laypeople. This changed in the twentieth century with the migration of Russians to Western Europe.

[20]"Western Christendom" is a shorthand way of speaking of the churches of the western Roman Empire in contradistinction to the churches formed in the eastern Roman Empire. To speak thus is to include the Roman Catholic Church with the churches of the Protestant Reformation in their theological understanding. Indeed, this is precisely how "the West" is viewed by the Eastern Orthodox.

and responsibility. In fact, it will be argued that personal sin is taken seriously in the Eastern Orthodox Church. But the main point must not be lost that the Orthodox Church is not shaped by Augustinian anthropology.

One could go further and discuss differences in soteriology (which are covered in the essays) and methodology. From an Orthodox perspective, the late Russian philosopher L. A. Zander set out these differences in the negative:

- The East was not influenced by Augustine; its anthropology is different from that of the West.
- The East was not influenced by Anselm; its soteriology is different from that of the West.
- The East was not influenced by Thomas; its methodology is different from that of the West.[21]

As anyone trained in theology will quickly understand, these are huge differences that also account for the congruence on certain issues between the Orthodox Church and certain Protestant traditions. For example, conferences have been held to examine the congruence between the Orthodox Church and the Wesleyan tradition. While Wesleyans start from a Western framework, their conclusions are more in line with the Orthodox Church's view of human nature.

The theological framework of Eastern Orthodoxy is described by the Orthodox as having a "Patristic mind" that considers "the Fathers ... as living witnesses and contemporaries."[22] This leaves open the question of whether the patristic tradition, and therefore the Tradition, continues to grow. Indeed, it is dangerous to view "the Fathers" as a closed cycle of writings belonging wholly to the past, for might not our own age produce a new Basil or Athanasius? To say that there can be no more Fathers is to suggest that the Holy Spirit has deserted the church.[23]

To claim that the Eastern Orthodox Church is predominantly a church of the Holy Spirit is misleading if the charismatic gifts are thought of in terms of Pentecostalism or the modern charismatic movement. While it's true that there have been charismatic priests and congregations within the Orthodox communion, what

---

[21]See L. A. Zander, *Vision and Action* (London: Gollancz, 1952), 59.
[22]Ware, *The Orthodox Church*, 204.
[23]Ibid.

is commonly known as "the charismatic movement" has not marked the Orthodox churches, nor has it had the organization and following of the Roman Catholic charismatic movement.[24]

There is, however, the sense of the Holy Spirit in the theology of the Orthodox Church. This aspect contributes both to the spirituality of the church and to its openness to change that is in accordance with Scripture and Tradition.[25] Orthodox doctrine maintains that the Holy Spirit resides in the entire people of God.[26] This gives, or should give, a very dynamic interpretation of Tradition. It also theoretically gives the congregation power, as seen in the consecration process of a bishop.

In the Orthodox Church, the bishop is the authoritative representative of Jesus Christ in governing the congregation. The congregation, through whom the Holy Spirit speaks, must affirm the candidate's worthiness by voicing aloud, "He is worthy; he is worthy." While this custom can be either perfunctory in its application or abused, the theological reference behind this requirement is the conviction that the Holy Spirit indwells the church and not merely the officeholders.

Another characteristic of Orthodox theology that has a bearing on the way theology is done is its method. Termed "mystical theology," this method was first worked out by Clement of Alexandria in the late second and early third centuries, further refined by Origen, and taken up by the Cappadocian fathers in the fourth century. It is characterized by an apophatic approach that describes God in negative rather than positive terms. The Orthodox believe this theology of negation to be more accurate in that the human mind cannot comprehend God. It is more authentic to speak of what we know God is

---

[24]For an evaluation of the charismatic movement from an Orthodox point of view see John W. Morris, *Charismatic Movement: An Orthodox Evaluation* (Boston: Holy Cross Orthodox Press, 1984). An opposing view is found in Father Eusebius A. Stephanou, *Orthodox Charismatic Renewal: A Response* (Orthodox Renewal Series Pamphlet, n.p., n.d.).

[25]Some Orthodox theologians would argue that it is really only Tradition that should be spoken of as the source of doctrine, since Scripture can be subsumed under the category of Tradition.

[26]This belief is dealt with in James J. Stamoolis, "Scripture and Tradition in the Orthodox Church," *Evangelical Review of Theology* 19 (April/June 1995): 131–43. See my Th.M. thesis for a discussion of the Holy Spirit in the Orthodox laity: James J. Stamoolis, "Scripture and Tradition as Sources of Authority in the Eastern Orthodox Church," unpublished thesis, Trinity Evangelical Divinity School, 1971.

not—reflecting the apophatic approach—than to overstate what we cannot comprehend God to be.[27] While the Orthodox emphasize the apophatic approach to theology, in the pictorial representation of the saints, Jesus, Mary, and the biblical stories they focus on what *can* be said.[28]

Icons are the most visible feature of any Orthodox church, and the devotion paid to the icons by Orthodox faithful is perhaps jarring to evangelicals. It is critical to understand the theological distinction between veneration *(proskynesis)* for the icon and worship *(latreia)*, which is reserved for God alone. Even then, the true object of veneration is the person depicted in the icon, not the image itself.[29] Despite the true purpose of the icons, often the externals of the Eastern Orthodox Church are more prominent in the minds of the Orthodox faithful and of outside observers.

The externals of evangelical churches are harder to define. The gathering places can range from simple meetinghouses to elaborate buildings. Worship can run the gamut from no musical instruments and a focus on preaching to detailed liturgies. Because of the breadth of worship styles within the evangelical movement, it's not easy to point to a common set of externals, unless it would be a priority on preaching the word of God as recorded in the Bible.[30]

---

[27]See Ware, *The Orthodox Church,* 63. Cf. Vladimir Lossky, *The Mystical Theology of the Eastern Church* (Crestwood, N.Y.: St. Vladimir's Seminary Press, 1976), 44–67.

[28]There are several books that describe the role of icons. One of the best treatments is found in Ernst Benz, *The Eastern Orthodox Church: Its Thought and Life* (Garden City, N.Y.: Doubleday, 1963). Benz begins his book by discussing the role of the icon in the devotional life of the Orthodox Christian. This phenomenological approach brings the reader to the heart of Orthodox devotion and thereby the heart of Orthodox "system." For an excellent introduction to icons, see John Baggley and Richard Temple, *Door of Perception: Icons and Their Significance* (Crestwood, N.Y.: St. Vladimir's Seminary Press, 1996). For the history and theology of icons, see Leonid Ouspensky, *Theology of the Icon, Volumes I & II* (Crestwood, N.Y.: St. Vladimir's Seminary Press, 1992). See also Leonid Ouspensky and Vladimir Lossky, *The Meaning of Icons* (Crestwood, N.Y.: St. Vladimir's Seminary Press, 1999). Russell M. Hart (*The Icon Through Western Eyes* [Springfield, Ill.: Templegate, 1991]) gives a Western Christian's appreciation for the icon. For a history of the controversy, see Edward James Martin, *A History of the Iconoclastic Controversy* (London: Society for Promoting Christian Knowledge, 1930).

[29]See the chapter titled "The Theology of the Image," in Vladimir Lossky, *In the Image and Likeness of God* (London: Mowbrays, 1975).

[30]Carnegie Samuel Calian (*Icon and Pulpit: The Protestant-Orthodox Encounter* [Philadelphia: Westminster, 1968]) makes a useful distinction between the two traditions, although as the Orthodox will point out, the pulpit was never entirely absent from their tradition.

Some observers would find the classic prohibitions against alcohol and certain social activities as distinguishing externals.[31] While some evangelical churches have these prohibitions, not all do. Fundamentalist churches are, in fact, more likely to have them. But as noted above, the close theological connection between evangelicalism and fundamentalism, as well as their shared history, is a cause for confusion to outside observers.

The problem with externals is that they are often mistaken for the core of the subject. The externals have meaning in both Eastern Orthodoxy and evangelicalism, but this meaning is derived from the theological principles at the center of each system. This book is an attempt to get beneath the outward practices to the heart of both Eastern Orthodoxy and evangelicalism.

---

[31]These prohibitions against movies, dancing, alcohol, and tobacco are beginning to disappear from prominent evangelical bastions.

Chapter One

ARE EASTERN ORTHODOXY AND EVANGELICALISM COMPATIBLE? YES

*The Evangelical Theology of the
Eastern Orthodox Church*

Bradley Nassif

ARE EASTERN ORTHODOXY AND EVANGELICALISM COMPATIBLE? YES

The Evangelical Theology of the Eastern Orthodox Church

Bradley Nassif

SETTING THE STAGE: A PERSONAL WORD

If postmodernism has taught us anything, it has made us aware that we always interpret reality through the eyes of our own history—our family upbringing, educational background, cultural context, and religious community. My background is deeply rooted in the Eastern Orthodox tradition. I am a Lebanese Christian who grew up in America in the Antiochian Orthodox Church (formally named the Greek Orthodox Church of Antioch and All the East, whose patriarch resides in Damascus, Syria). It is among the most ancient and revered patriarchates in the Orthodox world, dating back to the great christological controversies of the fourth and fifth centuries—and even back to the first century, where the New Testament reports in Acts 11:26 that "the disciples were called Christians first at Antioch." The late Father John Meyendorff was my doctoral mentor with whom I specialized in Greek patristic theology and exegesis.

I am also deeply indebted to evangelical Christians who helped bring me into a personal relationship with Jesus Christ during my high school years. Over the past decade I have been a visiting or adjunct professor of Orthodox studies at leading evangelical schools such as Fuller Theological Seminary, Regent College, Trinity Evangelical Divinity School, and The Southern Baptist Theological Seminary. Much of my work has been devoted to introducing evangelical students and faculty to the riches of the Eastern Orthodox tradition, and many of these evangelicals have become friends and colleagues. In the early 1990s I founded a Pan-Orthodox, Pan-Evangelical organization named the Society for the Study of Eastern Orthodoxy and Evangelicalism. For the past decade we've held annual meetings to explore the areas of convergence and divergence between our two traditions.

I share these brief biographical excerpts because readers may appreciate knowing that I have not just *thought* about Orthodox and evangelical compatibility, but I've *lived* it most of my life. I'm also convinced that my personal history has been a theological asset to the exposition of Orthodox theology, not a confessional liability, because it has given me firsthand knowledge of the very best and the very worst in the Orthodox and evangelical worlds. There are plenty of negative experiences one could point to on both sides, by virtue of which one could argue that the positive stance I've adopted here is nothing more than wishful thinking. I know as an insider how disillusioning it can be to see how deep and widespread the ignorance of Orthodox Church members can be concerning their own faith, how low their levels of personal commitment sometimes are, and how bigoted they sometimes act toward other Christians.

On the other hand, I have witnessed the hubris of some evangelical Christians, which is often tied to historical amnesia and an idolatrous self-confidence in their own exegetical skills. I've also been a deeply wounded casualty of the broken promises and highly unethical behavior of certain evangelical leaders. But I must quickly add that the good in both communities far outweighs the bad.

So I write this chapter under no romantic illusions. I bring to this essay both an intimate academic knowledge and an intimate experiential knowledge of both communities, from the top down and the bottom up. It is precisely because of—and in spite of—these many perspective-shaping experiences that I am quite certain our two traditions will never see full communion in my lifetime (barring an intervention by the Holy Spirit). I'm not sure there should even be full communion. But in order to lay a common ground for mutual exploration and to increase the level of theological communication between our two estranged communities, I accepted the invitation to participate in this volume by identifying areas of convergence and divergence through a brief overview of the evangelical theology of the Eastern Orthodox Church.

SETTING THE STAGE: WHAT I HOPE TO ACCOMPLISH

Goals

I have three goals for this chapter: (1) to define evangelical identity and use the definition to measure the common ground between Eastern Orthodox and Protestant evangelical theology;[1] (2) to see how the distinctive theological themes that comprise the identity of contemporary evangelicalism were interpreted by the classical tradition of the Greek church fathers from the fourth to the fourteenth centuries; and (3) to assess the similarities and differences between the classical and contemporary versions of the evangelical faith as the basis for viewing the extent of conflict and compatibility between both the Orthodox and the Protestant evangelical communities today.

Method

The strength of our conclusions will depend largely on the reliability of the research method applied. My procedure will not try to address the distressing diversity of evangelicalism but to constructively set forth our common consent to the evangelical faith in a way that is faithful to the Orthodox vision of life in Christ. I will contend that there are no core disagreements between evangelicals and Eastern Orthodox over the issues that define the evangelical movement, issues that are also present in the Eastern Orthodox Church. There are major differences, however, over the

---

[1]The best supplementary reading to this chapter is Donald Fairbairn's *Eastern Orthodoxy Through Western Eyes* (Louisville, Ky.: Westminster John Knox, 2002). A comprehensive summary in one convenient location of all known sources, leaders, and dialogues dealing with Orthodoxy and evangelicalism between 1990 and 2003 can be found in Bradley Nassif's "Eastern Orthodoxy and Evangelicalism: The Status of an Emerging Global Dialogue" in *Eastern Orthodox Theology: A Contemporary Reader*, rev. ed., ed. Daniel Clendenin (Grand Rapids: Baker, 2003).

extent to which the Orthodox understand and manifest, as evangelicals do not, those larger principles of evangelical identity through the church's incarnational Trinitarian vision of life.

I will first carefully define the meaning of the term *evangelical* and then measure the components of this definition against the theological norms that have guided Orthodox church life for nearly two thousand years: the dogmatic definitions of its church fathers and councils, liturgies, spirituality, iconography, architecture, and mission theology. I'll discuss contemporary ecumenical documents that have been produced by the Orthodox Church as their official responses to specific doctrinal issues raised in their dialogues with Protestants and Catholics—documents previously unexamined for their relevance to the evangelical movement. I will also briefly document how the current work of leading evangelical scholars has been inadvertently moving the evangelical movement toward a rediscovery of the creative relevance of the Christian East in its classical theology, spirituality, and worship—often far more attractively than we Orthodox are doing for ourselves!

Using simultaneously the historical and systematic disciplines to compare Orthodox and evangelical theology runs the obvious risk of generalizing at the expense of analytic research. Given the ecumenical task at hand, however, a panoramic overview of the evangelical theology of the Orthodox Church appears to be what is most urgently needed in order to correct the nearsightedness of those seemingly unable to see the forest for the trees.

Desired Outcomes

I hope this chapter brings new insight that will prompt a significant segment of the Orthodox and evangelical worlds to believe more positively about and act more constructively toward each other than they have to date. By showing how the evangelical faith is embraced and transcended by the Orthodox Church, I hope to provide the grounds for evangelicals to reassess the comprehensiveness of their own incarnational Trinitarian faith and implement an Orthodox reconstruction of the evangelical movement; conversely, I hope also to encourage a spiritual renewal of the Orthodox Church through a deeper appreciation of the evangelical character of our own theology, spirituality, and sacramental life.

EVANGELICAL IDENTITY

The criteria used to define the term *evangelical* will largely determine how one answers the question of conflict or compatibility between the Orthodox and evangelical traditions. In his newest study of evangelicalism, Mark Noll explains that evangelicalism "is a more complicated phenomenon than either its adherents or its foes usually admit. The complexity is immediately obvious when definitions are proposed."[2] Two pages later he adds, "Evangelicalism has been an extraordinarily complex phenomenon. Since its origins, the movement has always been *diverse, flexible, adaptable, and multiform* [emphasis his]."[3] In his next chapter Noll makes this observation:

> Precision in terminology is important. It is natural to use the term "evangelical" to mean those who hold certain Christian beliefs and exercise certain Christian practices. It is also legitimate to use the term historically for designating certain churches and religious traditions deriving ultimately from the Reformation and also identifying strongly with more recent revival traditions. But it is also precarious when those two usages are merged without discrimination. As the survey shows, considerable differences result from defining "evangelicals" as those who hold evangelical convictions when compared to defining as "evangelicals" those who identify with the historic Protestant denominations where those beliefs have been most prominent.[4]

Here Noll alludes to an extensive, highly sophisticated survey conducted by the Angus Reid Group of Toronto on the number of evangelical constituencies in thirty-three countries around the world. The questions were carefully worded so that respondents would be answering whether or not they adhered to the distinctive features of evangelical religion. The Angus Reid researchers admitted that their work touched only parts of the world, but even with its limitations the poll contains useful information related to Roman Catholicism and Orthodoxy. Noll

---

[2]Mark Noll, *American Evangelical Christianity: An Introduction* (Oxford, U.K.: Blackwell, 2001), 12.

[3]Ibid., 14.

[4]Ibid., 37.

observes that "the distribution of beliefs and practices traditionally known as 'evangelical' is surprisingly wide.... It is even more striking how much Roman Catholics contribute to the total of evangelical believers, especially in Canada."[5]

Two survey results pertained to Eastern Orthodoxy. In a 1996 survey of 6,000 Americans and Canadians, the number of respondents representing the "Other" grab-bag category—Mormons, Jehovah's Witnesses, Eastern Orthodox, Unitarian Universalists, Jews, and others not readily classifiable with the larger Protestant and Catholic groups—was "quite low."[6] In the 1997 "World Poll" conducted by the Angus Reid Group (where "Orthodoxy" was substituted for "Catholicism" for respondents in Greece, Russia, and the Ukraine), people were asked to affirm if "religion was very important *and* [they] prayed at least once a day *and* [they] attended church at least weekly *and* [they] have committed their lives to Christ and consider themselves converted Christians" ("True Believers"). Orthodox "True Believers" totaled 19 percent in Greece, 7 percent in the Ukraine, and 1 percent in Russia.[7]

The results of these studies show that the number of Orthodox "True Believers" is small. In addition, the relevance of this data for determining the "evangelical" identity of Eastern Orthodoxy appears to be threefold: First, it underscores how difficult it is to obtain reliable information from surveys of the general populace on the number of "True Believers" in traditionally Orthodox countries. Most of us who have traveled to those parts of the formerly Communist world know from experience that there is much more genuine faith there than what is reflected in these polls. Second, the comparatively high percentage of "True Believers" in Greece suggests that a significant number of Orthodox Christians readily identify themselves with evangelical faith, even though they do not know it by that name. Third, the fact that the global number of Roman Catholics who were "True Believers" greatly surpassed the number of the Protestant variety implies that a great many Catholics see the essential features of evangelicalism as compatible with their sacramental vision. Of course, high numbers in and of themselves do not guarantee confessional integrity, but they do indicate beyond a reasonable

[5]Ibid.
[6]Ibid., 32.
[7]Ibid., 40.

doubt that a great many Catholics in the world today closely qualify as traditional evangelical believers. This fact alone is a staggering indicator of the changing definition of evangelical identity at the beginning of the twenty-first century. If it were possible to survey traditional Catholics of the sixteenth century with this same poll, it is hard to resist the conclusion that the results would have been quite different.

When dealing with Orthodoxy and evangelicalism, therefore, it is especially important to identify what *kind* of evangelicalism we mean. We need to follow Noll's admonition to distinguish carefully between evangelical history and evangelical theology. No one who understands the history of the Eastern Orthodox Church would suggest that Orthodoxy is heir to the *history* of Protestant evangelicalism. But the question remains as to whether Orthodoxy shares a consistent pattern of *theological* convictions with evangelicalism.

The criteria I'll use to answer this question are provided in Noll's report of David Bebbington's fourfold definition of evangelical beliefs, which the Angus Reid Group survey used in formulating its questions.[8] This is what a firmly evangelical respondent would agree to with regard to beliefs:

- A respondent strongly agreed that "through the life, death, and resurrection of Jesus, God provided a way for the forgiveness of my sins" (crucicentrism).
- A respondent strongly agreed that "the Bible is the inspired word of God" or agreed to whatever degree that "the Bible is God's word and is to be taken literally, word for word" (biblicism).
- A respondent strongly agreed that "I have committed my life to Christ and consider myself to be a converted Christian" (conversionism).
- A respondent agreed or agreed strongly that "it is important to encourage non-Christians to become Christians" (activism).

Noll observed that "by tallying the number of those who responded positively to all four measures (sometimes three or

---

[8]See Noll, *American Evangelical Christianity,* 13, 31. Bebbington's four points are: (1) the centrality of the cross—crucicentrism; (2) the centrality of the Bible—biblicism; (3) the centrality of conversion—conversionism; and (4) the centrality of evangelism—activism.

four), it is possible to obtain a rough picture of the prevalence of traditional evangelical convictions."[9]

These features of evangelicalism appear to be the most critically reliable criteria for defining evangelical identity when assessing its theological compatibility with Eastern Orthodoxy. A lengthy but crucial excerpt from Noll's analysis of the history of evangelicalism from 1970 to the present elaborates Bebbington's four points and enables us to see the newest form of evangelicalism, which has arisen as "new leaders and new concerns have created a more pluralistic evangelicalism than has ever existed in American history."[10] It is this form of evangelicalism, states Noll, with which Orthodox Christianity is to be compared at the beginning of the twenty-first century:

> At the beginning of the twenty-first century, there are very few generalizations that apply to all American evangelicals. To be sure, David Bebbington's four defining characteristics are still generally valid. A *reliance on Scripture* remains, though how that reliance is expressed differs widely. Some evangelicals rejoice in themes they find in the Bible for the liberation of women. Others, by contrast, think that the Bible teaches traditional patriarchy. Some think that the notion of "inerrancy" is the best way to express the Bible's authority, while others look for doctrinal formulas less tied to the controversies from the late nineteenth century. . . .
>
> Concern for *conversion* also remains, though conversion is understood differently in, for example, charismatic, confessional, or Baptist circles. Sometimes conversion is even described with the language popularized by Alcoholics Anonymous's "Twelve Step" program to combat addiction. Yet the conviction that life-changing encounters with God can, do, and should take place remains a fixture in evangelical churches.
>
> Evangelicals are as *active* as ever, but that activity spreads over every point on the compass. . . .
>
> Finally, the *death of Christ on the cross* is still at the heart of evangelical religion, though the formal doctrines that once defined the message of atonement receive much less attention today than thirty or sixty or a hundred

---

[9]Noll, *American Evangelical Christianity*, 31.
[10]Ibid., 22.

years ago. The continuing spread of pentecostalism and the growth of the charismatic movement have meant more concentration on doctrines of sanctification (becoming holy oneself) than on doctrines of justification (how God accepts a sinner). In addition, an appeal to the consolations of redemption is now much more common than detailed theological exposition of its nature. In biblical terms, the Psalms have taken precedence over Isaiah, the gospels are edging out the epistles of Paul.

Much, in other words, separates contemporary evangelical Christians from the first modern evangelicals two-and-a-half centuries ago. . . .[11]

The above excerpts from Noll's analysis of the Angus Reid Group survey encapsulate what appears to be the most authoritative study on evangelical identity available, because this is what evangelicalism *is* today, for better or for worse, according to the best scholars and the best-supported strategies used to chart the character and constituencies of the evangelical faith. Laying aside the historical debates over the origins and Wesleyan departures from evangelicalism, the theological features of evangelicalism today embrace a wide array of denominations and churches, ranging from Reformed to Wesleyan, charismatic to Pentecostal, Baptist to Catholic, thus revealing evangelicalism as a transdenominational, transnational movement. To compare Orthodox theology with the theological emphases of only one of these Protestant groups to the exclusion of the others would alter evangelical identity from that of a transdenominational movement to that of a single denomination, thus subverting the meaning of the term "evangelical" and requiring as many comparative monographs as there are Protestant denominations.

Clearly, the evangelicalism of today is not the evangelicalism of yesterday. This is manifested in its changed emphases on conversion theology and the cross regarding such issues as "justification by faith" (the forensic notion, which the old evangelicalism used to emphasize), personal assurance (whether it is sudden or gradual), the means of conversion (in relation to baptism, particularly within the Anglican and Russian Baptist wings of evangelicalism), and substitutionary atonement (which used to explain the significance of the incarnation rather than the

---

[11]Ibid., 24–26 (emphasis added for clarity when referring back to Bebbington's four points).

other way around), as well as others noted above by Noll and Bebbington.

THE EVANGELICAL THEOLOGY
OF THE ORTHODOX CHURCH

The complexity of the comparison between Orthodoxy and evangelicalism is evident in the differing ways in which each appropriates the Christian past. As the Angus Reid Group survey indicates, the greater part of evangelicalism adopts a mentality that seeks no validation beyond the Bible due to the increasing influence of the Pentecostal and charismatic movements. Orthodoxy, on the other hand, views Scripture within the larger context of apostolic tradition handed down over the centuries in an unbroken succession of truth. Authentic tradition implies a personal acceptance of the gospel based on the historical tradition of the person and work of Christ, handed down and proclaimed in the church of the New Testament and successive generations and received by the enabling power of the Holy Spirit.[12]

In order for readers to see how the evangelical faith was understood and appropriated by the classical tradition of Eastern Orthodoxy, I will turn to a theological analysis of representative church fathers and central elements of the church's tradition from the fourth to fourteenth centuries that became constitutive of the evangelical identity of the Orthodox Church in its classical and contemporary forms. My analysis will follow the four distinctives of the evangelical faith as defined by Noll and the Angus Reid Group questionnaire.

---

[12]Ironically, this was evangelical scholar George Ladd's way of understanding "tradition," though he never saw how that definition was fleshed out in subsequent Christian history: "Tradition [in the NT] has a twofold character: it is both historical tradition and kerygmatic-pneumatic tradition at one and the same time. It is historical because it is tied to events in history, and the tradition preserves the report of these events. It is kerygmatic because it can be perpetuated only as *kerygma* [gospel] and received as a confession of faith. It is pneumatic because it can be received and preserved only by the enabling of the Spirit. Neither the historical nor the kerygmatic aspects of the word of God can be emphasized to the neglect of the other ... the gospel is both past event and present proclamation. When the kerygmatic aspect is neglected, the *kerygma* becomes a recital of facts and events lying in the past and thereby loses its character as salvation event. Both aspects must be retained" (George Ladd, *Theology of the New Testament* [Grand Rapids: Eerdmans, 1978], 390–91).

Evangelical Identity #1: "Through the Life, Death, and Resurrection of Jesus, God Provided a Way for the Forgiveness of My Sins" (Crucicentrism)

The evangelical emphasis on the work of Christ, which assumes his deity, was the first characteristic listed among the tenets of evangelical identity by the Angus Reid Group survey (Bebbington's "crucicentrism"). A brief history of soteriology in the Christian East will be explored by focusing on the principal theological controversies of the Byzantine Orthodox Church from the fourth to the fourteenth centuries. These developments continue to live at the center of Orthodox theology and piety today and reveal the church's disharmony with the evangelical movement.

The areas of difference that separate Orthodox soteriology from evangelical theories of the redemptive work of Christ lie chiefly in the way Orthodoxy has maintained the inseparable union between Christology and soteriology, and evangelicalism has not. As Noll noted (see pages 34–35), the older evangelical theories of substitutionary atonement and justification by faith are still very important but no longer serve as distinguishing features of the evangelical faith as they once did, so we are under no obligation to use these issues as a litmus test of Orthodox and evangelical compatibility. However, I realize there are still a large number of Calvinistically oriented evangelicals who insist on these positions, even if they no longer are the majority (who are now the charismatics and Pentecostals). The Calvinist critiques of Orthodoxy are still meaningful based on their own merits, so I will briefly address those concerns.

Atonement and Justification

The older evangelical interpretation of the death of Christ as a vicarious atonement traces its roots back to the Reformation emphasis on the biblical doctrine of justification by faith and the earlier formulation of atonement developed by Anselm of Canterbury at the end of the eleventh century in his *Cur Deus Homo (Why God Became Human).*

The main points centered on the relationship among sin, guilt, and divine satisfaction. God's mercy and justice needed to be satisfied in dealing with the guilt of human sin. The method by which God satisfied his justice and mercy was the death of Christ, whose humanity satisfied God's justice and whose divinity made that satisfaction universally applicable. Christ died in our place and for our sins.

The Reformers took up this theme and complemented it with Saint Paul's doctrine of justification by faith. Justification by faith meant that sinners could obtain a right standing before God only through the merits of the death of Christ, through faith alone and not by good works. The term "justification" was a metaphor taken from the legal realm, which conveyed the idea that justified sinners were "declared" righteous before God, much like a guilty criminal in a court of law was pronounced innocent before a civil judge. On the negative side of the ledger, guilt was legally removed in God's sight; on the positive side, Christ's righteousness was said to be imputed to the repentant sinner.

These doctrines were retained in the later history of nineteenth- and much of twentieth-century evangelicalism, especially among Calvinists. One of the main arguments for their validity, along with the scriptural texts that were cited, was that these doctrines reflected the essence of the gospel and thus belonged to the very definition of Christian orthodoxy (with lowercase "o"). Today these doctrines are less in evidence in modern expositions of the evangelical faith and, as we have pointed out, no longer qualify as benchmark criteria of evangelical identity.

By saying that they no longer qualify as benchmark criteria of evangelical identity, I do not wish to deny their centrality to noncharismatic evangelicals but to note that the wider evangelical family—especially those affiliated with and influenced by the Pentecostal and charismatic movements—simply does not give these doctrines a central place in their contemporary church life. As Noll pointed out, the *therapeutic* aspects of redemption are being stressed over the *transactional* aspects. Today, noncharismatic evangelicals are recognizing that there is more to Christ's atonement than just its substitutionary aspect and that justification by faith is not purely forensic but also personal. In so doing, they are broadening their views, but in fairness to them it does not constitute a departure from the centrality of these two doctrines within those particular evangelical communities.

Evangelicals who tend to interpret Scripture through the theological prism of justification by faith think of the Orthodox as not being sufficiently concerned with or able to adequately deal with the doctrine of justification due to undue concentration on the doctrine of *theosis*. While it is true that justification has not been as explicit a theme as *theosis* in Greek patristic theology, justification has by no means been bypassed. The Orthodox view baptism as both a justifying event and the beginning of *theosis*. As long as justification is proclaimed in terms of the "union with Christ" model for imputed righteousness from Christ's divinized humanity, without the basic assumption of an Augustinian anthropology with its inherited guilt, it comports well with today's emphasis on holiness, or sanctification, as one of evangelicalism's primary characteristics. Unfortunately, Orthodox theologians (particularly those who haven't studied the doctrine carefully in Scripture) have at times viewed justification in an exclusively forensic sense and wrongly rejected it chiefly on that basis.

Although conceptually distinct from justification, *theosis* may be regarded as including justification, though not exclusively in a forensic sense, and as happening simultaneously with it. The conception of justification as conformity to Christ in his righteousness maintains that, in the justification event, believers are given a new identity—are made Christlike *(theosis)* through their mystical union with him in baptism. Justification cannot be interpreted in any sense apart from the incarnation, from which it derives its benefits. Justification derives its forensic sense of imputed righteousness from the hypostatic union that united Christ's being with his redemptive acts in the context of a thoroughgoing Trinitarianism. In recent years, Lutheran-Orthodox conversations on the relation between "justification" and "deification" have witnessed a more positive appraisal of deification by Lutherans, initiated in large measure by the "new quest for Luther's theology" by the Mannermaa school at the University of Helsinki.[13]

---

[13]See Carl E. Braaten and Robert W. Jenson, eds., *Union with Christ: The New Finnish Interpretation of Luther* (Grand Rapids: Eerdmans, 1988); see the review of this book by John Pester, "Luther Reexamined," *Affirmation & Critique* (January 1999), 43–48; can be viewed on the Web at www.affcrit.com/pdfs/1999/01/99_01_br.pdf. See also A. N. Williams, *The Ground of Union: Deification in Aquinas and Palamas* (Oxford: Oxford Univ. Press, 1999).

When one states the Eastern Orthodox understanding of salvation in positive terms, the picture of human redemption that emerges complements rather than conflicts with evangelicalism's picture. It does not require an incompatibility with the evangelical interpretation of justification by faith or substitutionary atonement. Very simply, the classical evangelical tradition developed a "transactional" model of redemption in which emphasis is placed on *what* Christ did *for me* (i.e., the work of Christ on the cross and his substitutionary atonement), while the East adopted a "transformational" model that places emphasis on *who* Christ is (i.e., the person of Christ, his resurrection, and his triumphant victory over sin and death—the *Christus Victor* theme). Acknowledging this distinction goes a long way in explaining why each side emphasizes different aspects of salvation. Both Orthodoxy and evangelicalism recognize both aspects but focus primarily on one of them.

Orthodox Trinitarianism

In addition to the doctrine of *theosis* (to be explored more fully later in this chapter), the doctrine of the Trinity became central to the Orthodox understanding of salvation. Even though the Angus Reid Group survey did not include belief in the Trinity as part of the evangelical affirmation, most evangelicals would affirm this belief, as Noll pointed out. For these reasons I would like to explore the Orthodox doctrine of the Trinity and how it relates to our vision of salvation.

The reality of the Holy Trinity, of course, is a fundamental tenet of Orthodoxy. In the development of Eastern Orthodox dogma, the Orthodox Church gave official affirmation of the Trinitarian foundations of the church's evangelical faith principally through its development of the Nicene Creed in the fourth century. This ecumenical creed clearly connects to the characteristic evangelical interest in the identity, life, death, and resurrection of Jesus Christ.

Since the Nicene Creed is the most important ecumenical creed ever formulated, I doubt that a clearer, more universally confessed affirmation of evangelical identity could be given. The Nicene Creed forthrightly asserts the first distinctive of the evangelical identity given above: "Through the life, death, and resurrection of Jesus, God provided a way for the forgiveness of my sins."

Even the most ardent foes of Orthodox and evangelical compatibility cannot escape our centrally shared emphasis on *God's forgiveness in Jesus Christ.* It is the common ground of our Orthodox and evangelical identities. The historical circumstances surrounding the creation of this creed in its final form centered on Arianism (named after the heretic Arius, who denied the full divinity of God the Son). The first and second ecumenical councils of the church, held at Nicea in AD 325 and at Constantinople in 381, respectively, condemned the teachings of Arius and specified in detail how the Son of God and the Spirit of God were coequal with the Father within the mystery of the Holy Trinity.

The Nicene Creed remains unchanged by the Orthodox Church to this day. Its articles do not attempt to define the faith but to express it on behalf of the universal church. Anglicans, Wesleyans, Lutherans, and a few other Protestant denominations whose histories began centuries after the Nicene Creed's formation also quote it (usually with the later addition of the *filioque* clause—"who proceeds from the Father *and the Son*"); most evangelicals today, however, don't quote it because they fail to see the value of using creeds in worship.

The importance of the Nicene Creed in the Orthodox Church is witnessed to by the fact that by the fifth century it was used in all Sunday worship services and is still recited by parishioners every week and in the morning prayers of the faithful. It also served as a teaching tool for memorization by students in catechetical schools who were preparing for baptism, and it remains in use today as part of the baptismal liturgy when a convert gives his personal statement of faith in Jesus Christ as Lord and Savior. The Nicene Creed, therefore, is no incidental creed with which one may disagree on this point or that, but rather it is a universally agreed upon, authoritative consensus of the Eastern Orthodox faith throughout the world.

The Nicene Creed's basic soteriological assertion is that the Father, Son, and Holy Spirit are three persons who are fully equal in their commonly shared divinity within the eternal mystery of their inner Trinitarian relations. The fourth-century Cappadocian fathers—Saints Basil the Great, Gregory Nazianzus, and Gregory Nyssa—pointed out that the church's dogmatic creedal statements emerged out of worship and that it is supremely in worship that we are made aware of the element of mystery in our knowledge of God. Worship is the gift of participating through the Spirit in the incarnate Son's communion with the Father.

Following the language of the Nicene Creed, the Cappadocians discerned a double movement in the life of the Trinity—on the one hand, a movement of God toward humans, which operates from *(ek)* the Father through *(dia)* the Son in *(en)* the Spirit; and on the other hand, a movement of humans toward the Father through the Son in the Spirit. This double movement is the heart of the divine-human relationship in worship and is grounded in the very being of the triune God and his relationship with the world in creation, incarnation, and redemption. This Cappadocian understanding of the Trinity views God's primary purpose for humanity as relational and filial (i.e., humans are related to the Son of God, who brings our being into communion with God's being).

This Trinitarian approach to salvation has a direct bearing on the church's worship. It means that worship is the gift of participating in the incarnate Son's communion with the Father through the Spirit. It also means participating, in union with Christ, in what Christ has done for us in his self-offering to the Father in his life, death, resurrection, and ascension, and what he continues to do for us in the presence of the Father and in his mission from the Father to the world.

Our sonship and communion with the Father are our sharing by the Spirit of adoption in Christ's sonship and communion with the Father, and our sharing of that sonship and communion with one another. Nowhere is this communion better expressed liturgically than in the Eucharist (the Lord's Supper), for we are never more truly human than at the Eucharist, where Christ communicates his life to us while drawing us into his life of communion with the Father and into communion with one another.

The consequences of the Cappadocian approach to the Trinity, therefore, are far-reaching for Orthodox and evangelical understandings of salvation today. The Cappadocian approach is unifying, not divisive. It implies that the church is one, not many, and thus invites individuals to join in the

---

[14]Orthodox appeals to Protestant and Catholic communities in the past two decades to recover the centrality of the Cappadocian understanding of the Trinity have come most powerfully from Metropolitan John Zizioulas of Pergamon. Influential

church's participation in the Trinitarian life of God.[14] Moreover, the Cappadocian approach heals an unnecessary division that has been created by some one-sided evangelicals and misinformed Orthodox who wish to see the believer's receipt of the "imputed righteousness" of Christ as irreconcilable with the "participatory" language of the Cappadocians. On the contrary, the reason the righteousness of Christ can even be imputed to us in the first place is that we have been enabled by faith to "participate" in Christ, who is the righteous one. Both of these views ("imputed righteousness" and "participation") should be distinguished from "imparted righteousness," if it means that righteousness somehow becomes my own in a way that could be viewed apart from Christ himself.

What is noticeably lacking in the Nicene Creed is an explanation of *how* this salvation takes place.[15] The writings of the church fathers that surrounded the promulgation of the Nicene Creed throughout the fourth century did not take these statements as referring to the "substitutionary atonement" of Christ but rather utilized a variety of soteriological metaphors for how the Trinity, the Devil, and humans were engaged in the redemptive events. There is a formal absence of a universally authoritative theory on the death of Christ in the Nicene Creed, the later Chalcedonian Definition (AD 451), and all other authoritative documents of the early church. I agree with John McIntyre's explanation for the absence:

---

evangelical teachers and graduate students have begun to respond to Zizioulas's appeal, resulting in a clearly discernible intellectual movement within the evangelical community toward a recovery of Cappadocian theology in America and continental Europe (see John D. Zizioulas, *Being as Communion* (Crestwood, N.Y.: St. Vladimir's Seminary Press, 1985). In the academic world of evangelicalism see James Torrance, *Worship, Community and the Triune God of Grace* (Downers Grove, Ill.: InterVarsity Press, 1996). Unlike Zizioulas, with his penchant for dense writing, Torrance offers an intellectually rigorous exposition of Cappadocian theology but explains it in a clear manner alive with pastoral counsel; see also Colin E. Gunton, *The One, the Three and the Many* (Cambridge, U.K.: Cambridge Univ. Press, 1993) and his forthcoming sequel *From the Dust of the Earth,* which explores the relational nature of being—both divine and human; Thomas F. Torrance, *Trinitarian Perspectives: Toward Doctrinal Agreement* (Edinburgh: T & T Clark, 1994); and Miroslav Volf, *The Church as Communion* (Grand Rapids: Eerdmans, 1999), which offers a Free Church analysis of Zizioulas's and Catholic Cardinal Joseph Ratzinger's "communion ecclesiologies."

[15]The Greek preposition *dia* (*"for* us humans and *for* our salvation") gives us the reason for redemption, namely, "for our sake," not the manner of it, as would the preposition *anti,* meaning "in our place."

The first, and very important reason . . . must surely be the centrality not only of a soteriological theme, but of the direct connection between the death of Christ and the forgiveness of sins, to all the *eucharistic liturgies* of the Church [emphasis his]. . . .

The atonement effected by the death of Christ was more integral to the worship-life of the Church than to the thought-life of its theologians. . . .

The definitive text of 1 Cor. 11:24 ["Take, eat: this is my body, which is broken for you"] . . . has been enshrined at the heart of the eucharist from the earliest days of the Church. . . .

Another possible explanation of the difference in development between Christology and soteriology during the first five or six centuries of the Church's history may lie in the absence of protracted heretical attacks on established soteriological positions, to any degree comparable to the controversies which surrounded trinitarian and christological theories during the third to the fifth centuries.[16]

There is clearly a need for further study on the sacrificial vocabulary of the Eastern church in its eucharistic liturgies and patristic literature. Still, the evidence we have demonstrates that the Greek fathers went far beyond the sparse creedal statements in reference to the death of Christ and its relation to the forgiveness of sins, and that the Greek fathers' views often correlate with the Pauline views advanced by evangelical theologians today.[17]

This point is significant for our comparisons of Orthodox and evangelical soteriologies because, although there was unity in diversity among the Greek fathers, no single definitive theory of the atonement was advanced in the earliest tradition of the church to which Orthodox or evangelicals must give common

---

[16]John McIntyre, *The Shape of Soteriology: Studies in the Doctrine of the Death of Christ* (Edinburgh: T & T Clark, 1992), 8, 10, 14, 15.

[17]Very little research has actually been done on sacrificial terms in the Eastern fathers with the exception of Frances M. Young's doctoral thesis, *The Use of Sacrificial Ideas in Greek Christian Writers from the New Testament to John Chrysostom* (Cambridge, Mass.: Philadelphia Patristic Foundation, 1979). See Lars Koen's work on sacrificial terms in Saint Cyril of Alexandria (*The Saving Passion* [Philadelphia: Coronet Books, 1991], 122–31); and further patristic examples in *The International Standard Bible Encyclopedia*, fully revised, ed. Geoffrey W. Bromiley (Grand Rapids: Eerdmans, 1979), s.v. "Atone."

assent. And so we must ask, *Where lies heresy if there is no defined orthodoxy?*

The historical realities of the early church leave room for a variety of soteriological theories that, from the perspective of the Eastern church fathers, can accommodate a substitutionary view of the atonement. Nevertheless, there was clearly a widely held consensus on the primary connection between soteriology and the incarnation, and it is this connection that had such far-reaching consequences for the church's sacramental vision of redemption. In an assertion that became a classic summary of Orthodox soteriology, Saint Athanasius (c. 293–373), the chief adversary of Arius, declared that God became human so that humans might become divine.[18]

This statement encapsulates a very long tradition of Orthodox soteriology dating from at least the second century, as evidenced in Saint Irenaeus of Lyons if not in the New Testament documents themselves that contain the Pauline teachings on adoption, sonship, and the indwelling Spirit (Romans 8; Galatians 4) and John's promise of the gift of divine glory (John 17:5, 22–24). It assumes that the starting point of the fallen human predicament is *death* from sin, not *guilt*, and so *life* through Christ is the only appropriate redemption (Romans 5:12–21).

Athanasius's understanding of salvation as divinization, or deification (technically termed *theosis* as transliterated from the Greek language in other Greek patristic authors) provided the unifying theme underlying the entire history of Eastern Christian thought in the age of the ecumenical councils (AD 325–787) and even beyond through the writings of Saint Gregory Palamas in the fourteenth century, where the biblical story of the transfiguration becomes the dominant image for *theosis.* In fact,

---

[18]See Saint Athanasius, *On the Incarnation of the Word* (Crestwood, N.Y.: St. Vladimir's Seminary Press, 1976), par. 54. An ecumenical effort to recover the Eastern theme of deification for the Lutheran and Pentecostal traditions has been taken up recently by Dr. Veli-Matti Kärkkäinen, a systematic theology professor at Fuller Seminary who has been involved in Pentecostal-Orthodox dialogues (see his article "The Ecumenical Potential of *Theosis*: Emerging Convergences between Eastern Orthodox, Protestant, and Pentecostal Soteriologies," *Sobernost/Eastern Churches Review* 23:2 (2002): 45–77; see also his chapter "Salvation as Justification and Deification: The Ecumenical Potential of a New Perspective on Luther," in *Theology between West and East*, eds. Frank Macchia and Paul Chung [Lanham, Md.: University Press of America, 2002], 59–76). This is illustrative of an attempted soteriological rapprochement between Orthodoxy and evangelicalism.

it would not be an overstatement to assert that the entire history of Byzantine theology from the fourth to the fourteenth centuries constitutes an extended exegesis of the soteriological meaning of the incarnation in its great variety of implications relating to the doctrine of the Trinity, the church, the Bible, the sacraments, iconography, the spiritual life, and literally the entire material cosmos. The Johannine affirmation that "the Word became flesh and made his dwelling among us" (John 1:14) summarizes the revelatory content of that all-encompassing redemptive event.

What, then, did salvation as deification mean in the Greek patristic tradition? For Athanasius, the eternal relations between the Father and the Son had direct bearing on how one is to understand the person and work of Christ in human salvation. Athanasius argued that if the Son of God in his essential nature is "one with the Father" (*homoousios*, meaning "consubstantial") within the eternal being of the triune God, then there are far-reaching implications for our understanding of the incarnation and atonement. The incarnation must be regarded as falling within the inner life of God, and the atoning work of Christ must be connected to that reality. The atoning work of Christ, who is the mediator between God and humans, takes place within the incarnate person of Christ as the reconciling operation of the personal union of his divine and human natures. Hence the unity between Christ's incarnate "being" and his "acts" demands an integrated way of understanding the person and work of the Son in human salvation. On that basis, Christ's self-offering in death was a sacrifice in which he acted to pay the debts "on behalf of all" *(hyper panton)* and "in the place of all" *(anti panton)*[19]—an apparently clear reference to the doctrine of substitutionary atonement but not identical with the later medieval Roman version with its doctrinal corollaries of purgatory and indulgences.

There is no doubt that Christ "died for our sins" and that, in the words of Orthodox theologian Georges Florovsky, "the redeeming death is the ultimate purpose of the Incarnation."[20]

---

[19]See Saint Athanasius, *On the Incarnation of the Word,* par. 20. In their zeal to set in contrast the Orthodox and Protestant views of salvation, Orthodox writers have not always paid sufficient attention to the use of these prepositional distinctions *(anti, hyper).* Clearly there is a place for an Athanasian approach to substitutionary, or perhaps better to say "representative," atonement, through the incarnation, even if that approach differs from later Roman Catholic theories.

[20]Georges Florovsky, *Collected Works of Georges Florovsky,* vol. 3, *Creation and Redemption* (Belmont, Mass.: Nordland, 1976), 99. Protestant evangelicals sometimes

The redemptive work of Christ was fully representative and universal in its scope. Its vicarious efficacy derived from the union of his divine person with humanity in the incarnation, i.e., it was a vicarious humanity. Athanasius, therefore, closely linked together the personal with the ontological, creation with redemption, and incarnation with atonement. He took the atonement language of Scripture to refer to what takes place within the incarnate being of the Son of God in his ontological solidarity with humankind.

Athanasius is careful to point out that, when the Word became flesh, he did so in order that it would be possible for us to become divine—but not in the same sense in which Christ himself was God. Humans can never become God by nature, as though it were possible for us to become fourth persons of the

---

allege that the Orthodox reject the doctrine of substitutionary atonement. But the alleged lack of development of the doctrine of substitutionary atonement by Byzantine theologians appears to be due to the fact that the church's sacrificial terminology has not yet been sufficiently studied, especially in its liturgical usages. Florovsky acknowledges that "Christ did indeed take upon himself the sin of the world," but this is not "to be explained by the idea of a substitutional satisfaction, the *satisfactio vicaria* of the Scholastics. Not because substitution is not possible ..." (p. 102), and then Florovsky goes on to speculate against substitution in a fashion reminiscent of Abelard's opposition to Anselm. Florovsky, like John Meyendorff, Sergius Bulgakov, Timothy (Kallistos) Ware, John Karmiris, and other Orthodox theologians in the secondary literature of the past two or three generations, did not interact with the works of evangelical biblical scholars—or many other exegetes, for that matter—to interpret the death of Christ against the older Catholic theories. He appears, rather, to have consulted conservative biblical commentaries written by Anglican scholars such as B. F. Westcott, along with the works of New Testament lexicography written by sometimes liberal Protestant authors (such as F. Büchsel's article on Greek New Testament words for "redemption" in G. Kittel's *Theological Dictionary of the New Testament* [4:353–56]), to reject Anselm and the later Scholastics. But the biblical doctrine of the atonement espoused by evangelicals is not that of medieval Roman Catholicism, nor is it the same one necessarily rejected by the Fathers and modern Orthodox. Anselm's theory is not identical with the theories of the Reformers and their evangelical children. No single view of the atonement was ever elevated to the status of "orthodoxy" in Christian antiquity, nor does any have that status today, so that it is possible for some Orthodox to agree with the evangelical interpretation and others to disagree. Nevertheless, whether or not all Orthodox agree that Christ's sacrifice "satisfied divine justice by propitiating the Father," what is incontestable is that the consensus of the patristic tradition interprets Christ, the new Adam, as "representative" of humanity (by living, dying, and rising on behalf of the whole human race), and that his perfect sacrifice was offered "for our sins." On that there is no disagreement between Orthodox and evangelicals.

Trinity. On the contrary, humans become by grace what Christ was by his divinized human nature: "Christ deified that which he put on, and more than that, 'gave' it graciously to the race of humans."[21] We, then, can also be divinized by participating in the incarnate deified humanity of the Son.

Few evangelicals realize today that certain forms of popular evangelical worship reveal a surprising indebtedness to this Athanasian theme in Eastern Orthodox theology. The Orthodox emphasis on "Christ Is Victor" (*Christus Victor*) highlights Christ's death and resurrection as the conquest over the powers of evil and mortality. A number of Charles Wesley's hymns (e.g., "Love Divine, All Loves Excelling" and "O Thou Who Camest from Above") reflect the perspective of Greek patristic Christology, with its emphasis on human transformation through divinization.[22]

Orthodox Christology

Athanasius dealt masterfully with the divinity of Christ in human salvation. But in dealing with the problems of the Trinity, he raised all the more acutely a succeeding question over how the eternal Son of God could also be the human son of Mary. Saint Cyril of Alexandria (378–444), who also came out of the Alexandrian tradition, built the general platform of his Christology on that of Saint Athanasius. Cyril stressed the truth that Jesus Christ was one person and that the unity of Christ's divine

---

[21]Athanasius, *Against Arius*, bk. 1, par. 42. The motive for the incarnation was God's love more than his justice, honor, or glory. Anselm, John Calvin, and later evangelical writers certainly stress the love of God as a motive for redemption, but they seem to have lost the idea that humankind can still in any sense be "attractive" to God because of the ugly consequences of the fall. For Athanasius and the Greek fathers, love becomes the controlling imagery in the divine drama, even after the entrance of human sin, because, like a beloved garment that has been torn, fallen people remain attractive to God.

[22]The seventeenth-century Anglican authors Lancelot Andrewes (1555–1626) and Thomas Ken (1637–1710) influenced the theological perspectives of John and Charles Wesley. Some of Charles Wesley's hymns now popularized in evangelical worship emphasize the transformation of human nature into Christ's divinized humanity. The Orthodox writer Nicholas Lossky has demonstrated how the Greek patristic inheritance was mediated to the Anglican tradition in the work of Andrewes (see *Lancelot Andrewes the Preacher [1555–1626]: The Origins of the Mystical Theology of the Church of England* [Oxford: Clarendon, 1986]).

and human natures made possible salvation as deification *(theosis)*. God the Son brought together God and humanity within his own person, thereby making it possible for us humans to partake of the divine nature. The one person of Christ was the person *(hypostasis)* of God the Son, not a composite person created in Mary's womb from a union of two abstract natures. Here Cyril provides the grounds for contemporary Orthodox and evangelical unity. What sets us (and conservative Roman Catholics) apart from liberal Protestants (beginning with Friedrich Schleiermacher) is that liberals see the one person of Christ as a composite being, or (more likely) as being the man Jesus himself, rather than as "two natures in one divine Person" (as Cyril and the Council of Chalcedon maintained through their varied vocabularies).

The great strength of Cyril's Christology, however, lay in its strong sense of the sacramental. The sacraments of baptism and the Eucharist are ways in which the incarnate Christ communicates his divine life to believers in the church. Cyril's theology of the presence of Christ in the bread and wine is representative of contemporary Orthodox understandings of the Eucharist and takes on significant implications for ecclesiology. Cyril's eucharistic theology is best understood in the context of his attack against the accused heretic Nestorius, whose Christology was said to split Christ into two separate persons, one divine and the other human. One of Cyril's favorite biblical texts, which he used against Nestorius, came from verses 53 and 55 of the sixth chapter of John: "unless you eat the flesh of the Son of Man and drink his blood, you have no life in you. . . . Whoever eats my flesh and drinks my blood remains in me, and I in him."

This was a very powerful text for Cyril, who explained that this could not be "life-giving" flesh unless it had become the very flesh of the Lord who gives life to everything. Cyril argued that the Eucharist was a real participation in the life of the risen Lord. The consecrated bread and wine of the Eucharist were somehow really, yet mystically, the body and blood of Christ. It was not a memorial meal in the sense in which most evangelicals today view the Lord's Supper, but an eschatological presence in time and space of the risen, now present, and returning Lord.

Cyril did not try to explain the mystery but was content simply to affirm it as a long-standing apostolic tradition that even his adversaries had accepted.[23] That mystery was based on the foundation of the incarnation. If there were no real union between God and humans in the incarnation, then the Eucharist itself would be meaningless because the Eucharist must, in some way, be described as *God's* blood.

This differs markedly from the Christology of Cyril's opponent, Nestorius, which in reality tended to undermine the real union between the human and divine natures in Christ and instead "conjoined" or "juxtaposed" them. As Cyril was quick to point out, Nestorius's christological disjunction carried with it disastrous sacramental implications. Since there was no real union between the divine and human in the Nestorian Christ, neither could there be a real union between the divine and human in the Eucharist. Yet, Cyril insisted, the Eucharist was not just the blood of "a" man who happened to be "joined next to" the divine Christ. If pushed to the logical end of his Christology, Nestorius would have to admit that his Eucharist would not be the incarnate Christ's body and blood at all but simply human flesh, even a memorial meal in which the bread and wine remain unchanged and no real participation in Christ was possible or even necessary.

For Cyril, real communion with God was possible through the Eucharist because of the mystery that God ontologically united himself to humanity through the incarnation of Jesus Christ. The achievements of that union implied an inseparable connection between Christology and the Eucharist, and that connection correlates with the real presence of Christ in the Supper. In the Eucharist one mystically receives Christ through the bread and wine and is further united with him. A very serious difference exists at this point between the church fathers and modern evangelicals. Unlike the Orthodox, most evangelicals today have accepted Cyril's Christology while rejecting his corollary doctrine of the real presence of Christ in the Eucharist.[24]

---

[23]This view should not be confused with the later Catholic theories of "transubstantiation" or Post-Vatican II "trans-signification," but may be compatible with the Lutheran theory of a "real and bodily presence" (as distinct from the misleading label of the Lutheran view as "consubstantiation"). Orthodox eucharistic theology today retains its primitive simplicity. The church is content not to explain the mystery but to hymn and confess it doxologically.

[24]It is difficult to avoid observing a major theological inconsistency in evangelicals who give verbal allegiance to historic Christianity as represented by Cyril

In his replies to Cyril, Nestorius's Christology and anthropology also influenced his theology of good works in the Christian life. For Nestorius, and especially for his colleague Theodore of Mopsuestia, God created humans as a microcosm that held together the physical, intellectual, and spiritual worlds in one harmonious whole. The fall of humanity, however, introduced disharmony and death, which resulted in the separation of body and soul and the decay of the cosmos. The task of the incarnation of Christ, therefore, was to reintegrate and restore the old Adam to what he was before the fall. Christ enters the human race as our older brother and *moral example,* who leads the way in victory over the powers of death and the Devil. His strivings against the passions of the flesh and the forces of death become an example for our own moral strivings.

The obvious implication of this Christology is that it can easily lead to salvation by good works. It should come as no surprise that Nestorius later rehabilitated the heretic Pelagius, who taught precisely that belief. Cyril's rejection of Nestorian Christology, therefore, meant also the rejection of a "works righteousness" (to use the later language of the Reformers), and this goes far to answer some contemporary evangelical critiques of Orthodoxy as teaching salvation by works.[25]

These heresies, as well as those of Apollinarianism and Eutychianism that denied Christ's full humanity, eventually led to the famous Council of Chalcedon (AD 451). This council gave voice to the enduring standard by which Orthodox Christology would be measured to this day. The crucial section of the Chalcedonian Definition is as follows:

> Therefore, following the holy Fathers, we all with one accord teach men to acknowledge one and the same Son,

and the Chalcedonian Definition, while at the same denying the equally strong witness of the church's eucharistic doctrine of the real presence of Christ maintained by those same church fathers as a corollary to orthodox Christology and soteriology. Notwithstanding, here again we hear evangelical voices in high places calling the movement back to the historic faith of the undivided church. Along with the familiar works of Robert Webber, see Daniel H. Williams, *Retrieving the Tradition and Renewing Evangelicalism: A Primer for Suspicious Protestants* (Grand Rapids: Eerdmans, 1999).

[25]I agree with evangelicals who have noticed that some Orthodox writers provide evidence for a "works righteousness." Although some critiques are well grounded, such Orthodox writings should be regarded as christologically and anthropologically misguided and not representative of the central tradition itself.

our Lord Jesus Christ, at once complete in Godhead and complete in manhood, truly God and truly man, consisting also of a reasonable soul and body; of one substance (*homoousion*) with the Father as regards his Godhead, and at the same time of one substance with us as regards his manhood, like us in all respects, apart from sin; as regards his Godhead, begotten of the Father before the ages, but yet as regards his manhood begotten, for us men and for our salvation, of Mary the Virgin, the God-bearer (*Theotokos*); one and the same Christ, Son, Lord, Only-begotten, recognized in two natures, without confusion, without change, without division, without separation, the distinction of natures being in no way annulled by the union, but rather the characteristics of each nature being preserved and coming together to form one person (*prosopon*) and subsistence (*hypostasis*), not as parted or separated into two persons, but one and the same Son and Only-begotten God the Word, the Lord Jesus Christ; even as the prophets from earliest times spoke of him, and our Lord Jesus Christ himself taught us, and the creed of the Fathers has handed down to us.[26]

The Chalcedonian Definition provides the fundamental christological framework for Orthodox-evangelical compatibility as a substantially faithful rendition of the identity of Jesus Christ portrayed in Scripture. There is a strong bond of unity between us on the complete divinity and complete humanity of Jesus Christ that must not be taken for granted. Like assent to the Nicene Creed, assent to the Definition (as written, or in its Cyrillian expressions for the non-Chalcedonian Orthodox churches) requires an Orthodox Christian to give "strong agreement" to the statement in the Angus Reid Group survey of evangelical identity that "through the life, death, and resurrection of Jesus, God provided a way for the forgiveness of my sins." As an exegesis of the Nicene Creed, the Definition affirms that there are two natures (human and divine) in one divine person. This "hypostatic union," as it is technically known, set the boundaries within which the mystery of the incarnation is to be understood. Using both cataphatic and apophatic language,[27] the

---

[26]Cited in Henry Bettenson, *Documents of the Christian Church* (New York: Oxford Univ. Press, 1981), 72–73. The Definition is not a "creed," as it is so often wrongly called today, because it was never intended for liturgical use.

[27]The Greek church fathers distinguished two ways of theologizing about God: the *cataphatic* method, which proceeded by way of positive propositional affirmations

Definition affirms the mystery without offering a rational explanation as to how this is so.

As with the Nicene Creed, it is tempting to gloss over this authoritative document with a token, halfhearted recognition of its evangelical identity while maintaining an overriding voice of strong dissent over such differences as Mary's role as *Theotokos* and whether or not evangelicals really "follow the holy Fathers." However there is no difference between Orthodox and evangelicals over Mary's title as *Theotokos*, since the title says more about who the subject of Mary's birth was (i.e., the Word made flesh) than it does about Mary herself, and with this evangelicals concur, even if they know nothing at all about the history of the title itself. Their Mariological deficiencies in worship and piety have more to do with their failure to comprehend her christological significance in the Old and New Testaments than with any formal disavowal of her as the God-bearer. As the patristic tradition itself appears to indicate, the only dogmatic requirement of Orthodox Mariology is the *soteriological* confession of her as the birth-giver of the Son of God, and on this we strongly agree.[28]

---

about God, and the *apophatic* method, which proceeded by way of negative statements of what God is not, yet leading to a positive experience of the transcendent God. Apophatic language was the church's way of recognizing the inadequacies of human language in expressing the fullness of divine truth. The Definition acknowledges this inadequacy chiefly in its use of the four negative adverbs "without confusion, without change, without division, without separation." The mystical theology of the Orthodox Church is shot through with this sort of language. However, Vladimir Lossky's classic work *(The Mystical Theology of the Eastern Church)* appears to have overstated the apophatic character of the Greek fathers' method of theologizing, which can easily lead us to an "apophatic agnosticism"—a kind of "since we cannot know, we cannot say" position that leaves no room for revelation. Lossky did not deny cataphatic propositions in principle but appears to do so in his exposition. Saint Gregory Palamas denounced this position in his attack on the apophatic agnosticism of Barlaam the Calabrian and his excessive reliance on Pseudo-Dionysius the Areopagite.

[28]"The only doctrinal definition on Mary to which the Byzantine Church was formally committed is the decree of the Council of Ephesus [repeated by Chalcedon], which called her the *Theotokos,* or 'Mother of God'.... So the Byzantine church, wisely preserving a scale of theological values which always gave precedence to the *basic* fundamental truths of the Gospel, abstained from enforcing any dogmatic formulation concerning Mary, except that she was truly and really the *Theotokos,* 'Mother of God'" (John Meyendorff, *Byzantine Theology* [Bronx, N.Y.: Fordham Univ. Press, 1981], 148, 165). Leading Orthodox writers disagree on what is truly dogmatic on the issue of whether the epithets for Mary as "Ever-Virgin," "All Holy," and "New Eve" should also be considered as official church dogma that is necessary for salvation. See Vladimir Lossky, *In the Image and Likeness of God* (Crestwood, N.Y.: St. Vladimir's Seminary Press, 1981), 195–96; Florovsky, *Collected Works,* vol. 3, *Creation and Redemption,* 171.

As to whether evangelicals "follow the holy Fathers," both sides concur that nothing can contradict Scripture, and thus to follow the holy Fathers is to follow their interpretations and holiness insofar as they accord with biblical truth. Yet, as we observed earlier, nonsacramental evangelicals (as compared with Lutherans, Anglicans, and followers of some branches of the Reformed faith) are not consistent about this when it comes to embracing the fullness of holy tradition, particularly regarding the Fathers' understanding of the close connection between Christology, soteriology, and the real presence of Christ in the Eucharist.

Christological Maximalism

The enormous consequences of Chalcedonian Christology on the remainder of the history of Byzantine theology from the fifth to the fourteenth centuries were very far-reaching indeed. Unlike the Byzantine fathers, however, only a small number of influential evangelical thinkers have begun to grasp the depth of the inseparable connections between Christology and the whole of the Christian life. *Our greatest differences, therefore, can be seen in the tensions that arise between evangelicalism and Orthodoxy over what one could describe as "christological minimalism" versus "christological maximalism."* In the final remarks of this section, I can only provide a schematic outline of how the church's christological maximalism affected its vision of salvation and shaped its particular evangelical identity.

Following Athanasius, the Cappadocian fathers, the Nicene Creed, Cyril of Alexandria, the Chalcedonian Definition, and a great deal more than I can allude to here, the christological maximalism of the Orthodox Church in its Trinitarian framework takes the implications of the incarnation light-years beyond the christological minimalism of the evangelical movement! For the fathers of the Eastern church, the incarnation became the medium of theological integration in all its rich complexity. The mystery of the incarnation required a theological method that integrated the whole of Christian truth and spiritual experience in the person of Jesus Christ. We have already sketched how this was done when the Fathers integrated Christology and soteriology with its corollaries of eucharistic theology and good works. Further implications of this cosmic event were drawn out for the Christian understanding of creation, iconography, the knowability of God, and the role of the body in prayer. Literally, all creation was believed to have been affected by the salvation wrought by the incarnate Lord, and therefore everything material now carries with it the potential to be restored. The "goodness" of created matter has been sanctified through "the Word made flesh" and can thus become a vehicle of saving grace through the church's physical sacraments, by its audible proclamation of the gospel, by pen and parchment of the written Word, by the visible witness of the church's art, by the blessing of the physical body in prayer, as well as in the earthly routines of everyday life.

Several examples will illustrate the christological principle from which all of life finds its meaning. In biblical interpretation, the church fathers viewed Christ himself as the hermeneutical key who unlocks the meaning of the Old Testament and relates the promises of the old covenant to their fulfillment in the new. In Scripture itself, the human and divine natures of the written text were seen as similar to (but certainly not identical to) the coexistence of the human and divine natures of Christ. Eschatologically, the doctrine of "the last things" was not taken solely as the final stage in the temporal plan of redemption but also as the breaking in of the kingdom of God in preliminary form here and now in the earthly realities of bread and wine in the Eucharist in a manner analogous to the human and divine in Jesus Christ.

In Christian art, the incarnation formed the basis for the justification of icons in the iconoclastic controversy of the eighth and ninth centuries. Building on Scripture and the conclusions reached by the Council of Chalcedon nearly three hundred years earlier, the Orthodox drew out the implications of the incarnation for Christian art, arguing that icons function as educational tools, models of saints' lives, witnesses to the ultimate transfiguration of the cosmos, and, above all, dogmatic confessions in lines and colors that "the Word became flesh and made his dwelling among us" (John 1:14).

In the church's worship, the commemoration and celebration of redemption was further proclaimed in a conspicuously visible way in the development of the liturgy. In the church's symbolic and ritual proclamations of Christ, time and again the Byzantine liturgy communicated the message of salvation through the death, resurrection, and ascension of Christ. Even the church's architectural design witnessed to the redemption of the created order by stressing the immanence of God in Christ. The domed ceiling of the magnificent Church of the Holy Wisdom in Constantinople, adorned on the inside with a large icon of Christ—"the Ruler over All," who looks down from heaven—communicated the Good News that "God is with us!" by its very architectural embrace of the worshipers below. As worshipers enter the nave of the church, the salvific words of John 3:16 are at times inscribed on the inside of the domes of some churches. The church building gives worshipers an eschatological orientation by facing the people east toward the sanctuary, which is a witness that the kingdom of God is "already" inaugurated in the preaching of the Word and the giving of the Eucharist, but that it will "not yet" be fully realized until the last day when Christ returns. The priest's garments, the incense, the candles, and a myriad of other elaborate symbols in the Byzantine liturgy all testify to Christ's crucifixion, death, and resurrection, and the forgiveness of sins through him. Even the practice of venerating saints, relics, and holy places has no other foundation than the simple conviction of faith in the bodily resurrection of Christ.[29] In virtually all of the church's worship the great theological themes of the Trinity and Christ are transformed into doxological celebrations. Orthodox liturgiologist Alexander Schmemann described it this way:

> The Byzantine service, as already observed, is a blend of the dogmatic achievements of the preceding period in liturgical form. It is almost entirely adorned with the colors of the Trinity and of Christology.... For centuries these liturgical riches were to be the main source of knowledge and religious life and inspiration in the Orthodox world; and in the darkest ages, when traditions were broken and education became rare, people in the Church would rediscover again and again the spirit of universal, all-embracing, and inexhaustibly profound Orthodoxy in its golden age.[30]

---

[29]"We are *all* saints by grace, but we must *become* saints by our acts and in our whole being" (John Meyendorff, *The Orthodox Church: Its Past and Its Role in the World Today*, 4th rev. ed. [Crestwood, N.Y.: St. Vladimir's Seminary Press, 1996], 175 [italics in the original]). This is a close equivalent to the "indicative/imperative" or "positional/progressive" structure of Christian sanctification outlined in the New Testament in which believers are called to "be" by grace what we already "are" by virtue of our position in Christ.

[30]Alexander Schmemann, *The Historical Road of Eastern Orthodoxy* (Crestwood, N.Y.: St. Vladimir's Seminary Press, 1977), 227–28.

Finally, in the mystical theology of the Eastern church, great saints such as Symeon the New Theologian (949–1022) and Gregory Palamas (1296–1359) taught by word and life the need for a direct, personal experience of the triune God through Christ and his church. In particular, Gregory Palamas, the last great theologian and mystic of the church, synthesized the preceding centuries of patristic tradition concerning the knowledge of God, Christology, and anthropology. In what became known as the famous "essence/energies" distinction in the Trinity, Palamas clarified the difference between God's unknowable essence and his knowable energies.

Based on the earlier Council of Chalcedon, as well as on the theology of Saint Maximus the Confessor (c. 580–662), Palamas strenuously defended the church's teaching that a direct, personal experience of God himself *(theosis)* was accessible through God's energies made available through the hypostatic union of the two natures of Christ. The incarnate Word hypostasized human nature and acted in accordance with the divine and human wills. There was thus a sharing of attributes *(communicato idiomatum)* whereby the humanity of Christ was penetrated by the divine energies and thereby deified. Those divine energies, which we partake of, were not understood as an impersonal "something" from God but as God himself because Christ is consubstantial *(homoousios)* with the Father. Through the incarnate Christ, God gives himself to us in such a living, personal way that the gift and the giver are one and the same. This "union according to energy" becomes accessible to all those who are in Christ through repentance and faith. It was Palamas's defense of the knowability of God through participation in the sacraments of baptism and the Eucharist, and the monastic practice of *hesychasm* (stillness), with its psychosomatic methods of prayer (not to be confused with yoga), that gave to Orthodoxy its personalist emphasis on Christian spirituality.

In summary, the content of the evangelical soteriology of the Orthodox Church is Jesus of Nazareth, God's only-begotten Son, who became what we are by being born of the Virgin Mary, the *Theotokos*, and who suffered and died on the cross, rose from the dead, and ascended into heaven. He did this that we might by grace become what he is, so that all those who put their faith in him may be joined to him and participate in the fellowship he shares within the life of the Holy Trinity and be joined with one another in his body, the church.

The church preaches this Good News and celebrates the resurrection and its life-giving power in its sacramental life and its worship of God the Father through the Son in the Holy Spirit. It may be said, therefore, that over the entire course of Eastern Orthodox history, Christ himself, as one of the Holy Trinity, was the unifying medium through which the church interpreted the whole range of Christian doctrine, worship, and spirituality. Thus, it is precisely this incarnational Trinitarian model that unites Orthodoxy and evangelicalism in a christological minimalism and at the same time sharply divides them in their understanding of the larger consequences of a christological maximalism that embraces and sanctifies the entire cosmos as an eschatological presence and promise of the kingdom of God.

Evangelical Identity #2: "The Bible Is the Inspired Word of God and Is to Be Taken Literally, Word for Word" (Biblicism)

Following a consistently incarnational Trinitarian approach to salvation, which I have outlined above, Orthodoxy's understanding of the Bible and its authority in the life of the church is equally personalist in its emphasis. As in salvation, so also in theological authority, the correct starting point for answering the question of Orthodox-evangelical compatibility is not "What?" but "Who?" Just as the question, "What is salvation?" was answered by the prior question, "Who is Christ?" in the church's Trinitarian and christological reflections from the fourth to the fourteenth centuries, so also the question, "What is the authority of Scripture?" is resolved in the prior answer to "Who is truth?" We do not begin our theological inquiries with abstract questions over the possibility of belief in God, arguments for his existence, and the grounds for belief, which are all outside of divine revelation, and then, only after those questions have been answered, proceed to the Christian doctrines of the Trinity and the incarnation. On the contrary, Orthodoxy begins where the New Testament and the church's liturgy would have us begin—with the reality of the Father-Son relationship given to us in Christ and into which we are drawn by the Spirit. In the words of the Nicene Creed, "I believe in one God, the Father Almighty, . . . and in one Lord Jesus Christ."

Doctrinal authority, like salvation itself, begins not with a verification of possible belief in God as a hypothesis but with trust in a person. This may seem a very natural perspective to the great majority of common believers because it accords well with the experience of countless Christians down through the centuries. But this simple and direct approach to knowing God is quite central, even though much of evangelical scholarship today has turned it upside down, notably within the Reformed wing of evangelicalism—which is often more representative of seventeenth-century Reformed Scholasticism than it is of John Calvin himself. Rational propositions *are* necessary to inform us of how we may be saved, but they need not be developed the way the Scholastics did in order to be theologically valid.[31]

Today the Scholastic perspective is slowly being challenged by trusted voices within the evangelical community. James Torrance, for example, has admitted the fatal error of Reformed Scholasticism and is calling evangelicals back to the church fathers and to an authentic recovery of John Calvin's historic

---

[31]In Europe (and to a lesser extent in America) the traditional pattern of theological education begins in the first year with a study of the philosophy of religion in which students consider arguments for the existence of God, the meaning of miracles in a scientific age, the nature of verification and falsification, and so on. Once a rationale for believing in God has been established outside of revelation, only then, in the second year, are the Christian doctrines of the incarnation and the Trinity taught, as though tacked on to a previous conception of an Aristotelian abstraction about God. I once had a conversation with the late evangelical theologian Carl Henry about the role of reason. I'll never forget his comment about what a Christian college curriculum would look like if he were to construct it: "I would start the curriculum with a study of the Greek philosopher Plato and from there move eventually into the study of Christian theology." Now I have nothing but the highest admiration for Dr. Henry, but I couldn't help wondering, *How in the world did the person of Jesus Christ fail to outdo Plato!* Dr. Henry would no doubt have provided a plausible answer to this question if I had thought to ask him just then, and I'm sure it would have focused on our differing presuppositions about theological epistemology. Nevertheless, the contrast in our approaches to authority was illustrative of the wider epistemological gulf that began in the early centuries between the Cappadocian East and the Augustinian West. The development of the Scholastic method in the West began as early as the second century with Tertullian and continued with Augustine, then Aquinas, and on through the analytical tradition that comes from Descartes and the way of thinking in external relations embodied in Isaac Newton and Immanuel Kant (i.e., the Enlightenment). In the end, Scholasticism alone is the culprit, not the Augustinian tradition or the Reformers per se. See the critique of Scholasticism by Thomas F. Torrance, *Karl Barth: Biblical and Evangelical Theologian* (Edinburgh: T & T Clark, 1990), 213–40; see also the defense of Reformed Scholasticism through a hostile and dismissive critique of Torrance by Richard A. Muller, "The Barth Legacy: New Athanasius or Origen Redivivus? A Response to T. F. Torrance," *Thomist* 54 (1990): 673–704.

approach to theology—which Torrance sees as being consistent with the Cappadocian fathers. Even though Torrance represents a distinctively Scottish voice in modern theology, his book *Worship, Community and the Triune God of Grace* challenges evangelicals across the continents to reconstruct the manner in which they worship and think about God, so they can more appropriately reflect who God is and what he has done for us in Christ by the Holy Spirit.[32] Similarly, from within the Evangelical Free Church denomination, Ray Anderson has advocated an incarnational approach, particularly as it relates to the person and ministry of Christ, as the basis for both revelation and reconciliation.[33]

So when we compare Orthodoxy with evangelicalism, the two methodological forms and norms with which we are working are these (even if they are not always in evidence): (1) the Orthodox, with their belief that all genuine theological knowledge is to be ontologically grounded in a person vis-à-vis an incarnational Trinitarian approach to Scripture that both "witnesses to" and "propositionally informs us about" God's revelation in Christ, and (2) most Protestant evangelicals, with their generally dualistic—if not epistemologically Nestorian—methodology inherited from the Scholastic heritage, which starts not with a person but with a written text, the Bible, telling us about the person of Jesus Christ (although trusted voices are slowly being heeded within the evangelical movement—voices calling for theological reform in a Nicene and Chalcedonian direction).[34]

---

[32]See James Torrance, *Worship, Community and the Triune God of Grace* (Downers Grove, Ill.: InterVarsity Press, 1997).

[33]See Ray Anderson, *The Shape of Practical Theology: Empowering Ministry with Theological Praxis* (Downers Grove, Ill.: InterVarsity Press, 2001), especially chapters 5 and 8.

[34]The differences are reminiscent of the contests between "personal" (Christ himself) and "propositional" (Scripture) forms of revelation within the evangelical community in its reaction to Karl Barth. It would be an overstatement to label Orthodox theology as "Barthian," but the similarities are clearly there, because Barth was essentially a "catholic" theologian of the wider church, including the patristic tradition. But the connection between personal revelation and propositional revelation hasn't been adequately explored by Orthodox theologians, past or present; writers such as Georges Florovsky and Dumitru Staniloae have written on the subject but have not, in my opinion, adequately understood the inseparable relationship between these two forms of revelation. The problem itself derives from making a disjunction between personal and propositional revelation, which itself is but a further instance

Interpretation and Inspiration

With that general orientation stated, and since the limitation of space prevents us from analyzing patristic texts, liturgical prayers, and the hymnography of the Orthodox tradition, we will limit our remarks to the more specific areas of compatibility in matters of biblical exegesis and inspiration. In the area of biblical exegesis, Orthodoxy consistently manifests and tolerates a hermeneutical pluralism that generally falls within the third- and fourth-century Alexandrian school of *allegorical exegesis* or the Antiochene school of *literal exegesis* (which recognized metaphorical language and figures of speech as part of the literal sense). If one were to use the creation narrative of Genesis as a test case to find a homogeneous Orthodox position, evidence from either of these two schools would be seen, depending on which patristic author was consulted (Augustine and Basil the Great following a generally allegorical approach, and Chrysostom following a more literalist interpretation). The church's liturgical rites and ascetical writings generally follow a blend of Alexandrian allegory and Antiochene typology or *theoria* (the "fuller sense" of Scripture, which at times overlaps typology but can also be a separate principle of patristic exegesis). Yet it was the Antiochene literalist, Saint John Chrysostom, who was venerated as the greatest preacher and exegete of all the patriarchs in the Byzantine Empire. Contemporary Orthodox exegetes most often utilize the literal approach of Antioch without requiring a strict twenty-four-hour interpretation of the Genesis account of creation.

Since evangelicalism today does not specify any particular brand of literalism as constitutive of its identity (unlike certain strands of its fundamentalist wing), and the historic definition of Orthodoxy does not oblige one to follow any particular school

---

of the false dichotomy set up by the Protestant Scholastics and others between Scripture and tradition, a dichotomy that implies an adversarial relationship between the two. The answer one gives to the relation between Scripture and tradition, therefore, will essentially be that which applies to the question of personal and propositional revelation. The Orthodox understanding of Scripture and tradition given in this section provides the foundation for the church's answer, which will see personal and propositional revelation not entirely as either/or but both/and with God's *primary* revelation of himself being *personal* through Jesus Christ, which is witnessed to by the ongoing apostolic preaching and worshiping tradition of the church, yet which is also *propositional* through the written Word which tells us *about* the personal Word.

of exegesis but embraces both the Alexandrian and Antiochene models as useful in varying contexts, Orthodoxy's marriage with evangelicalism on this subject is harmonious. This is particularly evident in the shared preferences of modern Orthodox and evangelical authors for the literal method. Commonly used textbooks on Scripture by Orthodox and evangelical biblical scholars show that both endorse the use of historical criticism in the modern writing of biblical commentaries and monographs, and to that extent, both may be considered biblical literalists.

In the area of biblical inspiration, among the most authoritative documents we can consult to assess Orthodox-evangelical compatibility are the "Agreed Statements" between Orthodox and non-Orthodox Christians in their ecumenical dialogues over the past thirty years. These statements do not enjoy the authority of the early ecumenical councils, but because of their communal character they represent the response of the church's living tradition in the face of contemporary Christian pluralism and are therefore more officially representative of Orthodoxy than are the opinions of any single theologian. An Orthodox theology of biblical inspiration and interpretation is well expressed in the "Common Declaration" of the Anglican-Orthodox Joint Doctrinal Commission adopted in Moscow during the Commission's session in the summer of 1976:

> The Scriptures constitute a coherent whole. They are at once divinely inspired and humanly expressed. They bear authoritative witness to God's revelation of himself in creation, in the incarnation of the Word and in all the history of salvation, and as such they express the Word of God in human language. We know, receive, and interpret Scripture through the church and in the church. Our approach to the Bible is one of obedience so that we may hear the revelation of himself that God gives through it. The books of Scripture contained in the canon are authoritative because they truly convey the authentic revelation of God....
>
> Any disjunction between Scripture and Tradition such as would treat them as two separate "sources of revelation" must be rejected. The two are correlative. We affirm (1) that Scripture is the main criterion whereby the church tests traditions to determine whether they are truly part of Holy Tradition or not; (2) that Holy Tradition

completes Holy Scripture in the sense that it safeguards the integrity of the biblical message.[35]

In addition to the Moscow Statement, the "Agreed Statements" of the more recent international Lutheran-Orthodox Joint Commission add further points of consensus:

> The decisions of the ecumenical councils and local synods of the church, the teaching of the holy fathers and liturgical texts and rites are especially important and authoritative expressions of this manifold action of the Holy Spirit. However, not every synod claiming to be orthodox, not every teaching of an ecclesiastical writer, not all rites are expressions of the holy Tradition, if they are not accepted by the whole church. They may be only human traditions, lacking the presence of the Holy Spirit. That is why the problem of the criteria for determination of the presence of the holy Tradition in the traditions of the churches is of great importance and needs further study....
>
> The function of holy scriptures is to serve the authenticity of the church's living experience in safeguarding the holy Tradition from all attempts to falsify the true faith (cf. Heb. 4:12, etc.), not to undermine the authority of the church, the body of Christ.
>
> Regarding the relation of scripture and Tradition, for centuries there seemed to have been a deep difference between Orthodox and Lutheran teaching. Orthodox hear with satisfaction the affirmation of the Lutheran theologians that the formula *sola Scriptura* was always intended to point to God's revelation, God's saving act through Christ in the power of the Holy Spirit, and therefore to the holy Tradition of the church ... against human traditions that darken the authentic teaching in the church....

---

[35]*Anglican-Orthodox Dialogue: The Dublin Agreed Statement 1984* (Crestwood, N.Y.: St. Vladimir's Seminary Press, 1985), 50–51. Over twenty "Agreed Statements" have been put out by the Orthodox in their relations with the Oriental Orthodox, Catholics, Old Catholics, Anglicans, Reformed, and Lutherans, not to mention papers given in the Faith and Order Commission of the World Council of Churches. The Orthodox are currently seeking ways to open a dialogue with Methodists and Baptists. For a historical overview of the dialogues, see Günther Gassmann, ed., *International Bilateral Dialogues, 1965–1991, Fifth Forum,* Faith and Order Paper No. 156 (Geneva: WCC Publications, 1991); Alan D. Falconer, ed., *Seventh Forum on Bilateral Dialogues,* Faith and Order Paper No. 179 (Geneva: WCC Publications, 1997).

Inspiration is the operation of the Holy Spirit in the authors of the holy scripture so that they may bear witness to the revelation (John 5:39) without erring about God and God's ways and means for the salvation of humankind....

Expressions and concepts of biblical authors about God are inspired because they are unerring *guides* [emphasis theirs] to communion with God....

Authentic interpreters of the holy scripture are persons who have had the same experience of revelation and inspiration within the body of Christ as the biblical writers had. Therefore it is necessary for authentic understanding that anybody who reads or hears the Bible be inspired by the Holy Spirit. The Orthodox believe that such authentic interpretation is the service of the fathers of the church especially expressed in the decisions of the ecumenical councils.[36]

These ecumenical documents demonstrate compatibility between Orthodoxy and evangelicalism on the inspiration of Scripture, especially since inerrancy is not a required hallmark of evangelical identity today (though in Orthodoxy one can be an inerrantist, as were some of the Fathers). The disagreement within evangelicalism is over what the reliability of Scripture means rather than over whether Scripture is reliable. One cannot disbelieve the Bible and still be an evangelical. So Orthodox and evangelical Christians share a common allegiance to the evangelical identity described by Bebbington's "biblicism," namely, that "the Bible is the inspired Word of God." As quoted above, the delegates of the Moscow conference specifically state that the Scriptures are "at once divinely inspired and humanly expressed." Likewise the Lutheran-Orthodox agreement maintains, "Inspiration is the operation of the Holy Spirit in the authors of the holy scripture so that they may bear witness to the revelation (John 5:39) without erring about God and God's

---

[36]*Lutheran-Orthodox Dialogue: Agreed Statements 1985-1989* (Geneva: Lutheran World Federation, 1992), 11, 15–17, 26. Although few Orthodox seem to be aware of it, the confessional debates within Lutheranism have influenced some of the theological vocabulary of these ecumenical documents, which supports more liberal Lutheran positions that may become problematic for some Orthodox in the future. The failure to qualify the distinction between biblical inspiration and contemporary personal inspiration is a case in point. The use of the term "guides" also subtly leads the Orthodox away from accepting the notion of propositional revelation.

ways and means for the salvation of humankind." Moscow further qualifies Scripture as the "main criterion" for testing truth and error in church tradition, while the Lutheran-Orthodox agreement also sees no discord between the Lutheran doctrine of *sola Scriptura* and Orthodoxy's view of the relation between Scripture and tradition.

Orthodoxy and Sola Scriptura

These agreements have not been sufficiently appreciated by members of either the evangelical movement or the Orthodox Church. It is an ecumenically hazardous exercise when Orthodox and Protestant theologians who are experts on their own traditions engage in dialogue without defining their terms or having a responsible understanding of the other's theological vocabulary and the diversity of opinions that exist within it.

In few places is this more evident in the secondary literature than when comparisons are made with reference to the doctrine of *sola Scriptura* (generally viewed as Scripture being the main criterion for faith and practice). Different assessments result from different definitions of this phrase.[37] The key problem is over how the various Reformers interpreted *sola Scriptura* in relation to church tradition.

Members of the Radical Reformation (Anabaptists) maintained that the Bible is all that is needed and that church councils, creeds, church fathers, and liturgies have no significant role to play in the theological formulation of the faith. The private judgment and conscience of an individual's interpretation of Scripture stand above the corporate judgment of the church. The Magisterial Reformation (Luther, Calvin, and Anglicans), however, upheld

---

[37]Orthodox authors: "for [the Orthodox] the Christian faith and experience can in no way be compatible with the notion of *Scriptura sola*" (John Meyendorff, "Light from the East? 'Doing Theology' in an Eastern Orthodox Perspective," in *Doing Theology in Today's World*, ed. John D. Woodbridge and Thomas Edward McComisky [Grand Rapids: Zondervan, 1991], 341); Sergius Bulgakov, *The Orthodox Church*, trans. Lydia Kesich (Crestwood, N.Y.: St. Vladimir's Seminary Press, 1988, from 1935 original), 21ff. An evangelical use of the Anabaptist definition of *sola Scriptura* with divisive results can be seen in the unpublished *Eastern Orthodox Teachings in Comparison with the Doctrinal Position of Biola University*, prepared by Robert L. Saucy, John Coe, Alan W. Gomes (April 13, 1998). The common definition of *sola Scriptura* assumed by the authors was that of the radical wing of the Reformation in which the Bible was not just the final authority but the exclusive authority.

the church's traditional interpretation of Scripture and viewed the church fathers, councils, creeds, and liturgies as valuable guides to the correct understanding of Scripture. They were not ambivalent toward tradition, but stood only against its abuses. Scripture was still the primary authority for faith and practice, but it was not the only authority.

The Reformers' diversity of attitudes toward the abiding values of Christian history has left their modern evangelical children with no commonly developed theology of tradition. The lack of clarity over which Protestant definition of *sola Scriptura* is in use when comparing evangelical and Orthodox views of Scripture has resulted in an ambivalent legacy of tensions that has contributed to its perception as an irreconcilable issue.

The ecumenical documents quoted above acknowledge the church as the final interpreter of the Bible, while Scripture itself is the main criterion of the church's authority. The Moscow document explains that "Holy Tradition completes Holy Scripture in the sense that it safeguards the integrity of the biblical message." This does not forbid individuals from making personal judgments or discourage them from engaging in critical scholarship, but it does mean that private opinions, as learned as they might be, are not to be preferred to the experience of the saints and the church's rule of faith down through the centuries. The church, the Bible, and Holy Tradition form an unbreakable unity of checks and balances wherein Scripture is given the most authoritative voice on matters of faith and practice.

To add further historical reflections of my own on this subject, it is relevant to point out that, chronologically, tradition is anterior to Scripture because it transmitted the gospel within the liturgical community of the church. By the end of the first century that apostolic tradition was enshrined in written texts. The church later decided which texts constituted the canon of Scripture by "recognizing" their apostolic origins, content, and usage within the worshiping community. This did not mean that Scripture owed its *inherent* authority to the church—which comes only from the Spirit of God and not a legal institution such as the pope or conciliar institutions[38]—but that the church was inseparably

---

[38]For Orthodoxy, the ecumenical councils were not viewed as legal institutions but as charismatic witnesses to the unity of the faith accepted by the people of God in communion with their local bishops according to no formal criteria of reception other than an organic, Spirit-illumined insight into the matters of faith. In an

united with its sacred texts as the *mediating* authority that simply authenticated what was already there within its own life.

Whether they are aware of it or not, when evangelicals give assent to the canonical texts, they are simultaneously validating the church's tradition as an *authoritative norm of canonicity*, just as it has actually functioned within the life of the Orthodox Church itself. A consistent application of the Anabaptist meaning of *sola Scriptura* would seem to permit individual believers the freedom to include or to exclude whatever books of the Bible they felt so led by the Spirit to remove. It also abducts the Bible from the very church that acknowledged the canon, by saying, in effect, "Thank you, early church, for recognizing which books belong to the Bible. Now give it here, and I'll tell you what it all means and how wrong you've been in interpreting it!" The irony of this disdain is that evangelicals rely on the church's authoritative charismatic judgment on the colossal issue of canonicity but not on its consensual agreement on fundamental matters of historic interpretation, such as the sacramental meaning of baptism and the real presence of Christ in the Eucharist (however differently that real presence was defined by the Latin and Greek traditions). *In contrast to nonsacramental forms of Protestant evangelicalism, the Orthodox perspective is more internally consistent: To accept the books of the canon is also to accept the ongoing Spirit-led authority of the church's tradition, which recognizes, interprets, worships, and corrects itself by the witness of Holy Scripture.*

Evangelical Identity #3: "I Have Committed My Life to Christ and Consider Myself to Be a Converted Christian" (Conversionism)

The redemptive purposes of the Holy Trinity and incarnation of Christ are eloquently expressed in the conversion theology of the Orthodox Church. This conversion theology is manifested through the prayers that are offered to God in the church's baptismal rites of initiation.

---

illuminating essay on this subject, Georges Florovsky states that the "ultimate authority [of Church councils] was still grounded in their conformity with the 'Apostolic Tradition.'. . . It will be no exaggeration to suggest that Councils were never regarded as a canonical institution, but rather as occasional *charismatic events* [emphasis his]" (Georges Florovsky, *Collected Works of Georges Florovsky,* vol. 1, *Bible, Church, Tradition: An Eastern Orthodox View* [Belmont, Mass.: Nordland, 1972], 95–96).

Baptism and Faith

The Orthodox baptismal liturgy is an evangelical sacrament of the church's symbolic and ritual proclamation of Christ that summons us and our children to costly faith and discipleship. Because of its enormous influence on the evangelical identity of the Orthodox Church, I will cite the questions and answers and quote the central prayers of the baptismal rite that every repentant sinner confesses upon his or her entrance into the church, thereby showing what conversion to Christ entails.

> *The sponsors with the child [or adult] . . . stand facing the priest. The priest asks the following question three times:*
> Do you renounce Satan and all his angels and all his works and all his service and all his pride?
> *The sponsor or adult to be baptized responds each time:*
> I do.
> *The priest asks the next question, likewise three times:*
> Have you renounced Satan?
> *Again the sponsor or adult to be baptized responds each time:*
> I have.
> *Then the priest says:*
> Breathe and spit on him. (*Spit*)
> *The priest asks three times:*
> Do you unite yourself to Christ?
> *Each time the sponsor or adult answers:*
> I do unite myself to Christ.
> *The priest then asks:*
> Have you united yourself to Christ?
> *The sponsor or adult answers:*
> I have united myself to Christ.
> *The priest asks:*
> Do you believe in him?
> *The sponsor or adult answers:*
> I believe in him as King and as God.
> *The candidate then recites the Nicene Creed.*

After the recitation of the creed, the priest again asks the sponsor or adult (three times) whether they have united themselves to Christ. He then asks them to bow down before God. The priest then leads in this prayer:

O Master, Lord our God, call thy servant _____
to thy holy illumination and grant him/her that great
grace of thy holy baptism. Put off from him/her the old
man, and renew him/her unto life everlasting; and fill
him/her with the power of thy Holy Spirit, in the unity
of thy Christ, that he/she may be no more a child of the
body, but a child of thy kingdom. Through the good will
and grace of thine Only-begotten Son, with whom thou
art blessed, together with thy most holy and good and
life-creating Spirit, now and ever and unto ages of ages.

The priest then blesses the water by dipping the fingers of
his right hand into it and tracing the sign of the cross three times.
He breathes on the water and says:

Let all adverse powers be crushed beneath the sign
of the image of thy cross. *(Repeat three times.)* We pray
thee, O God, that every aerial and obscure phantom may
withdraw itself from us; and that no demon of darkness
may conceal himself in this water; and that no evil spirit
which instills darkening of intentions and rebelliousness
of thought may descend into it with him/her who is
about to be baptized.

But do thou, O Master of all, show this water to be
the water of redemption, the water of sanctification, the
purification of flesh and spirit, the loosing of bonds, the
remission of sins, the illumination of the soul, the bath
of regeneration, the renewal of the Spirit, the gift of
adoption to sonship, the garment of incorruption, the
fountain of life. For thou, O Lord, has said: 'Wash and
be clean; put away evil things from your souls.' Thou
has bestowed upon us from on high a new birth through
water and the Spirit. Wherefore, O Lord, manifest thy-
self in this water, and grant that he/she who is baptized
therein may be transformed; that he/she may put away
from him/her the old man which is corrupt through the
lusts of the flesh, and that he/she may be clothed with
the new man, and renewed after the image of him who
created him/her: that being buried, after the pattern of
thy death, in baptism, he/she may, in like manner, be a
partaker of thy resurrection. . . .

After the one being baptized is anointed with oil through the sacrament of chrismation, the priest then dips a sponge in pure water and sprinkles the candidate, saying, "Thou art justified! Thou are illumined! Thou art sanctified! Thou art washed in the Name of the Father, and of the Son, and of the Holy Spirit. Amen."[39]

In this liturgical setting the evangelical theology of the Orthodox Church is very vividly confessed. The conversion theology of the liturgy is directly tied to the incarnational Trinitarian understanding of salvation previously analyzed in this chapter. The necessity of personal faith in Jesus Christ as Lord and Savior is made absolutely clear through the direct questions that are powerfully addressed to the candidate no less than three times by the priest, along with the candidate's public declaration of Jesus as his/her personal King and God and a solemn confession of the Nicene faith. No mistake can be made about the free gift of salvation given by the unmerited favor of God's grace, or the sufficiency of the redemptive work of Christ on the cross[40] and his triumph over sin, death, and the Devil.[41]

Reflecting a strongly Pauline and Johannine theology, the liturgy confesses that through baptism we enter into the inner life of the Trinity (Matt. 28:19–20) and thus are saved (1 Pet. 3:21), regenerated (John 3:5; Titus 3:5–6), united with Christ in his death

---

[39]See Antiochian Orthodox Archdiocese, *Service Book of the Holy Eastern Orthodox Church*, 3d ed. (1960), 146–65.

[40]Literally, every time an Orthodox believer sincerely crosses himself, from the moment of his baptism to the time of his death, he reaffirms the life-giving power of the cross. Through this very meaningful symbol of dedication and confession, the pious believer daily recalls his baptismal vows of personal commitment to and co-crucifixion with Christ. "Make this sign as you eat and drink, when you sit down, when you go to bed, when you get up again, while you are talking, while you are walking; in brief, at your every undertaking" (Cyril of Jerusalem, "Catechetical Lectures," 4.14, in *Library of Christian Classics*, vol. 4 (Philadelphia: Westminster, 1963), 106.

[41]"Deep-level healing" and spiritual "power encounters" between Satan, God, and believers, rediscovered relatively recently by Protestant evangelicals, have long been recognized in the ancient liturgies and monastic spirituality of the Orthodox Church. They are recognized, for instance, in the baptismal service through the rite of exorcism and the personal renunciation of the Devil and all his works. Once again we see the evangelical community rediscovering the richness and relevance of Christian antiquity and inadvertently moving ever closer to a more Orthodox holistic vision of life in Christ. See Charles Kraft, ed., *Behind Enemy Lines* (Ann Arbor, Mich.: Servant, 1994); Charles Kraft, *Deep Wounds, Deep Healing* (Ann Arbor, Mich.: Servant,

and resurrection (Rom. 6:3–8; Gal. 3:27), adopted (Rom. 8:23; Gal. 4:5), justified (Rom. 5:12–6:12), incorporated into his body, the church (1 Cor. 12:13), and made partakers of the divine nature (2 Pet. 1:4). All these biblical and liturgical images are different ways of showing how God makes us his own through Jesus Christ.

Unlike the baptismal theology of nonsacramental evangelicals, who think that baptism is an outward picture of one's previous conversion experience apart from baptism, the baptismal language of the Orthodox service sees the Holy Spirit as the divine agency of redemption in water baptism, though the water itself does not save. Through the work of the Holy Spirit, water baptism is the occasion at which time God brings about the believer's co-death and co-resurrection with Christ, so that the physical symbol and spiritual reality are inseparably and efficaciously united.[42]

Is baptism unconditionally efficacious in the performance of the rite? No. Faith is needed, both Christ's and our own (or that of the baptismal sponsors in the case of infants). This faith is exercised within an ecclesial context by the covenant community of faith. Baptism is linked to the covenant community of the faithful. Personal faith is expressed by the godparents, who belong to the covenant community, on behalf of the child. After

---

1993); and Janice Strength, "From Conflict to Love: Suggestions for Healing the Christian Family," in *God in Russia: The Challenge of Freedom,* ed. Sharon Linzey and Ken Kaisch (Lanham, Md.: University Press of America, 1999). Janice Strength is a family therapist with self-consciously Orthodox leanings. Cf. Timothy Warner, *Spiritual Warfare* (Wheaton, Ill.: Crossway, 1991) and Neil Anderson, *Victory Over the Darkness* (Ventura, Calif.: Regal, 1990).

[42]Due to the strong influence of Orthodoxy in Russia, Russian Baptist evangelicals, in contrast to their American counterparts, endorse much of this same sacramental theology but exclude infant baptism. In America, see similar sacramental views expressed by the Baptist G. R. Beasley-Murray (*Baptism in the New Testament* [Grand Rapids: Eerdmans, 1962]), the famous Anglican from Fuller Seminary G. W. Bromiley ("Baptismal Regeneration," in *The International Standard Bible Encyclopedia,* vol. 1 [Grand Rapids: Eerdmans, 1979], 428–29; Geoffrey Bromiley, *Children of Promise* [Grand Rapids: Eerdmans, 1979]), and the Anglican Michael Green ("Baptism," in *The Complete Book of Everyday Christianity* [Downers Grove, Ill.: InterVarsity Press, 1997], 58–62). Tensions over the meaning of baptism remain unresolved, if largely avoided, by the evangelical community. The problem is a perennial one among Anglican evangelicals because the Book of Common Prayer declares that infants are regenerated through baptism. One conclusion to be drawn is that, if solid sacramental Anglicans such as Bromiley and Green, who believe in the regeneration of infants in baptism, are considered card-carrying evangelicals, nothing should prevent evangelicals from recognizing the same in the Orthodox.

being baptized, the child himself is to be spiritually nurtured by his parents, godparents, and the covenant community. He or she must deliberately choose to follow Christ and accept the church's faith at every step of his or her life, from infancy onward.

This is one reason why the Orthodox Church is theologically self-consistent by practicing infant communion. The communion service is a time of continual renewal through self-examination, repentance, and genuine faith, which the child is supposed to learn from the earliest years of life. Clearly, the vast majority of evangelicals would be extremely uncomfortable with this Orthodox perspective on baptism, since evangelicals stand in sharp contrast to anything close to baptismal regeneration, let alone infant baptism.[43] So the problem of compatibility between Orthodox and evangelicals is very serious in this area and should not be minimized for the sake of unity.

Nevertheless, the late Orthodox liturgiologist Alexander Schmemann provides an explanation for the church's sacramental theology: "According to the Church's teaching, the *validity* of sacraments does not, in any way, depend on either the holiness or the deficiencies of those who perform them [i.e., the priest]."[44] Later in his book he writes, "Baptism does not and indeed cannot 'depend' for its *reality* (i.e., for truly being our death, our resurrection with Christ) on personal faith. This is not because of any deficiencies or limitations of that personal faith, but only because Baptism depends—totally and exclusively—on Christ's faith."[45] Schmemann also makes this observation:

> There is a difference—not only in degree but also in essence—between the faith which *converts* an unbeliever or a non-Christian to Christ, and the faith which constitutes

[43]Yet evangelicals should acknowledge that even one of their staunchest conservative defenders of the doctrine of biblical inerrancy, Dr. Gleason Archer, professor emeritus of Old Testament and Semitic Languages, Trinity Evangelical Divinity School (Deerfield, Illinois), supports the practice of infant baptism from a Calvinist perspective with its stress on the importance of the covenant community. Paradoxically, while Archer does not believe in baptismal regeneration per se, he does accept the validity of infant baptism and the role of sponsors in nurturing the (unregenerate?) faith of a baptized child.

[44]Alexander Schmemann, *Of Water and the Spirit* (Crestwood, N.Y.: St. Vladimir's Seminary Press, 1974), 44.

[45]Ibid., 68.

the very life of the Church and of her members.... But the former is a *response* to the call while the latter is the very *reality* of that to which the call summons.... It is his personal faith in Christ which brings the catechumen to the Church; it is the Church that will instruct him in and bestow upon him Christ's faith by which she lives. Our faith in Christ, Christ's faith in us: the one is the fulfillment of the other, is given to us so that we may have the other. But when we speak of the Church's faith—the one by which she lives, which truly *is* her very life—we speak of the presence in her of Christ's faith, of Him Himself as perfect faith, perfect love, perfect desire. And the Church is life because she is Christ's life in us, because she believes that which He believes, loves that which He loves, desires that which He desires. And He is not only the "object" of her faith, but the "subject" of her entire life [emphases his].[46]

The Orthodox view of the candidate's ability to believe is not based on Augustinian anthropology, which renders human beings incapable of making a positive spiritual response to God's call, but on the conviction that humans possess a capacity for freedom of choice even after the fall.[47] In the words of Saint Maximus the Confessor, sin is a "personal" or hypostatic choice ("gnomic" will) based on the exercise of free will given to every human person, rather than a function of "nature" ("natural" will), which is the common characteristic of all human nature that is intrinsically inclined toward God, though weakened by the fall. The will is "in bondage" (to use Martin Luther's terminology), but that bondage is limited. Repentance remains an enduring possibility, even in the darkest of hearts.

The Orthodox understanding of free will rejects the need for a special act of God's prevenient grace, because grace belongs to the image of God himself, which includes the freedom of

---

[46]Ibid., 67–68.

[47]Augustine's doctrine of inherited guilt was disharmonious with the wider "catholic" tradition of Greek and Latin patristic theology before and during his time. See Bradley Nassif, "Towards a 'Catholic' Understanding of St. Augustine's View of Original Sin," *Union Seminary Quarterly Review* 39, no. 4 (1984): 287–300; David Weaver, "From Paul to Augustine: Romans 5:12 in Early Christian Exegesis," *St. Vladimir's Theological Quarterly* 27 (1983): 187–206; idem, parts 2-3, "The Exegesis of Romans 5:12 Among the Greek Fathers and Its Implications for the Doctrine of Original Sin: The 5th–12th Centuries," *St. Vladimir's Theological Quarterly* 29 (1985): 133–59, 231–57.

choice given to humans in creation and remaining within them in a dysfunctional condition even after the fall. Our basic orientation, or compass, toward God and the freedom to choose him remains intact, yet we fail to see that compass clearly or to exercise that freedom to believe and obey properly, because our will is now wayward and because sin has dramatically blurred our ability to see God and know ourselves.

For the Greek church fathers, sin was understood not primarily as a deliberate act of willful disobedience (which it is) as much as the inability to see and know God and ourselves clearly (which is the fundamental meaning of the Greek term *hamartia* in the New Testament, literally rendered "a missing of the mark") because of a misguided will that has freely chosen to leave the path of union with God. Freedom and orientation is not the problem; recognizing and acting obediently on that orientation is.

In Orthodox baptismal theology, therefore, salvation is accomplished only through the paradox of divine initiative and a non-Pelagian human response. The candidate for baptism merely responds to and cooperates with that divine grace by actively welcoming it into his or her heart by faith and then living out this baptism through active obedience on that same principle of unmeritable synergism. Divine grace and human cooperation are never read in opposition to one another or viewed as mutually exclusive. Faith is both a divine gift and the free response of the human person. Saint John Chrysostom aptly affirms, "All indeed depends on God, but not so that our free will is hindered."[48] This is the basis for Orthodox asceticism and its goal of deification *(theosis)* as the content of salvation.[49]

Saint Mark the Ascetic (c. 390) offers perhaps the clearest statement in all of Orthodox literature showing that we are not made righteous by our good works but that true faith will man-

---

[48]John Chrysostom, "Homily 12 on The Epistle to the Hebrews," in Philip Schaff, *Nicene and Post-Nicene Fathers*, ser. 2, vol. 14 (Grand Rapids: Eerdmans, 1974), 425.

[49]The intersection between Orthodoxy and evangelicalism in the area of Christian spirituality is very likely the most dynamic manifestation of their common ground. Like evangelicalism, "mystical theology" for the Orthodox Church implies an inseparable union of *doctrine* and *experience* in the Christian life, not a subjective spiritual experience apart from God's revelation in Christ. Nicene Trinitarianism and Chalcedonian Christology provide the common theological foundations for Orthodox and evangelical spirituality, though evangelicals generally have not been consistent in the outworking of these foundations for their understanding of creation, the sacraments, iconography, and related areas. Once more, however, evangelicalism

ifest itself in good works—and that without good works a person does not have genuine saving faith. In his treatise "On Those Who Think They Are Made Righteous by Works," he achieves the balance between Jesus, Paul, and James:

> When Scripture says "He will reward every man according to his works" (Mt 16:27), do not imagine that works in themselves merit either hell or the kingdom. On the contrary, Christ rewards each man according to whether his works are done with faith or without faith in Himself; and He is not a dealer bound by contract, but God our Creator and Redeemer.[50]

The "Necessity" of Baptism

Further questions arise over the Orthodox understanding of baptism and redemption: How does baptism relate to Orthodox-evangelical unity in light of the candidate's confession of the Nicene Creed, which relates Jesus' death and resurrection to the "one baptism for the remission of sins"? Is baptism *necessary* for salvation? Can non-Orthodox, nonsacramental evangelical people of genuine faith—Presbyterians, Baptists, Methodists, Evangelical Free Church members, Mennonites, charismatics, nondenominational groups, and so on—be considered as members of the "one holy catholic and apostolic church," which the

at the beginning of the third millennium is correcting itself in an Orthodox direction by redefining evangelicalism chiefly as a movement united by a common life-changing experience of spiritual transformation that is cradled in a shared theology, which differs from the older emphases of evangelical identity described by Mark Noll and the Angus Reid Group report. Stanley Grenz and Donald Bloesch are the prominent systematic theologians for this approach, while evangelical spiritual writers such as James Houston, R. Paul Stevens, Eugene Peterson, Dallas Willard, Rodney Clapp, and Jennifer Bakke apply those concepts to their advocacy of spirituality as growth into Trinitarian love and the incarnational covenant community. Charles Metteer, adjunct professor at Fuller Seminary, teaches courses on "Desert Spirituality for City Dwellers" in an attempt to reappropriate the ancient monastic ideals for evangelical spirituality today.

[50]Saint Mark the Ascetic, "On Those Who Think They Are Made Righteous by Works: Two Hundred and Twenty-six Texts," #22, in *The Philokalia*, vol. 1, trans. G. E. H. Palmer, Philip Sherrard, and Kallistos Ware (London: Faber and Faber, 1979): 125–46. The centrality of the evangelical emphasis on the role of Scripture in Eastern Christian spirituality is amply documented in Douglas Burton-Christie, *The Word in the Desert: Scripture and the Quest for Holiness in Early Christian Monasticism* (New York: Oxford Univ. Press, 1993).

Orthodox Church believes itself to be? Can even the Quakers, who do not believe in celebrating physical sacraments at all, be considered as members of the body of Christ? Are there members of the Orthodox Church who, by their confession of the Nicene Creed, are not visibly connected to the Orthodox Church?

Bishop Kallistos Ware puts into perspective the relation between the unity of the church and the doctrine of salvation as he comments on Saint Cyprian's famous dictum, "Outside the Church there is no salvation":

> Does it therefore follow that anyone who is not visibly within the Church is necessarily damned? Of course not; still less does it follow that everyone who is visibly within the Church is necessarily saved.... While there is no division between a 'visible' and an 'invisible Church,' yet there may be members of the Church who are not visibly such, but whose membership is known to God alone. If anyone is saved, he must *in some sense* be a member of the Church; *in what sense*, we cannot always say....
>
> Different Orthodox would answer in different ways, for although nearly all Orthodox are agreed in their fundamental teaching concerning the Church, they do not entirely agree concerning the practical consequences which follow from this teaching.[51]

Orthodox "rigorists" hold that anyone who is not Orthodox cannot be a member of the church. However, "moderate" Orthodox theologians, including this author, adopt an affirmative stance toward the ecclesial status of non-Orthodox Christians because we believe this has been the church's historic position. There are also other compelling reasons one can point to that arise from an exegesis of Scripture's teaching about the relation between baptism and the reception of the Holy Spirit, the rites for receiving converts, the tension held by Orthodox mystical writers between "Spirit" and "institution," and the close personal contacts many of us have had with evangelical Christians that tell us this must be so. Only a few words can be said concerning the reception of converts into Orthodoxy and concerning the biblical and patristic testimony, which form the basis of my convictions.

---

[51]Timothy (Kallistos) Ware, *The Orthodox Church* (Baltimore, Md.: Penguin, 1997), 247–48, 308.

The liturgical reception of converts into the Orthodox Church today does not usually require historic Protestants or Catholics to be rebaptized if their previous baptism was done in the name of the Holy Trinity, because there is only "one Lord, one faith, one baptism" (Eph. 4:5). The question is not rebaptism at all, but whether or not the person was truly baptized in the first place. If they were, then no second baptism is required,[52] but only a public confession of the Orthodox faith and a blessing on the convert with oil and prayers through the sacrament of chrismation (the Eastern equivalent of the Western "confirmation").[53] Chrismation, therefore, is intended not as a *negative* judgment against the convert's past but as a *positive* blessing on their past conversion as authentic and the joyful celebration of their entrance into the church as the fulfillment and completion of the fullness of the Orthodox faith that was previously lacking.

The ecumenical consequences appear to be highly relevant to Orthodox-evangelical unity. If there is only one authentic baptism possible for each person, then Orthodox and evangelical believers are either in the body of Christ or out of it. If someone has come to Christ with a sincere heart of repentance and faith and has been baptized in the name of the Holy Trinity, then they are clearly "in Christ." And if they are "in Christ," they can be nowhere else but "in the church"! If the Orthodox accept as valid the baptism of Baptists and other Free Church types of evangelical converts who come into the church, but deny that other Protestant evangelicals from these same denominations, who have had the very same baptism as its converts

---

[52]The unconditional baptism of all converts by some rigorist Orthodox ministers today is actually an innovative departure from the well-established practice of the Orthodox Church, which has always accepted as valid the previous Trinitarian baptism of its converts. The same is true with the reception of Catholic priests: no second ordination is required because the first one performed in the Roman Church is viewed as valid.

[53]Baptism-Chrismation-Communion all form a unified rite of initiation in the Orthodox Church. Theologians have differed over whether the Holy Spirit is given in baptism or chrismation. John Zizioulas dismisses the importance of prioritizing one over the other because the work of the Spirit and the work of Christ are inseparably united: "there is … evidence suggesting that baptism itself was inconceivable in the early church without the giving of the Spirit, which leads to the conclusion that the two rites were united in one synthesis both liturgically and theologically, regardless of the priority of any of the two aspects over the other" (John D. Zizioulas, *Being as Communion* [Crestwood, N.Y.: St. Vladimir's Seminary Press, 1985], 128–29).

have had, are also in the same body of Christ, then we are denying the reality of our common "one baptism in Christ." To some extent, therefore, the consistent application of our conversion theology impels us to have a visible manifestation of the common life and witness we already possess with each other, even if we are not and cannot be in full communion because there is not yet full agreement in the faith.

As to whether baptism is "necessary" for salvation—in the sense that if one is not baptized, one cannot experience the forgiveness of sins and the gift of the Holy Spirit—the most truthful answer has to be both yes and no, even if the question itself would have been unnatural in the apostolic age. This is a sticking point for evangelicals, but it's important for the Orthodox as well, because baptism is intimately connected with repentance and faith. The answer is yes in the sense that baptism was the necessary concomitant to repentance and faith in the preaching and practice of the apostolic age, but no in the sense that God's sovereignty in bestowing forgiveness and the gift of the Holy Spirit at times transcends the normally necessary occasion for receiving the redemptive benefits given at the time of baptism.

I realize that few Orthodox have so plainly acknowledged this and that some will even take offense at my answer. It is sometimes said that the word "necessary" is misguided because it is reductionistic, seeking only the bare minimum of what a person must do to be saved rather than embracing the wider ramifications of soteriology inherent in the gospel, or that the question itself derives from "the West," as if to imply that it has theologically defective DNA since it comes from a Scholastic mentality foreign to the mind of the Eastern church. In truth, however, the question is very helpful because it forces us to be faithful to the maximalist vision of the church's theology. The question does not just arise from the West but is also related to our current practices of the reception of converts; the New Testament's teaching on the meaning of salvation as it relates to repentance, faith, and baptism; and the church fathers' commitment to the mystery of divine sovereignty in human salvation.

The first thing that must be said is that there is little question that the New Testament knows of no unbaptized Christian. Repentance, faith, and baptism were viewed as an inseparable trilogy. It is "normally necessary," not in the sense of "causation," as though the water itself automatically produces redemption, but it is necessary in the sense of "concomitance," meaning that repentance, faith, and baptism all naturally belong together (e.g., Acts 2:38; 22:16) and that baptism is not an optional extra but is that which goes along with repentance and faith. Ultimately, it is the grace of God that saves, not any one of these apart from the other (or isolating redemption to any one moment connected with the three), so that we can say it is the whole triad together that constitutes the time of Christian initiation.

A careful reading of the book of Acts makes it immediately apparent that there was never a presentation of the gospel without a reference to baptism, or else we could never explain the immediacy with which people were baptized as was quite dramatically seen in Acts 16:25–34. Baptism follows faith both naturally and necessarily. Thus Paul can say that both belief with the heart and confession with the lips (at baptism) are the prerequisite of salvation (Rom. 10:9–10). As its natural expression, faith demands baptism; for its validity, baptism demands faith. Two dangers to be avoided are faith without baptism, and baptism without faith (cf. 1 Cor. 10:1–6). Thus the New Testament evidence may be summarized as follows: Repentance, faith, and baptism leads to salvation as forgiveness and the receipt of the Holy Spirit (Acts 2:38; 16:31).

In addition, not only was baptism the "normally necessary" rite of Christian initiation universally practiced during the apostolic age; it was also employed as such throughout the universal church, East and West, until the time of the Protestant Reformation. One must neither reject nor relativize baptism for cultural or theological reasons. But neither can we restrict the sovereignty of the Spirit by putting God in a sacramental box. To say that baptism is always and unconditionally "necessary" would be to denounce our own liturgical rites in the reception of nonsacramentalist converts whose baptism was done in the name of the Trinity but who did *not* believe in its soteriological benefits at the time they were originally baptized because they did not know it to be efficacious. Yet the Orthodox Church accepts their baptisms as valid, even though at the time of their original baptism many believed that they had been given new life through Christ at some time before or, rarely, during or even after being baptized.[54] If the church today were suddenly to disavow this established

---

[54]Orthodoxy does not automatically acknowledge the validity of these and other denominations' baptisms apart from a pastoral inquiry of converts on an

practice, it would pronounce a negative judgment on itself by calling into question the salvation of those who have already been granted entrance into the church on the basis of their previous Protestant baptism and subsequent confession of the Orthodox faith.

The wisdom of the church's flexibility in this matter is borne out by Scripture. The book of Acts shows that all statements about the action of God in baptism must make allowance for the divine freedom in bestowing salvation and the Spirit. This is illustrated at Pentecost when the Spirit was poured out on men and women who had not previously received Christian baptism in "the name of Jesus Christ" (Acts 2:38; possibly shorthand for the Trinitarian formula of Matthew 28:19). The accounts of the Samaritan believers (Acts 8:14–17), Cornelius and his company (Acts 10:44–48), and the Ephesian "disciples" (Acts 19:1–7) who received the Spirit before or after being baptized (not during) were also not likely solitary examples of divine sovereignty in the complex relationship between baptism and the bestowing of the Holy Spirit in the early church.

These incidences remind us that life is more complex than formulations of doctrine and that the church recognizes that God is able to meet every variation from the norm in the apostolic age and subsequently throughout church history. Even Saint Gregory Nazianzus recognized important exceptions to the normal necessity of receiving baptism in the case of martyrs whose baptism was made valid by desire or by fire.[55]

Moreover, a post-baptismal personal experience of the Spirit coming and flooding the life is not denied by the Orthodox understanding of baptism. In fact, the greatest spiritual writers of the Eastern church speak of it as the antidote for nominal faith and liturgical legalism. Such experiences are recognized as the genuine fulfillment of baptism by Saints Makarius of Egypt (c. 300–390) and Symeon the New Theologian (949–1022),[56] who acknowledged that any water baptism that is unaccompanied by a conscious experience of God's presence in the heart cannot save. Makarius's and Symeon's witness successfully navigates

---

individual basis. But such inquiries still have not prevented the church from accepting these baptisms as valid.

[55]Gregory Nazianzus, *Oration* 39:17; 40:23.

[56]See *The Pseudo-Makarius: The Fifty Spiritual Homilies and the Great Letter* (New York: Paulist, 1992); *Symeon the New Theologian: The Discourses*, trans. C. J. DeCatanzaro (New York: Paulist, 1982).

the tension in Orthodoxy between "the Spirit" and so-called "institution" by carrying an evangelical message of genuine conversion for those Orthodox who have undergone the formality of baptism but live in an experiential denial of its life-giving power through their failure to repent and follow Jesus as Lord of their lives. Paradoxically, therefore, the church contains within itself the internal resources for spiritual renewal and internal evangelism, because the cure for both nominality and ecclesial idolatry does not come from ecclesial minimalism or ecclesial dissent but from ecclesial authenticity.

Evangelical Identity #4: "It Is Important to Encourage Non-Christians to Become Christians" (Activism)

Is there any evidence that an Orthodox incarnational Trinitarian approach to life has had a positive, lasting influence on any given culture or community? Has the church's spiritual communion with God been translated into an evangelistic concern for the salvation of its neighbors?

The evangelical message of repentance and faith in Jesus Christ is supremely revealed in the mission theology of the Orthodox Church. The soteriology implicit in the Trinitarian life of God, the incarnation of the Son, and the conversion theology of the church's baptismal liturgy and mystical writers, described all throughout this chapter, lies at the heart of Orthodoxy's missionary activity and social action. The spiritual and material vitality of the Orthodox Church in the Byzantine Empire (fourth to fifteenth centuries) is a case in point. The Byzantine church and state organized the first Christian social welfare system devoted to caring for the sick, the needy, and the disabled. In "imitation of Christ," the "human-loving Lord," the attribute of divine philanthropy (*philanthrōpia*, Titus 3:4) was emulated and enculturated throughout the empire by establishing hospitals and homes for the poor, orphaned, blind, aged, mentally ill, and repentant prostitutes—all under the care of ecclesiastical units. In all this, the spiritual salvation of both the giver and the beneficiary was stressed.[57]

Outside the empire, the history of missions in Russia, Eastern Europe, and the West provides ample evidence of Orthodoxy's evangelical conviction that "it is important to encourage

---

[57]See D. J. Constantelos, *Byzantine Philanthropy and Social Welfare* (New Brunswick, N.J.: Rutgers Univ. Press, 1968).

non-Christians to become Christians." The church's principles of carrying out evangelism wherever it went were almost universally applied: using the vernacular in preaching and translating the Bible, liturgy, and the Fathers; implementing indigenous clergy; and eventually establishing the local autonomy of a national church.

A key missions method was the use of the liturgy, i.e., the church itself as witness. During the Middle Ages the results of missionary work often included a package deal of political and religious alliances with the Byzantines, yet on the deeper level the missionaries sought the personal conversion of the people and the founding of local Orthodox churches. The goal of evangelism was to convert people to Christ and to the fullness of truth, as it is known in the Trinitarian God.[58]

The Orthodox witness today, however, is admittedly weak throughout the world, due in part to the legacy of Communist and Islamic domination over the church as well as to an internal emphasis on ethnic traditions more than the transcultural message of the gospel. The situation is very gradually improving but still has a long way to go in terms of economic recovery as well as in Christian education and spiritual adjustments to the religious and social effects of globalization, pluralism, and the challenges of Western missionary activity. At the same time, some renewal movements within the Orthodox Church itself have brought people to personal faith in Jesus Christ as Lord and Savior as well as to a revived interest in worship, Bible study, preaching, and the study of the church fathers.[59]

In America, a pan-Orthodox mission organization, founded in Florida under the name Orthodox Christian Mission Center, sends missionaries to poor and underdeveloped countries. Related expressions of spiritual and social concern can be found in the outreach ministries of the Orthodox Christian Prison Min-

---

[58]For a brief survey of the history and theology of Orthodox missions, see Bradley Nassif, "Orthodox Mission Movements," and James Stamoolis, "Orthodox Theology of Missions," with bibliographies, in *Evangelical Dictionary of World Missions,* ed. A. Scott Moreau (Grand Rapids: Baker, 2000), 413–15; Luke Veronis, *Missionaries, Monks, and Martyrs* (Minneapolis: Light & Life, 1994).

[59]For example, The Lord's Army in Romania, the Zoe movement in Greece, the Orthodox Youth Movement in Lebanon, the Brotherhood of Saint Symeon the New Theologian in America, and the evangelical missionary work of the Antiochian Orthodox Church in America headed by Peter Gillquist, a former Campus Crusade for Christ leader.

istry and the International Orthodox Christian Charities. There is also a clearly "American Orthodox theology" that is emerging among some of its theologians in response to both positive and negative forms of evangelical influence, as well as in reaction to American religious pluralism and the ethical challenges of postmodernism. The Standing Conference of the Canonical Orthodox Bishops in the Americas (SCOBA) recently christened the third millennium with a public assessment of the spiritual darkness of the human condition and an exhortation to their flock in America to fulfill the church's missionary vocation to preach the gospel and renew itself through personal repentance.[60]

In these few representative examples of how Orthodoxy has been communicating the gospel to both body and soul, Eastern Orthodoxy expresses its commonly held belief with evangelicalism that "it is important to encourage non-Christians to become Christians."

CONCLUSION

I have maintained in this chapter that Orthodoxy and evangelicalism are largely compatible according to the criteria of evangelical self-definition; however, they are significantly less compatible according to Orthodox self-definition. Indeed, if I had used the Orthodox self-definition as my criterion for answering the larger question of compatibility, my response would have been a carefully qualified no. It would have been a carefully qualified no, not because we fail to share the very same principles of the evangelical faith as our Protestant brethren, but because the Orthodox Church has comprehended the larger cosmic and ecclesial consequences of that commonly shared faith in a way evangelicalism has not. Orthodoxy embraces all the principles of the gospel that evangelicals hold but transcends them in the outworking of their implications.

I would like to offer two analogies in an attempt to summarize my vision of the relationship between Orthodoxy and evangelicalism. First, the core doctrines of Orthodoxy and evangelicalism can be seen as two concentric circles, with the smaller circle (evangelicalism) being inside and embraced by the other

---

[60]SCOBA, "And the Word Became Flesh and Dwelt Among Us: A Pastoral Letter on the Occasion of the Third Christian Millennium," available on the Web at www.antiochian.org/News/SCOBA_MillenniumPastoral20001217.htm.

larger one (Orthodoxy). The inner circle includes doctrines that both groups hold as essential; the larger outer circle includes doctrines the Orthodox hold to be essential but evangelicals generally do not.

In my second analogy, the differences in doctrinal development can be compared to the relationship that exists between a seed (evangelicalism) and the more developed and mature tree (Orthodoxy). Great theological potential exists in the seed of evangelicalism, which has much (if not all) that is needed for developing into the fuller tree of Orthodox life and thought; likewise, the tree of Orthodoxy has developed from the seed of evangelical faith contained in the gospel of Jesus Christ. (These analogies are not intended to be developed beyond these simple comments, lest they inadvertently muddy the very waters we are trying to clear up.)

Now, if evangelicals are going to be self-consistent, they have no other choice but to strongly affirm and support the Orthodox Church, because all that they are is abundantly present in it. Likewise, if the Orthodox are going to be self-consistent, they have no other alternative but to strongly support and affirm evangelicals, insofar as the fundamental tenets of evangelicalism are deeply embedded within the doctrine, sacraments, and liturgical life of our church. The evangelical faith lies at the very heart of all the church's dogmatic definitions, ecumenical councils, liturgies, sacramental theology, teachings of the Fathers, iconography, architecture, spirituality, and mission theology.

Serious problems remain, however, and must not be minimized for the sake of goodwill. If each side is willing to listen to the voice of the other, mutual challenges can bring about the rapprochement of an Orthodox reconstruction of evangelicalism and an evangelical renewal of Eastern Orthodoxy.

Evangelicals have a message the Orthodox Church needs to hear, and it is this: Orthodox bishops, pastors, and lay leaders need to make the gospel much clearer and more central to our parishioners than we are now doing. Despite the evangelical theology of the Orthodox Church we've discussed throughout this chapter, it would be a tragic mistake to maintain that all this is clearly obvious in traditionally Orthodox countries or in the Orthodox churches in the West. The dim religious light that scarcely illumines some segments of the church is not entirely the result of the continuing legacy of Communist and Islamic domination. We have to be honest enough to admit that it is also due to the predominance of nominal faith, biblical illiteracy, ethnic nationalism, folk religion, and just plain human sin.

The bishops and priests are spiritually and theologically more accountable to God for their flock than are the lay theologians and parishioners, while together all of these are supposed to take responsibility for the faith. But each must bear faithful witness to Christ, according to the gifts and opportunities he or she has been given. There seems little doubt that the most urgent need at this time in history is for the Orthodox Church to engage in an aggressive "internal mission" of spiritual renewal and conversion of its own people to Jesus Christ. We need to recognize and preach the gospel that is already there in our own church, because it is not always shown and proclaimed to us by our leaders. Just because the gospel is *in* the life of the church does not mean that Orthodox parishioners have *understood and appropriated* its message!

Church leaders must never take the gospel of Jesus Christ for granted but must freshly proclaim its saving message anew for each person, in each generation, in each sacramental act, in each liturgy, and in each period of fasting and prayer. The basic elementary principles of the gospel must be proclaimed in many and various ways in the totality of the church's life, since they form the foundation of all spiritual renewal and growth. One of the most effective missionary principles I have tried to convey to my students in evangelical seminaries who are preparing for work in Orthodox lands is that the best tool to use when witnessing to Orthodox Christians is our own theology.

When properly understood, the Eastern Orthodox Church is, I am convinced, the most thoroughly evangelical church in all the world because of its incarnational Trinitarian vision of life. It is not without reason that the Book of the Gospels rests on the center of the communion table in every Orthodox place of worship. But, alas! There is a tragic gap between Orthodox principles and Orthodox practice. If only we Orthodox would study and live the Bible as Protestant evangelicals do!

If we Orthodox wish to truly manifest our incarnational Trinitarian faith, we will need to constantly recover the personal and relational aspects of God in every life-giving action of the church. Failure to do so will constitute an experiential denial of our own Orthodox faith. Even if we Orthodox find evangelicals theologically deficient in a number of areas, evangelicals can rightly find us existentially deficient in the practical outworking of our faith. Perhaps if we humble ourselves before our evangelical brethren, we will learn the true meaning of our own faith and, in the process, bring them with us into the fullness of the life of the church.

Conversely, the Orthodox have a message evangelicals need to hear, and it is this: Evangelicals need a deeper understanding of their own religion. They need to more fully comprehend the soteriological consequences of the Christian doctrines of creation, the Trinity, and the incarnation; the inseparable union between the incarnation and soteriology; and how these realities impact the nature of the church, its pastoral structures, and the physical ways in which God works to bring about human redemption.

Evangelicals have everything to gain from learning about the Orthodox incarnational Trinitarian vision of life, and they need to heed the calls for reform that are coming from respected voices within their own academic institutions—calls we've highlighted along the way. Because God declared that his creation was "very good" (Gen. 1:31) and that in Christ "the Word became flesh" (John 1:14), the entire cosmos is blessed and usable as a sacramental vehicle of the divine presence. Bread, wine, water, oil—all of these are created means of the uncreated grace of God given through the sacramental life of the church. Even the role of Mary and the veneration of the saints find their deepest meaning, not in Mariolatry, but in the central revelation of the incarnation, death, and resurrection of Christ.

Moreover, the evangelical emphasis on personal salvation needs to be balanced by the Orthodox vision of corporate communion in Christ. The individualistic, experience-centered worship of many evangelicals needs to be augmented by a more focused emphasis on the Trinitarian God himself. Even in the area of Christian spirituality, the monastic tradition of the Orthodox Church has much to say to modern evangelicals about the primacy of love, with humility and prayer as its servants. In short, evangelicals are in need of developing a *theology of tradition*, and this theology must be more fully reflective of the fullness of biblical and Christian history.

The principles of a christological minimalism in evangelicalism, described earlier in this essay, need to be more fully developed into the christological maximalism of Orthodoxy that embraces and transcends those very principles of evangelical theology. Perhaps if evangelicals are willing to humble themselves before their Orthodox brethren, they will see more clearly the full implications of their own incarnational Trinitarian faith.

In this chapter, I have tried to map out the theological terrain of some of the major issues that unite and divide the Eastern Orthodox and evangelical traditions. It is only an outline—hopefully a substantive one—that points the way for further dialogue. The next step will be to evaluate the conclusions and explore how our commonly held beliefs and values can be visibly expressed in our local communities.

> For by [Christ] all things were created: things in heaven and on earth, visible and invisible. . . . And he is the head of the body, the church. . . . For God was pleased to have all his fullness dwell in him, and through him to reconcile to himself all things, whether things on earth or things in heaven, by making peace through his blood, shed on the cross.
>
> Colossians 1:16, 18–19

A RESPONSE TO BRADLEY NASSIF

Michael Horton

First of all, it is a privilege to dwell on this learned piece and to be a part of a conversation with Professor Nassif, known far and wide to students of the Orthodox-evangelical dialogue.

The chapter begins with the rather frank statement of the author's suspicion that full communion between the two traditions is highly unlikely, perhaps even undesirable. Nevertheless, his hope is that the Orthodox and evangelicals will "act more constructively toward each other than they have to date" (page 30). This expresses both the assumption and the goal of my own essay and my personal prayers for fruitful future dialogue. As we are learning, even where institutional convergence is unlikely, grassroots ecumenism continues, and this may, over time, constitute God's quiet means of bringing about the agreement that we need for unity with integrity.

Professor Nassif's awareness of the complications involved in defining evangelicalism is sympathetic and nuanced. He appeals to a study indicating that the label "evangelical" has expanded significantly in recent history to include many Roman Catholics, encouraging him to attempt a more precise distinction between various types of evangelicalism, following David Bebbington's four criteria used by this survey: a Christ/cross-centered orientation; biblicism; conversionism; and evangelistic activism. This still seems at great distance from the criteria that would have defined the movement, say, in the sixteenth century or among its present-day heirs among card-carrying confessional Protestants. Nevertheless, it is more definite than the witty and no less accurate definition offered by George Marsden, namely, "someone who likes Billy Graham."

As Nassif reports Mark Noll's conclusions, evangelicalism retains these emphases to some degree, but, in Noll's words, "the formal doctrines that once defined the message of atonement receive much less attention today than thirty or sixty or a hundred years ago" (pages 34–35). In addition, "The continuing spread of pentecostalism and the growth of the charismatic movement have meant more concentration on doctrines of sanctification (becoming holy oneself) than on doctrines of justification (how God accepts a sinner). In addition, an appeal to the consolations of redemption is now much more common than detailed theological exposition of its nature.... Much, in other words, separates contemporary evangelical Christians from the first modern evangelicals two-and-a-half centuries ago" (page 35).

Nassif is undeniably correct to follow Noll in concluding that evangelicalism has shifted its emphases considerably—from justification to conversion, for instance. Among others, I have argued that modern evangelicalism represents the uneasy alliance of the Reformation and Puritanism on one side, and radical Anabaptism, Arminianism, pietism, and revivalism on the other. To some of us, it would appear that the latter wing has now come to dominate the movement.

The author follows the same criteria in exploring and defining the Orthodox heritage. First, with respect to the emphasis on the cross, Nassif holds that evangelical theology, in contrast to Orthodoxy, fails to recognize the unity of soteriology and Christology. On this point, there seems to be some justification. I do not believe this holds for Martin Luther, John Calvin, Thomas Cranmer, or others in the Reformation traditions who have seen themselves to be in self-conscious continuity with the ancient church. It is difficult to imagine a heated debate in modern evangelicalism over the nature of Christ's presence in the Eucharist, for instance. "*What* presence?" I hear some evangelical brothers and sisters saying! This controversy, the earliest Protestants correctly perceived, was at once soteriological and christological; hence, it really mattered.

The dominant expressions of evangelical theology today, including some from those who would identify themselves as moderately Reformed, tend to reduce soteriology to the so-called *ordo salutis* (the application of redemption to the individual believer). While this is not wrong in itself, it is hardly the whole story, and when it is treated as such, even the *ordo salutis* is impoverished. Calvin is at one with Athanasius and Chalcedon here: the belief in the two natures of Christ hypostatically united is not simply a corollary of or prelude to soteriology, but is its heart. As a student of Calvin and an adherent of the Reformed tradition, I cannot help but endorse Nassif's observation here and would expect us to find greater understanding and convergence here than even he might anticipate.

While recognizing that such emphases as forensic justification and substitutionary atonement are now often regarded as peculiarities of Calvinism, Nassif regards them as worthy of being addressed "on their own merits." He rightly sees the emphasis on vicarious atonement as inextricably linked to the Reformation's doctrine of justification and the Anselmic tradition of interpretation. He also rightly sees this emphasis fading in evangelical circles; such doctrines "no longer qualify as benchmark criteria of evangelical identity" (page 38), but often yield to therapeutic categories. We also agree that Orthodoxy has never bypassed the doctrine of justification, but because it denies that this is a purely forensic declaration based on the imputation of Christ's "alien righteousness," we have historically regarded the Orthodox position, like Rome's, as constituting a denial of the doctrine as it is presented in Scripture.

Reformation Christianity has never denied or undervalued the corporate, ecclesial, sacramental, sanctifying, or cosmic aspects of this redemption, as (in our view) other traditions have. While we do affirm good works as the necessary and inevitable fruit of genuine justifying faith (and thus the positive thrust of *theosis*), we do not believe that Orthodoxy affirms justification but that it simply collapses it into sanctification. Like other Orthodox accounts, Professor Nassif's essay seems to hold that Orthodoxy simply does not make justification or the legal aspect central. However, we have yet to see it affirmed at all.

Reformed theology does set its exploration of justification in the context of its overarching covenantal scheme of "union with Christ." This, in fact, is at least methodologically somewhat in contrast to the Lutheran approach, which may tend to abstract this purely forensic declaration from the whole Christ and all of his benefits. When the focus shifts from Christ to conversion, as it often does in later evangelicalism, this becomes all the more dangerous. Justification is increasingly treated as an impersonal judicial transaction between God and the believer rather than as the effect of being united with Christ. Salvation, therefore, as an all-encompassing category for God's redemption and restoration of his creation, must be seen as the fruit of union with Christ that produces both the purely forensic imputation of Christ's righteousness *and* the personal reconciliation with God, triumph over the powers, growth in holiness, and final glorification that awaits us. Nevertheless, from our perspective, justification cannot be treated as anything but a forensic reality. Again, we cannot be faulted for reductionism here, since we insist that this forensic declaration, though foundational, is not all that is meant by "salvation." On the other hand, it seems that Orthodox theology does collapse all of soteriological reality into the category of transformation.

Professor Nassif refers to the "Mannermaa school" and its revisionist Lutheran theology and concludes that as a result of recent discussions there is reason to believe that a convergence is possible that "does not require an incompatibility with the evangelical interpretation of justification by faith or substitutionary atonement" (page 40). Although I am less enthusiastic about the current results of the Finnish interpretation, I find Nassif's assertion here quite encouraging and suggestive of further conversation. His summary of the contrasting emphases of transaction and transformation, Christ's work and Christ's person (without either side denying the doctrine emphasized by the other), seems accurate, as does his suggestion that the traditions can help each other develop a fuller appreciation for what we might characterize as *Agnus Dei* and *Christus Victor.* As the author recognizes, neither side disallows the other. In fact, we could support this claim, at least as Protestants, with ample testimonies to the *Christus Victor* theme especially from Luther but also from Calvin and others in the Reformed tradition. A genuinely evangelical theology must not only be a theology of the cross but also a theology of the resurrection, taking seriously not only the "not yet" of glorification but the "already" as well.

The author's exploration of the unity we have in the Nicene Creed (which, by the way, we also cite regularly—although with the *filioque,* but with sympathy for the Orthodox protest against altering an ecumenical creed) is heartwarming, especially in the face of renewed Arian threats. As one who introduces Reformed students to the Cappadocian fathers in a patristics course, I share Professor Nassif's appreciation for the importance of the doctrine of the Trinity in understanding the God-world relationship. The vast implications of our union with Christ for renewal of liturgical and ecclesiastical life are an often forgotten treasure of our Reformed tradition that we, no doubt, learned to value at least in part from the church fathers. Many of the themes with which Nassif whets our appetite in his comments on the Nicene Creed (pages 40–44) are thoughtfully developed in our tradition, often to the surprise of many contemporaries within as well as without. We could no doubt do even better if we read the Fathers with as much sympathy and depth as our forebears. Happily, there are signs of this renewed attention taking place in our circles. As I mention later in one of my responses, Irenaeus's *Adversus Haereses* represents a remarkable resource for Reformed-Orthodox convergence (pages 186–87). And the fact that Nassif refuses to force a choice between participation and imputation encourages me in my confidence that such readings are not only possible but required by at least some of these classic texts.

It is undoubtedly true that Western theology has tended to regard the incarnation as a necessary preamble to the rest of the story. There are, however, notable exceptions to that general oversight. For instance, John Calvin writes, "Christ aggregated to his body that which was alienated from the hope of life: the world which was lost and history itself."[1]

I am not so dedicated to the theology of John Calvin out of nostalgia or devotion to a person, but precisely because I see in his work an attempt to wrestle with these very themes—with explicit appeal to the church fathers. We need a robust theology of the incarnation to remind us that creation, redemption, and consummation are all linked and that grace restores nature rather than replaces it. Parallels between recapitulation and covenant theology (a union with Christ at once organic and federal) could serve as the basis for further exploration between our traditions. Roman Catholic scholar Kilian McDonnell notes that, despite their differences, Luther and Calvin both were deeply grounded in a Chalcedonian theology: "Like Calvin [Luther] rejects both Nestorius and Eutyches, and he proceeds from the unity of the natures in the person of Christ. He could not abide the thought that the whole Christ did not save us."[2] McDonnell cites Calvin's *Institutes* to this effect:

---

[1]John Calvin, *Corpus Reformatorum,* 55:219.

[2]Kilian McDonnell, *John Calvin, the Church, and the Eucharist* (Princeton, N.J.: Princeton Univ. Press, 1967), 63.

We therefore hold that Christ, as he is God and man, consisting of new natures united but not mingled, is our Lord and the true Son of God even according to, but not by reason of, his humanity. Away with the error of Nestorius, who in wanting to pull apart rather than distinguish the natures of Christ devised a double Christ! Yet we see that Scripture cries out against this with a clear voice.... Hence, just as Nestorius had justly been condemned at the Synod of Ephesus, so Eutyches was afterward justly condemned.... For it is no more permissible to commingle the two natures of Christ than to pull them apart.[3]

The theology of Chalcedon is at the heart of Reformed treatments of the Eucharist, although the claim to Chalcedon's mantle was disputed between Lutherans and the Reformed during the sixteenth century and since. In fact, "Both Luther and Calvin move from union with Christ in faith to the eucharistic union with Christ, and from there to communion-fellowship."[4] As far as the real presence is concerned, "None of the reformers defended it more forcibly than Calvin."[5] McDonnell writes, "Calvin says explicitly that we receive more than the effect of Christ's body; we receive the body itself," and then he quotes Calvin: In the Supper, "Christ does not simply present to us the benefit of his death and resurrection but the very body in which he suffered and rose again."[6]

Although I have been appealing to constructs familiar to me as a Reformed theologian, it is obvious where Lutheran theology would join fruitfully in this conversation as well. The author index to Calvin's *Institutes*, supplied in the McNeill/Battles edition, lists (including notes) at least ten explicit references to Athanasius; nine to the Council of Chalcedon; fifty-seven to Chrysostom; seven to Clement of Alexandria; eight to the Council of Constantinople; seventy to Cyprian; eight to Cyril of Alexandria; six to Cyril of Jerusalem; five to Gregory Nazianzus; three to Gregory Nyssa; and sixteen to Irenaeus.[7]

---

[3]Cited in McDonnell, *John Calvin, the Church, and the Eucharist*, 214.

[4]McDonnell, *John Calvin, the Church, and the Eucharist*, 71.

[5]Ibid., 224.

[6]Ibid., 243.

[7]See John Calvin, *Institutes of the Christian Religion*, ed. John T. McNeill, trans. Ford Lewis Battles (Philadelphia: Westminster, 1960).

In fact, Calvin's view of the Supper has been regarded by many (including some dissenting Reformed interpreters!) as suspiciously similar to that of Eastern Orthodoxy. Not only Christ's divinity, but his humanity in union with his divinity, is communicated in the Supper. And communicants receive life not only for their souls but even for their bodies. After all, "the flesh of Christ is like a rich and inexhaustible fountain that pours into us the life springing forth from the Godhead into itself."[8] When Nassif writes, "It was not a memorial meal in the sense in which most evangelicals today view the Lord's Supper, but an eschatological presence in time and space of the risen, now present, and returning Lord" (page 49), we can only nod in enthusiastic agreement.

Nassif's explanation of Cyril's controversy with Nestorius reminds us of Luther's and Calvin's criticisms of Zwingli's understanding of the Supper—and, therefore, of Christology itself. "In the Eucharist," says Nassif, "one mystically receives Christ through the bread and wine and is further united with him" (page 50). While he is correct to observe a serious cleavage with current evangelical sacramentology and Christology at this point, the view here stated is identical to that of Calvin and the Reformed confessions.

Even on the point of the *Theotokos* (page 53), there is unanimity. (In the ancient church history course at our seminary, every first-year student is treated to a pop quiz in which Professor Robert Godfrey "traps" his prey with this question, as he goes on to explain the significance of this affirmation for orthodox Christianity.)

I am tempted to respond to nearly every sentence of Nassif's exceptional chapter. On the goodness of the material creation, eschatology as the in-breaking of Christ's kingdom here and now and not just "last things," and related issues, I can only indicate wholehearted support. In many respects, this represents greater convergence than many of us experience in relation to contemporary evangelicalism, particularly in the latter's apparent preoccupation with quasi-gnostic anthropologies and eschatologies. Despite obvious and deep differences, we share with the Orthodox a suspicion of a naive biblicism that ignores the communion of saints in its reading of sacred Scripture, as well as sharing an affirmation of the creeds and an aiming at

---

[8]Calvin, *Institutes of the Christian Religion*, 4.17.9., 1369.

the simplicity of ancient practice rather than the innovations of the fertile human imagination.

In our estimation, *sola Scriptura* has been misinterpreted within evangelicalism to mean something that the Reformation never intended. Nassif's illuminating description of the baptismal liturgy is in many respects familiar to our own liturgies, which were patterned on the ancient practice. In fact, his description of baptism (with repeated references to the covenantal context) bears striking similarities with Reformed understandings as formulated in our confessions, catechisms, and liturgical forms.

Reformed Christians, however, do not extrapolate from these essential agreements even the veneration (as distinguished from the worship) of icons. As I maintain later in another response (page 256), we do not argue from the incarnation to a general "incarnational" philosophy. Instead, we regard the incarnation of the God-Man as a unique (though not antithetical) "intrusion" in redemptive history. Hence, we regard the temple in Jerusalem and its temporary worship as a system of shadows and types that gave way to the True Temple, Christ's own flesh and blood, which believers together join as living stones, filled by the Glory-Cloud, which is the Holy Spirit. Our rejection of icons is not due to a matter-spirit dualism, since we do believe that God unites us to Christ and preserves us in faith through the earthly means of preaching, water, bread, and wine. But lest we be led by these signs to someone other than the Reality they signify, we are compelled to adopt with reverence the simplicity of God's commanded worship.

Like Professor Nassif, I am convinced that, despite important agreements (and I have argued that there is probably more agreement between confessional Protestants and Orthodoxy than is often suspected), we remain necessarily separated by outstanding differences. These differences should not be treated as insurmountable obstacles, but they should also not be regarded as insignificant details. Our disagreements lie at the heart of our confession, not at the periphery. Too often, the choice in ecumenism is either ignoring each other or joining each other. But, with this author, I am convinced that the best way forward is to accept our division for the time being and exploit the opportunity afforded by a "no risk" ecumenism that values sympathetic study and conversation. Professor Nassif's contribution is a superb example of what that might look like.

A RESPONSE TO BRADLEY NASSIF

Vladimir Berzonsky

My initial impression after reading Dr. Nassif's chapter is that it is written by a believer and theologian who is in relationship and mutual understanding far ahead of the place that the Orthodox Church and evangelicalism are at present—a place they may not achieve for decades. A similar spirit resided in the famous Russian thinker Vladimir Soloviev. People like Soloviev and Nassif see the possibilities of union that others not only miss but challenge and reject. Dr. Nassif courageously asserts, "I have not just *thought* about Orthodox and evangelical compatibility, but I've *lived* it most of my life" (page 28).

Of course, compatibility is not unity as much as it is tolerance. It is a very American attitude—live and let live. But if we mean more when it comes to relationships, then even Nassif's chapter qualifies such ambition. Yet he is no wishful romantic. He realizes the chasm separating Orthodoxy and evangelicalism. His indictment follows: *Ignorance* on the part of Orthodox Church members, along with *bigotry,* is matched by "the hubris of some evangelical Christians, which is often tied to historical amnesia and an idolatrous self-confidence in their own exegetical skills" (page 28). Such charges one might imagine would all but preclude any rapprochement.

But one must read on. Nassif suggests that "no core disagreements [exist] between evangelicals and Eastern Orthodox over the issues that define the evangelical movement, issues that are also present in the Orthodox Church" (page 29). The differences come about when the Orthodox Christians understand and manifest greater principles of the definitions evangelicals use for themselves—principles that emerge in a vision of life based on the church's incarnational Trinitarian perspective. Indeed, the writer proposes an emerging awareness, within some areas of current evangelical theology, of creative and relevant treasures of the East in theology, spirituality, and worship that the Orthodox themselves often fail to see.

In his winsome optimism, Nassif selects those aspects of evangelicalism that, in the words of one of their own, Mark Noll, are *"diverse, flexible, adaptable, and multiform"* (page 31). Nassif warns that it is imperative "to identify what *kind* of evangelicalism we mean" (page 33). Precisely. And with regard to the earmarks of evangelicalism, the Orthodox will walk along at least part of the way: salvation through the forgiveness of sins; the Bible as the inspired word of God; a commitment to Jesus Christ—who would argue with such proclamations? But Nassif goes on to explain that, beyond the basic tenets of all or most evangelical groups, evangelicalism today is not any one communion of the past; their theological features "embrace a wide array of denominations" (page 35). There are new emphases. How is the Orthodox Church, which is and announces itself to be the whole Truth about God in Christ Jesus, to form some relationship with mere emphases?

Regarding salvation, the author asserts honest differences between the two regarding the way a Christian is saved. For the Orthodox, salvation involves a cooperation between the two agents or arms of the Father, namely, the Word and the Spirit, who act inseparably yet distinctively in bringing the believer to the kingdom. From the evangelical side, while Nassif acknowledges that older evangelical theories of substitutionary atonement and justification by faith are yet important, they no longer have the importance they once did (page 37). In response one need only read Michael Horton's chapter elsewhere in this book (pages 117–43).

Nassif points out what he terms the "christological maximalism" of Orthodoxy in the matter of soteriology, as opposed to evangelical "christological minimalism" (page 54). He means by this that the fathers of the Eastern church worked out the implications of the incarnation of Christ, explaining the impact of Christ's birth, ministry, crucifixion, and resurrection on creation itself, sanctifying the earth and touching with goodness all that exists. The cosmic event had an impact on everything, making iconography, access to the Holy Trinity, worship, even the role of the body in prayer, realized in a new light. Even time itself is transcended, with the kingdom of the future, or rather eternity, bursting into the present in the Eucharist, drawing the believer forward into life everlasting. This, and more, is experienced in liturgy.

The writer uses an analogy to summarize what he understands to be the relationship between Orthodox Christianity and evangelicalism (pages 83–84), namely, that of a small circle (evangelicalism) inside a larger circle (Orthodox Christianity). It's as though the first were a seed that has the potential to grow into a full theological fruit. The premise is this: according to the evangelical self-definition, evangelicalism is compatible with Orthodoxy; the converse, however, is not the case.

I wonder how many evangelical scholars would be comfortable with this image. The Reformation was a cutting away of all that was considered historical accretions, a movement to refine and redefine the essential elements of pure Christianity, much like a Giacometti sculpture as opposed to a Rubens painting. Whatever we struggle to overcome between the two theologies, the basic approach to God and the way to the kingdom remain; essentially, Orthodox are iconodules, and evangelicals are iconoclasts. The one utilizes every opportunity to enhance thought, meditation, spirituality, and worship, while the other searches for ways to reduce them to the basic essentials. For the one, creation is blessed with the incarnation, the angel guarding Eden turns back the flaming sword, Mary is granted the dignity of speaking for all humankind when asked to play a role in salvation, humanity is given the opportunity to share—albeit "with fear and trembling"—in our salvation. For the other, such a statement is pure hubris, Pelagian, and indeed presumptuous; indeed, for Christ to have an absolute role in human salvation, the man must be a spiritual corpse.

Nassif is convinced that the Eastern Orthodox Church "is the most thoroughly evangelical church in all the world because of its incarnational Trinitarian vision of life" (page 85). After enumerating many faults of the Orthodox Church, he ends with the observation that "evangelicals are in need of developing a theology of tradition" (page 86). I should imagine that most evangelicals would claim to have a clear awareness of tradition—Reformation tradition—and they would thank Dr. Nassif but disassociate themselves from the tradition found within Orthodoxy.

A RESPONSE TO BRADLEY NASSIF

George Hancock-Stefan

What can one say about the scholarship of Dr. Bradley Nassif? One can begin by saying that Dr. Nassif is currently the best scholar on the Orthodox-evangelical dialogue. During the last twenty years he has been involved in this dialogue many times, either as the initiator of various forums or in the center of the ongoing discussions. He has lived and experienced both sides. He is meticulous in his research, knows the existing dialogue and its participants globally, has read and understood patristic and evangelical theology, and is able to summarize it accurately and fairly. In this dialogue one wishes to be in the Nassif corner.

Since he is optimistic that, if not in his lifetime, sooner or later, the dialogue will become fruitful and evangelicals will not have problems becoming Orthodox, I will raise some of my concerns about this well-researched and well-presented essay.

1. CONTEMPORARY ORTHODOX REALITY

The first issue appears on the opening page of his essay. It has to do with the fact that it was evangelicals "who helped bring [Dr. Nassif] into a personal relationship with Jesus Christ during my high school years" (page 27). One of the primary reasons so many people leave the Eastern Orthodox Church is that, in spite of all the liturgy presentations, many do not have an inkling about what it means to have a personal relationship with God. If a relationship with God is important, and if one finds God outside of the Eastern Orthodox Church, it logically follows that the Eastern Orthodox Church should rejoice greatly when her sons and daughters find Christ!

2. THE THEOLOGICAL CENTER AND PERIPHERY

There are a number of issues of accord that are undeniable between Eastern Orthodox and evangelicals. The theology of the evangelicals is incarnational and Trinitarian. The majority of evangelicals will agree with the conclusions of the six ecumenical councils. The departure from the center takes place when Eastern Orthodoxy defines its ecclesiology.

Dr. Mark Saucy from Kiev Theological Seminary (Ukraine) read a paper at the 1998 Evangelical Theological Society meeting titled "Evangelicals, Catholics, and Orthodox Together: Is the Church the Extension of the Incarnation?"[1] In this paper he presents some of the uncomfortable points for evangelicals in regard to Christology and ecclesiology. Starting with a quote from former Lutheran theologian and now Catholic priest Richard John Neuhaus that "faith in Christ and faith in the church is one act," Saucy argues against this Christology extended in ecclesiology beyond the intentionality of the biblical text. Saucy succinctly points to numerous exegetical passages in which the equal sign is placed between Christ and the church by the Orthodox and Catholics. The Orthodox and Catholic Christology and ecclesiology is of such an indistinguishable unity that one has difficulty seeing a difference between who Christ is and who the church is and what Christ does and what the church does. Saucy urges evangelicals, Catholics, and Orthodox to continue working together and proposes as a working model the perichoretic Trinitarian view.

While Saucy presents this strictly on a theological level, Romanian pastor and president of the Romanian Missionary Society Josef Tson has documented how this controversy was carried on between Romanian Orthodox theologians and Romanian poet Ioan Alexandru in the national press, where the theologians argued that one does not need to know God as long as they know the church.[2]

3. CHURCH TRADITION AND SCRIPTURE

This Eastern Orthodox position is held only by the Roman Catholic Church and by some in the Anglican Church. The

---

[1]Presented at the annual meeting of the Evangelical Theological Society, Orlando, Fla., November 1998.

[2]Josef Tson, "Individualizing a Person's Relationship with God," unpublished article.

authority that the church exercises in the creation of the canon, as presented by Dr. Nassif, is not accepted by the majority of evangelical historians and theologians. No one outside of the three traditions mentioned accepts the position that Dr. Nassif is presenting. In fact, many would argue the opposite, namely, that Scripture is always the judge of the church. The church accepted the Scriptures, but it did not create them or give them their authority.[3]

4. THE LORD'S SUPPER

Eastern Orthodoxy has never defined specifically what it holds with regard to the Lord's Supper. Nevertheless, one can surmise that it is closer to the Roman Catholic position. It is precisely with the concept of the Lord's Supper that all the sixteenth-century Reformers struggled. Luther's consubstantiation, Calvin's spiritualization, and Zwingli's and Menno's memorialization have been departures from a position they deemed indefensible. Thus, at this point, the evangelical Lutherans, Calvinists, and Anabaptists are no longer participating in the dialogue.

5. BELIEVERS' BAPTISM

On this point the Lutherans and the Calvinists are siding with the Eastern Orthodox. The Anabaptists have argued that the magisterial Reformers did not go far enough. Whenever the Eastern Orthodox are arguing against their members being proselytized, it is an argument against the Baptists and Pentecostals, who have placed a great emphasis on a personal encounter with Christ and a conversion experience, followed by a baptism. Surprisingly, in the twentieth century, Karl Barth came to the defense of the Anabaptist position on baptism, demonstrating succinctly

---

[3]See Wayne Grudem, *Systematic Theology* (Grand Rapids: Zondervan, 1994, 2000), 67–68; David Wells, "Word and World: The Biblical Authority and the Quandary of Modernity," in *Evangelical Affirmations*, ed. Kenneth Kantzer and Carl F. H. Henry (Grand Rapids: Zondervan, 1990), 161; Kenneth Scott Latourette, *A History of Christianity*, vol. 1 (Peabody, Mass.: Prince Press, 2000), 135; Alister E. McGrath, *Historical Theology: An Introduction to the History of Christian Thought* (Malden, Mass.: Blackwell, 1998), 29.

[4]See Karl Barth, *The Teaching of the Church Regarding Baptism* (London: SCM Press, 1948).

that the only type of baptism defensible on solid exegetical ground is believers' baptism.[4] The Eastern Orthodox Church and the magisterial Reformation are using words that become senseless—hearing the Word, believing the Word, repenting—for an infant cannot do any of these actions.

Dr. Nassif devotes a long section of his presentation to the subject of conversionism. Yet, for all practical purposes, one cannot talk about conversion in the Eastern Orthodox service. How often have we Protestants participated in the baptismal services where the godparents know nothing about Jesus Christ or his salvation? The godparents were not converted, the child was not converted, and on rare occasions the priest was not converted either. Declaring conversionism under these circumstances is like the Pharisees declaring themselves to be the children of Abraham. Jesus replied to them, "If you were Abraham's children, then you would do the things Abraham did" (John 8:39).

The succinct expression "Believe in the Lord Jesus, and you will be saved" (Acts 16:31) is not extended through the Lord's Supper, and the Supper is not given to someone who cannot believe. It is a belief in a historical act of God appropriated to the individual by the Holy Spirit. It is Dr. Nassif's encounter with evangelicals that brought him into a personal relationship with Jesus Christ. Was this his conversion, or was he converted when he was baptized and chrismated?

During the Communist regime in Eastern Europe, people would joke about the Communist economy by saying that the Communist government pretended to pay the workers and the workers pretended to work for the government. The production numbers were always inflated, which is one reason why the Communist regime collapsed. The same idea used to be applied in the numbering of Protestants and Orthodox. The Orthodox claimed the millions, but on Sundays the Protestant churches were filled, and the Orthodox churches were empty. The local Protestant church would declare that it had four hundred members, but over twelve hundred would be present. The Orthodox church would declare that it had twelve hundred members, but only four hundred would be present. Moreover, where the Orthodox churches were full, it was with the people from The Lord's Army, whom the Orthodox hierarchy often scorned as Protestants.

6. THEOLOGICAL PROGRESSION

From the sixteenth century on, whenever a theologian would move beyond the fourteenth-century theological perimeters, he would immediately be accused of being a Calvinist or a Latinist. The hierarchical reactions were violent—either excommunication or voluntary or forced recantation. I am not aware of an ecclesiological mechanism that allows the Eastern Orthodox Church to recant of a position or change a position because there is more light from the Holy Spirit. In view of the fact that this mechanism is not available, I wonder if there can be a dialogue between evangelicals and Orthodox, or if the sixteenth-century Constantinopolitan dictum is still in effect: When you change, you can come home. Until then, we have nothing to discuss!

A RESPONSE TO BRADLEY NASSIF

Edward Rommen

From an Orthodox perspective there is very little in Bradley Nassif's chapter that could be objected to, corrected, or even expanded on. The presentation of patristic understanding of select theological themes is thorough and certainly supports the author's contention that, at least in the four areas addressed, Orthodoxy and evangelicalism are compatible. That, in turn, would seem to justify his contention that self-consistency leaves evangelicals and Orthodox alike with no alternative but to support and affirm one another. Yet, few evangelicals and even fewer Orthodox believe that self-consistency compels them to mutual support and affirmation.

One problem seems to be the standard against which self-consistency is being measured. As the author himself admits, had he used an Orthodox self-definition question of compatibility, it would have been answered in the negative. For the theologically uninitiated, the encouraging fact of faith principles shared with evangelicals and the benefits of the dialogue-facilitating concept of concentric circles of theological content are likely to be overridden by a prior commitment to the unity of the one true church. In this case, self-consistency would require just the opposite of the support and affirmation of those who have separated themselves from the church.

The theologically astute would, of course, recognize the theological content shared with evangelicals but would ask why the consistency with the principles governing the theological subsets alone should be that which determines their approach to theological dialogue with evangelicals. Convinced that a subset divorced from the whole set cannot be properly understood, they would insist that consistency be judged on the basis of faithfulness to the larger cosmic and ecclesial context. While not eliminating the possibility of discussion, this commitment to faithfulness would place some limits on the degree and kind of theological agreement an Orthodox theologian would be willing to acknowledge.

The prospects of evangelicals being compelled by consistency with the self-definition to support and affirm the Orthodox are not significantly higher. The four theological themes that make up the definition amount to an abstracted lowest common denominator that does not define any evangelical group in particular. As is the case with all such theoretical constructs, they do not actually define an existing group but rather an imaginary entity used for the purpose of discussion. Yet, given the individualism and diversity of the evangelical community, individual representatives are going to measure consistency according to the principles that define their own subgroup.

This phenomenon is clearly visible in this volume, where a Calvinist contributor speaks of theological concessions that could easily be made by an Arminian. Perhaps it would have been better to choose another standard, such as the statement issued by the 1989 "Evangelical Affirmations" conference or the "Cambridge Declaration" of the Alliance of Confessing Evangelicals (April 1996). But this would certainly limit the range of theological agreement and the number of evangelicals represented by such agreement.

While a minimalist evangelical self-definition is useful at an abstract level, holding participants to its logical implications may not lead to the desired results. Mutual support and affirmation may be better served by engaging in limited discussions based on some degree of known agreement rather than attempting an inclusive dialogue that will highlight differences. The four theological themes could be used as an agenda, an indicator of interests, a measure of possible agreement, rather than as self-definition. With that in mind, an Orthodox theologian could consider a sequence of discussions—beginning with Wesleyans, with whom we may have the most in common,[1] followed by Lutherans,[2] and then perhaps Calvinists.

---

[1]See *Wesleyan Theological Journal* 26, no. 1 (Spring 1991); *The Asbury Theological Journal* 45, no. 2 (1990).

[2]Consider the Lutheran-Orthodox dialogue (*Lutheran-Orthodox Dialogue: Agreed Statements 1985–1989* [Geneva: Lutheran World Federation, 1992]) referenced by Bradley Nassif (page 64).

CONCLUSION

Bradley Nassif

In the remarks that follow, I will focus only on the responders' arguments that seem to be the strongest challenge to my thesis that Orthodoxy and evangelicalism are largely, but by no means entirely, compatible. My thesis has been that the Orthodox Church does indeed have an evangelical identity, and that this identity embraces the same evangelical identity of Protestant evangelicalism today, but that it also transcends it and contrasts with it in significant ways.

The major argument of Father Edward Rommen's critique of my essay is that he believes it is more theologically self-consistent for us who are Orthodox to emphasize our disunity with evangelicals than it is for us to support and affirm them because of our commitment to the unity of the church and the larger theological principles that govern its life. While recognizing a degree of theological commitments shared with evangelicals, Father Edward asks "why the consistency with the principles governing the theological subsets alone should be that which determines their approach to theological dialogue with evangelicals. Convinced that a subset divorced from the whole set cannot be properly understood, [the Orthodox] would insist that consistency be judged on the basis of faithfulness to the larger cosmic and ecclesial context" (pages 105–6). He further recognizes that there remains the possibility for discussion, but believes that "this commitment to faithfulness would place some limits on the degree and kind of theological agreement an Orthodox theologian would be willing to acknowledge."

In response, I would agree that a subset cannot be properly understood apart from the whole set of one's theological vision of truth. This is precisely why I have repeatedly drawn attention in my essay to our known and continuing differences over the meaning of tradition, baptism, the Eucharist, sin, salvation, justification, and other vital areas of theology. I hope not to have "divorced" these larger principles in my analysis, as Father Edward has alleged; on the contrary, I have tried to keep the church's maximalist vision clearly in mind when showing how the larger theological vision of Orthodoxy is inseparably related to the evangelical faith we hold in common. I was not attempting to find the "lowest common denominator" between Orthodoxy and evangelicalism but to be faithful to those principles that constitute the self-definition of each group.

From an evangelical perspective, this means that Orthodoxy shares the core principles of that which constitutes Protestant evangelical identity; from an Orthodox perspective, however, evangelicalism is seen as deficient in the outworking of those commonly held evangelical principles, particularly in the church's vision of the relation between Scripture and tradition, the sacraments, iconography, spirituality, and other vital areas that are inseparably connected to the Orthodox understanding of the incarnation and Trinity. I agree that the comparison I drew was not with any particular group (such as Baptists, Pentecostals, Methodists, and others) but with the whole of the evangelical movement *as a movement, not as a denomination.* Within that larger movement, however, I extended my analysis to include specific areas of theology that *divide* us from the Reformation traditions, since most evangelicals adhere to the classical distinctives of the Protestant faith. The relation I have drawn between the core principles of our shared theology in the area of Christology and its connection to iconography is but one example of many I discussed to illustrate the character of our compatibility (in doctrine) and incompatibility (regarding the implications of the doctrine).

So perhaps Father Edward did not fully understand what I was trying to say, or, more likely, I did not emphasize it sufficiently. He admits there is indeed a "degree and kind" of theological agreement we have with evangelicals, but instead of explaining and affirming this agreement in a qualified manner, he seems to have committed the same error he alleges I commit, namely, divorcing the subset from the whole set of the church's faith. Contrary to his assertion that my emphasis lies too strongly on the subset (the inner circle of commonly held beliefs), it seems as though he would like to emphasize the larger principles (the outer circle of the unity of "the one true church") so much that he ends up either minimizing or divorcing them from the major theological core that constitutes our shared faith with evangelicals. Thus, a more balanced view that keeps them together in a carefully qualified manner would seem to be required.

Our differences in evaluating Orthodox-evangelical compatibility appear to center on whether we are willing to keep the smaller and larger circles of faith together, understanding their logical relationships to each other and then, finally, carefully and critically measuring the theological value of those smaller principles of commonly held beliefs as they relate to the larger principles of the church's faith. Those theological issues, logic, and values are what finally constitute the content and kind of compatibility that the Eastern Orthodox and evangelical traditions do, in fact, share in common. If I am right, the next step will be to mutually affirm this commonly held evangelical faith, explore further our known and continuing differences, and then explore ways in which these common beliefs and values can be visibly expressed in our local communities throughout the world without compromising our doctrinal integrity.

As for Dr. Horton's response, I can only rejoice in the common ground we share, especially with the Reformed tradition. The Reformed tradition is not as opposed to Orthodoxy as many have imagined. The Scottish brothers Thomas and James Torrance have tried to show us some of these convergences from across the ocean; Dr. Horton is doing the same from a more conservative but ecumenical platform here in the United States. So the stage is set for deepening our dialogue with the more conservative Reformed denominations as well as the mainline Reformed body (as has already begun in Europe over the past decade or so).

The only clarifications I want to make concern the methodology I used in my essay and the need to put out a reminder of what Orthodoxy has done with the doctrine of justification. In defining evangelicalism, I utilized a study by Mark Noll in which certain criteria defined the movement. I grouped them under four categories. These categories, however, were not intended to be rigidly applied but simply to be indicators of the major theological commitments that define the evangelical movement.

Within these four categories, I went much farther to include specific doctrines many Reformed-minded groups consider as central to the gospel (such as justification, substitutionary atonement, and other themes). So I only wished to use the four major themes as rubrics that embrace the whole of the evangelical movement and at the same time can be used as an umbrella to include more specific doctrines many Reformed-minded evangelicals have deemed important. I did not, however, wish to use the same criteria to define the Orthodox heritage. Those four criteria alone would have been much too confining, reductionistic, and misleading. I tried to take that which defines evangelicalism and ask how the classical tradition of the first thousand years of Christian theology handled those contemporary themes. In so doing, I showed how Orthodoxy embraces yet transcends these four distinctives in a way that makes Orthodoxy both similar to and different from the modern evangelical movement.

As for the doctrine of justification itself, let me reiterate. There is no question that popular expressions of Orthodox belief by Orthodox Christians themselves often are not representative of the church's true faith. Too often the Christian faith is seen as a journey whose end may be crowned with the reward of justification after a lifetime of good works and church participation. As the baptismal liturgy makes clear, however, justification is an act that takes place at the beginning of the Christian life, not at the end. As the evangelical ecumenist Donald Fairbairn has acknowledged, for Orthodoxy "Christian life is not a means to an end, but is the ongoing result of a change that God has already made in one's status before God, in one's relationship with God, and in one's inner nature."[1] Mature Orthodoxy believes in "justification by faith" as a declarative act by God, but it is also personal and relational. It is God's acceptance of

---

[1]Donald Fairbairn, *Eastern Orthodoxy Through Western Eyes* (Louisville, Ky.: Westminster John Knox, 2002), 124; see also 122–27, 175–78. Orthodox and evangelicals should read these sections to see the full extent and nature of our compatibility on the issue of justification. Throughout his book, Fairbairn makes a helpful distinction between the views of "mature" Orthodoxy and "popular" or "unsophisticated" Orthodoxy.

sinners into fellowship with him as though we were righteous. This fellowship is a lifelong process of *theosis* rooted and grounded in the person and work of Christ, made accessible to the believer in the justifying event of the baptismal liturgy.

As for the rest of Dr. Horton's critiques, he agrees that Orthodoxy is more compatible with the Reformed faith than first appears. He spells out shared themes in some detail and indicates which themes would be fruitful for a future Orthodox-Reformed dialogue. He thus underscores my thesis that Orthodoxy and evangelicalism are largely compatible, though major obstacles remain to be addressed.

Concerning Father Berzonsky's response, I am grateful for his openness to my thesis. If any constructive changes occur in Orthodox-evangelical relations, it will not come without the positive attitude of faithful Orthodox priests such as him. I can only hope and pray that more Orthodox clerics will demonstrate a willingness to learn and be changed from the truth of the church's faith, even if such a relationship and mutual understanding with evangelicals are far ahead of where we now are (and may be for decades). Still, Father Berzonsky rightly questions whether the Reformation tradition would be willing to embrace the same tradition that is found within Orthodoxy. I do appreciate this observation, which summarizes the concerns of his response to my essay. The Orthodox tradition and the Reformation traditions are in no way completely compatible. What is important, however, is to see the common threads that comprise the evangelical identity of the Protestant Reformation, and then to see how this compares with the evangelical identity of the Orthodox Church.

In the process of my analysis, I tried to identify key areas of difference between the Lutheran and Reformed understandings of tradition and that of the Anabaptist wing, which defined the relation between Scripture and tradition very differently from their Lutheran and Reformed brethren. When navigating between those differing views on the relation of Scripture and tradition, I sought to be faithful to the Orthodox vision, and thus I contrasted it with the Anabaptist view. But the Anabaptist view also differed from the Reformed and Lutheran views, which were actually more Orthodox than Anabaptist.

My point is simply this: When asking how Orthodoxy and evangelicalism compare, we must highlight those features that constitute a common evangelical identity shared across the board by all our theological traditions, yet at the same time identify those areas that make us different and then assign to those differences a theological value that may or may not be church dividing. This requires a spiritually unified effort of the head, heart, and hands. It demands a mind that employs critical thinking and careful nuancing, a heart that is open to God and filled with love for the brethren, and hands that are eager to work side by side with Protestant evangelicals in the preaching of the gospel and in social outreach to the oppressed and needy. Berzonsky clearly shares this goal, and so whether or not I have convinced him of the limits within which it may be achieved will be for him and other Orthodox readers to judge.

Finally, Dr. Hancock-Stefan raises numerous theological issues that have already been addressed, though my treatment was not as systematically structured as was his response. In short, these issues reflect the concerns of an Eastern European Baptist: nominalism and its relation to the necessity of personal faith for salvation, the relation between Christ and the church, the church and the canon of Scripture, and the sacraments of the Lord's Supper and believers' baptism.

I sincerely support Dr. Hancock-Stefan's concern for genuine faith in all the sacramental acts of the church. Too often Orthodox parishioners have gone through the motions, with very little apparent faith or understanding of what it all means. To that extent, evangelicals could help the Orthodox by utilizing our own theology as a friendly tool for education and evangelism. The entire monastic tradition stands precisely as an abiding spiritual movement within the church to correct the sins of nominalism and folk religion. One need not be a Baptist to agree with Dr. Hancock-Stefan; one needs only to be a faithful Orthodox.

There will be continuing differences, of course, over infant baptism and similar issues. The way I have interpreted the church's practice of the reception of nonsacramental converts, however, should at the very least open the door to dialogue with nonsacramental evangelicals. If we accept the validity of a Baptist's previous baptism in the name of the Holy Trinity upon his or her conversion to the Orthodox faith—from a person who did not originally know or understand the efficacy of the rite, or who received the Holy Spirit before or after it after the fashion of the exception passages I've noted from the book of Acts—then this means that the boundaries of the church are not strictly limited to the canonical borders of the Orthodox Church. Just how far this goes and what it means for compatibility and visible unity remain to be explored. But clearly if one denies altogether the efficacy of baptism and faith, he is not a faithful spokesman for the Orthodox Church. Dr. Hancock-Stefan is a good Baptist and a faithful and kind Christian, but his view of evangelicalism is too parochial to be truly representative of the wider evangelical family or that of mainstream historic Christianity, whether it be in the Orthodox, Catholic, or magisterial Reformation traditions.

In conclusion, I am grateful for all the responders who have graciously reflected on my work. I am convinced that the Orthodox and Protestant evangelical communities are at a momentous turning point in church history. I have tried to provide the groundwork for a new paradigm of ecumenical relations that will offer hope for transforming our past tensions into positive resources for realignment and renewal. Depending on how each side responds to this emerging global dialogue, our relations will either return to the isolationism of a pre-ecumenical era or change the course of history. I hope it will be the latter. If so, the next courageous step will be for Orthodox and evangelicals to reach out to each other (from the top down and the bottom up), refine our conclusions, and explore how our common beliefs and values can be visibly expressed in our local communities throughout the world.

Chapter Two

ARE EASTERN ORTHODOXY AND EVANGELICALISM COMPATIBLE? NO

An Evangelical Perspective

Michael Horton

ARE EASTERN ORTHODOXY AND EVANGELICALISM COMPATIBLE? NO

An Evangelical Perspective

Michael Horton

One of the best ways to recognize the different linguistic paradigms of Eastern Orthodoxy and evangelicalism is to examine the indexes of any number of primary and secondary works on Eastern Orthodoxy. One will find such entries as chrismation, deification, energies of God, recapitulation, *theosis,* and the like, but notable absences will include original sin, grace, justification, sanctification, substitutionary atonement, and related terms that are familiar to Protestants—or at least once were.

It is an oversimplification, but it may be said generally that, while Western theological systems often follow a Trinitarian pattern reflected in the Apostles' Creed, the focus is often more on the work of the persons than on their perichoretic unity and the nature of the hypostatic union of the God-Man. This becomes most apparent in the second article, where Western theology tends to regard Christology as an essential means to the end of soteriology. Thus, there is an emphasis on the cross and resurrection as the apex of human redemption. In Eastern patristic and Byzantine theology, however, the accent falls on the incarnation itself. Jesus Christ the God-Man is not only who he is in order to be a Savior; he is a Savior precisely in being who he is.

Regarding the first five centuries as definitive, Orthodox theology revolves around christological issues, and this is why one may find teeming citations for hypostasis, Arianism, and the *filioque,* but few for guilt, Pelagius, forgiveness, reconciliation, and propitiation. In many cases, further conversation between Eastern and Western partners reveals considerable agreement in substance despite different taxonomies. In other cases, however—and not insignificant ones—the differences are clear and unambiguous. It will be the argument of this paper that (1) fruitful ecumenical dialogue has revealed considerable agreement between Orthodoxy and evangelical Protestantism and that (2) these results nevertheless have not overcome the disagreements that keep us from visible ecclesiastical communion.

RANGE OF AGREEMENTS

Scripture and Liturgy

Whatever may be lacking in the formal statements of Orthodox theology, the Orthodox liturgy often contains evangelical substance and even direct biblical citations. Protestant criticisms of the Roman canon of the mass as a corruption of the ancient liturgy are far less capable of being leveled at Orthodoxy, although disturbing features remain, such as prayers for the dead. The Orthodox realize that faith is shaped by practice as well as by belief: *lex orandi, lex credendi*—as we pray, so we believe.

Evangelical Protestants have tended—at least in the English-speaking world—to have a reductionistic view of the relation of Scripture and tradition. Because of this general tendency, the Reformers are often inaccurately regarded by friend and foe alike as forerunners of modern individualism. Forgetting that the context of Martin Luther's famous "Here I stand" was a court trial and not a march for individual rights, critics often suggest that the Reformers wanted to sit alone with the Bible and discover by themselves its meaning from scratch. While this impression is consistent with certain tendencies in fundamentalism and evangelicalism, it is nowhere close to the intention of the Protestant Reformation itself.

In addition to the ecumenical creeds, both Lutheran and Reformed traditions developed their respective confessions and catechisms, which had a binding status on their entire communions. Although secondary standards (Scripture being primary), these symbols took for granted that believers are formed in community and not as discrete individuals. John Calvin's writings are so replete with citations from the ancient church that he is justly regarded as a patristic scholar in his own right. During his exile from Geneva in Strasbourg, Calvin began to prepare a French edition of Chrysostom's sermons, Chrysostom being perhaps Calvin's nearest patristic influence next to Augustine.[1] He was also partial to Irenaeus, John of Damascus *(De fide orthodoxa)*, Athanasius, Cyprian (on whom Calvin draws throughout his *Institutes of the Christian Religion*), and others. It is not surprising that an evangelical patristic scholar like Christopher A. Hall would credit his appreciative introduction to the church fathers to his reading of Calvin, Luther, and Wesley.[2]

Once it has been acknowledged that tradition is to be tested by Scripture, recognizing that the former includes even contradictory decrees at times, Calvin is quite prepared to be guided by ancient reflection in his interpretation of Scripture. The ancient councils were carefully studied and appealed to by Calvin: "For I venerate them from my heart, and desire that they be honored by all."[3] "In this way, we willingly embrace and reverence as holy the early councils, such as those of Nicaea, Constantinople, Ephesus I, Chalcedon, and the like, which were concerned with refuting errors—in so far as they relate to the teachings of faith."[4] That last cavil was concerned with intramural practical debates that were often a part of those councils but were never regarded by Western Christians as particularly relevant. More recent (i.e., Western medieval) councils lacked the piety, attention to biblical exegesis, and love for the truth that the earlier ones displayed, according to Calvin.[5]

One might say that Scripture is the teaching, and tradition is the teacher. In one sense, of course, Scripture is both the teaching and the teacher *(analogia fidei)*, but in another sense tradition may be seen as what philosopher Alasdair MacIntyre has called "the long conversation" of the people of God as they are led into the Scriptures by their teaching officers. In addition to the creeds

---

[1]See Richard A. Muller, *The Unaccommodated Calvin: Studies in the Foundation of a Theological Tradition* (Oxford: Oxford Univ. Press, 2000), 27.

[2]See Christopher A. Hall, *Reading Scripture with the Church Fathers* (Downers Grove, Ill.: InterVarsity Press, 1998), 200.

[3]John Calvin, *Institutes of the Christian Religion,* ed. John T. McNeill, trans. Ford Lewis Battles (Philadelphia: Westminster, 1960), 4.9.1., 1166.

[4]Ibid., 4.9.8., 1171.

[5]Ibid.

and confessions, doctors of the church, pastors, and teachers have been held in high esteem by Lutheran and Reformed traditions. And yet, the church—its constitutions and officers—is regarded as having a ministerial rather than magisterial function. No conscience may be constrained beyond the Word, but the faithful acknowledge the importance of submitting to the church and agreeing together in a unity of confession. "Free spirits" were disciplined, not encouraged, in Reformation churches. The Reformers were in close contact with this patristic and, to a lesser extent, Byzantine, tradition, and whereas we sometimes begin church history with them, they were concerned with their connection to the church fathers of the East and West.

Creation and Fall

With Orthodox theologians contributing to this volume, it is hardly necessary for an outsider to attempt an explanation of their tenets. At the same time, it may help to describe areas of potential agreement, and in doing so it is helpful, at least for me, to state what I take to be some of the leading motifs. Misunderstandings on my part will hopefully be corrected by others in their responses.

One of my favorite sections in the patristics course is the one on Irenaeus, the second-century church father who led the struggle against Gnosticism. At stake in that controversy was the integrity of creation and its creator. In the various gnostic sects, "nature" was an inherently negative category, and salvation was conceived in terms of escape from temporal, physical, transient existence. Mani's gospel was a cosmic struggle between the bad god of creation and the good god of redemption from the material world. Pulling especially from Johannine and Pauline emphases, Irenaeus defended the goodness of the one God who created the world and redeems the world rather than redeeming divine sparks from their natural bondage to the world.

Nature never was perfected, according to Eastern theology (as I understand it), but was also not corrupt. Depending on human choice, nature could continue in its course toward completion and consummation or it could be corrupted. But there is nothing like the opposition of nature and grace that one finds in Augustine and in the most formative Western writers. All human beings even after the fall retain the divine image, but participation in the divine likeness is the hope that is central to the Orthodox vision of eschatological transformation. John Meyendorff summarizes this contrast:

> The view of man prevailing in the Christian East is based on the notion of "participation" in God. Man has been created not as an autonomous, or self-sufficient, being; his very nature is truly itself only inasmuch as it exists "in God" or "in grace." Grace, therefore, gives man his "natural" development....
>
> Maximus, in a famous passage of *Ambigua* 41, lists five polarities which are to be overcome by man [as microcosm]: God and creation, the intelligible and the sensible, heaven and earth, paradise and world, man and woman. The polarities have been sharpened by sin and rendered insuperable by human capabilities alone. Only the man Jesus, because He is also God, was able to overcome them. He is the new Adam, and in Him, creation again finds communion with the creator and harmony within itself.[6]

While there is a danger of drawing East-West contrasts too sharply, the influence of Augustine's Neoplatonism is at times more pronounced in Western than in Orthodox writers. Both traditions, to my mind, are too dependent on Plato and Neoplatonism at times, and it is difficult to fault the West with a depreciation of created nature given the abundance of Origenist and Alexandrian tendencies in much of Eastern theology. At the same time, the triumph of the Augustinian nature-grace antithesis has always given many Lutheran and Reformed dogmaticians an appreciation for the Eastern critique. "Patriarch Photius even goes so far as to say, referring to Western doctrines, that the belief in a 'sin of nature' is a heresy," Meyendorff reports.[7] Byzantine historian Constantine Tsirpanlis observes that Gregory Nazianzus places the blame for the fall not on Adam's flesh but on his mind.[8] Calvin criticizes as Manichaean any confusion of created nature and a propensity for sin (i.e., concupiscence):

---

[6]John Meyendorff, *Byzantine Theology: Historical Trends and Doctrinal Themes* (London: Mowbrays, 1974), 138, 142.

[7]Ibid., 143.

[8]See Constantine N. Tsirpanlis, *Introduction to Eastern Patristic Thought and Orthodox Theology* (Collegeville, Minn.: Liturgical Press, 1991), 50.

Now away with those persons who dare write God's name upon their faults, because we declare that men are vicious by nature! They perversely search out God's handiwork in their own pollution, when they ought rather to have sought it in that unimpaired and uncorrupted nature of Adam....

Therefore we declare that man is corrupted through natural vitiation, but a vitiation that did not flow from nature. We deny that it has flowed from nature in order to indicate that it is an adventitious quality which comes upon man rather than a substantial property which has been implanted from the beginning. Yet we call it "natural" in order that no man may think that anyone obtains it through bad conduct, since it holds all men fast by hereditary right.... Thus vanishes the foolish trifling of the Manichees, who, when they imagined wickedness of substance in man, dared fashion another creator for him in order that they might not seem to assign the cause and beginning of evil to the righteous God.[9]

It is significant that this older criticism of the Western Catholic tradition is essentially repeated, *mutatis mutandis* (with the necessary changes), by the Reformers and their successors.

The theology of the Christian East has been generally more attentive to the cosmic and communal aspect of creation and salvation—keeping both together—while Western theology has tended to concentrate more on natures in and of themselves, apart from the eschatological scheme. Thus, Orthodoxy has been more likely to see nature and grace as interdependent rather than as ontological strangers or even enemies. (We will argue below that Reformation theology, at its best at least, has mounted a similar critique of Roman Catholic theology, attempting to shift the antinomy from nature-and-grace to sin-and-grace—that is, from ontological to ethical categories.)

Despite the serious differences that will be explored, there is also a great deal of agreement between Orthodoxy and confessional Reformation theology on the nature of sin. It seems to me that there is a significant degree of diversity on this subject among Orthodox writers. Vsevolod Palachovsky, a priest and theologian of the Russian Orthodox Church of Paris, explains:

---

[9]Calvin, *Institutes*, 2.1.10–11, 253–55.

Our entire life is conditioned by our initial disobedience, which is not only that of Adam, but our own as well, for in him and through him we have all sinned. Alongside this state of sin, which we can all call ontological sin, we also have sinful acts, or actual sin.... It is man's fundamental corruption from the time of the fall which ultimately gives rise to sins. Man sins because he has become sin.[10]

This understanding is thus far identical with the Western view, particularly in its Reformation formulation. Father Palachovsky goes so far as to make this assertion: "Original sin has introduced corruption into man's nature."[11] He cites the Byzantine liturgy (itself a quote from Ecclesiastes): "There is no man who lives and does not commit sin."[12] In the contest between Orthodoxy and Romanism with respect to the *donum superadditum* (added gift), Reformation theology has consistently sided with Orthodoxy:

According to Orthodox teaching, man before the fall was neither mortal nor immortal; both possibilities were his, or perhaps we should say that if his life had unfolded according to the divine plan, he was necessarily immortal. In Orthodox teaching, the fall of man is not a lack of subordination of the lower powers to reason, but rather an about-face of man's being, which having been turned toward God, is now turned toward nature.[13]

The catechism published by the Greek Archdiocese of North and South America in 1960 declares this:

The most woeful thing of all is that these double results of the original transgression of our father, which are generally known under the name of moral evil and physical evil, were not confined to the person of the delinquent only, but were handed down as an hereditary disease to all his descendants, who, being the rotten fruits of a rotten tree, are born children of wrath and damnation.[14]

---

[10]V. Palachovsky and C. Vogel, *Sin in the Orthodox Church and in the Protestant Churches*, trans. Charles Schaldenbrand (New York: Desclee, 1966), 9–10.

[11]Ibid., 35.

[12]Ibid., 17.

[13]Ibid., 34–35.

[14]Constantine N. Callinicos, *The Greek Orthodox Catechism* (New York: Greek Archdiocese of North and South America, 1960), 23.

While the East did not embrace the full understanding of original sin as including guilt as well as corruption, these agreements are significant, and they serve favorably as an answer to the perennial charges of Pelagianism from Western theologians.

Incarnation and Redemption

Christian orthodoxy is known by its enemies, and, as everyone knows, the particular heresies confronted by a particular church in its time and place have something to do with the emphases of the resulting orthodoxy. Poised between the most decisive battles in church history—Antiochene and Alexandrine excesses—incarnation is the lodestar for Christology as much for Western Protestant theology as for Eastern theology. Orthodoxy has never separated the work of Christ from the person of Christ, as has often been done in the West. The incarnation is not merely a prerequisite for our redemption but is its beginning. Furthermore, Orthodoxy has tended to limit formulation to the most essential terms of christological and Trinitarian debates, in contrast to the high medieval speculations of the West.[15]

The close link of Christology and soteriology as well as creation and redemption is a helpful corrective to some of the reductionistic tendencies in Western formulations that miss the eschatological and cosmic dimensions of the incarnation and other saving events of Christ's work. As Irenaeus and the Cappadocian fathers recognized, there is an unmistakable emphasis in Scripture on the cosmic conquest of the God-Man over "the powers and principalities" that have held God's world in bondage. The position that Gustav Aulen would identify as the *Christus Victor* motif is an essential feature of biblical theology, and it has often been neglected in Western soteriology.

And yet, other equally important biblical motifs have been acknowledged in the Christian East. Western Christians (and perhaps some Eastern Christians) may be surprised to see in Irenaeus, for example, an emphasis not only on recapitulation but on the cross as a sacrifice and satisfaction for sin's guilt as well as a victory over sin's power. Callinicos's catechism answers the question "And why this death on the Cross?" with this reply:

---

[15]As, for instance, in the *asinus* controversy within late nominalism, as to whether the Son might have just as easily been incarnated as a donkey to attain human redemption. Cf. Heiko Augustinus Oberman, *The Harvest of Medieval Theology* (Cambridge, Mass.: Harvard Univ. Press, 1963), 250, 255–58.

For the expiation of the divine wrath against us. As a fact, we were the culprits and we should have been punished, that the moral order of the world, which had been disturbed by our transgression, might be re-established. But to propitiate the Infinite God, an infinite victim was also necessary; and such the earth could not provide, in spite of her never ceasing to offer bloody sacrifices, which spoke of an universal guilt. For that reason our Savior offered himself in atonement on the cross. By his human nature, he stood as the representative of the guilty; by his divine nature, he offered the ransom due to God; and being crucified for us, he satisfied the divine justice, reconciled all things unto himself and gave to us redemption "through his blood" (Eph. 1:7).[16]

Finally, there are areas of agreement on the relationship of the church to this deliverance that God has achieved in Christ. In much of popular evangelicalism, ecclesiology (the doctrine of the church) has fallen on hard times. Often, the church is seen as little more than a voluntary association of individuals rather than as a visible institution through which its sole mediator and head saves, sanctifies, and extends his community. Here the churches of the Reformation occupy a position between the sacerdotal error on the one hand and the generally low esteem for the role of church and sacraments within mainstream evangelicalism on the other. Adding to the connections between creation and consummation, incarnation and redemption, nature and grace, and Christology and soteriology is the close link between this last pair and ecclesiology. The church is not merely the sum total of the saved but is, in its visible ministry of word, sacrament, and discipline, the earthly theater of God's grace. Hence, Calvin approvingly cites the familiar line from Cyprian, "Outside the church there is no salvation," and the Reformation confessions and catechisms concur. "He cannot have God as his Father who takes not the Church for his mother," Calvin warned. "Furthermore, away from her bosom one cannot hope for any forgiveness of sins or any salvation, as Isaiah and Joel testify."[17]

While Orthodoxy holds views of the priesthood that must be rejected on the same grounds as criticism of Roman Catholic dogma, there is a greater tendency among the former to regard

---

[16]Callinicos, *The Greek Orthodox Catechism*, 29.

[17]Calvin, *Institutes*, 4.1.4., 1016.

the role of the church as ministerial (i.e., evangelical) rather than magisterial (i.e., legalistic), and this represents an interesting area for further discussion. In his catechism Father Callinicos asks, "How does the Church succeed in sanctifying us?" His answer, "By the Word of God and the Sacraments,"[18] is identical to the reply of the Lutheran, Reformed, and Presbyterian catechisms. The similarities between Calvin's understanding of the Lord's Supper and that of Orthodoxy, especially in relation to the *sursum corda* ("Lift up your hearts") and the eschatological feeding through mystical union with Christ, are profound.

RANGE OF DISAGREEMENTS

Having too briefly observed some areas of agreement that are being fruitfully explored in our day, I will now attempt a similarly disappointing strategy in discussing disagreements. More satisfying treatments are needed, but we will concentrate on those at the heart of what evangelical Christianity has most cherished.

Scripture and Tradition

Many evangelicals have witnessed the bewildering proliferation of sects claiming to be unearthing the real meaning of the Bible that has been forgotten by everyone else for most of church history. Nowhere has free-enterprise religion more characterized a people than in American church history. In the face of this scandal, it is not at all surprising that many evangelicals are attracted to the stability of Orthodoxy as an institution. Furthermore, an understandable antimodernist reaction against Heraclitean flux (what author and psychiatrist Robert Jay Lifton has called the protean self) may incline some toward a Parmenidean stasis—in order to regain one's balance in a sea of change.

It is certainly the case, however, that Eastern Orthodoxy and orthodox Protestantism approach Scripture and tradition, as well as their coordination, rather differently. Like Rome, the East has generally accepted at least certain post-apostolic traditions as equal in authority to Scripture. Daniel Clendenin is quite justified in reminding Protestants of the historical context for

---

[18]Callinicos, *The Greek Orthodox Catechism*, 39.

Orthodoxy's view on this point.[19] Irenaeus, for example, developed a rigorous view of episcopal authority (though not papal authority, as our Orthodox interlocutors will agree) and the external criteria for identifying the true church and distinguishing it from the false church. The gnostics, of course, claimed the authority of Scripture as well, but when they traced their lineage back to its origins, they could not claim a single apostle. As a second-century bishop, Irenaeus could claim a direct line of descent, as could other orthodox bishops. This test is absent from Scripture and probably was, even for Irenaeus, more of an argument from common sense than a dogma.

In the face of heresies, the claims of tradition and apostolic succession became more pronounced, despite the New Testament emphasis on the succession of apostolic ministry rather than apostolic men. Still, Irenaeus did not appear to hold the view that became standard among both Orthodox and Roman Catholic writers since the fifth century. Writing against the heresies, he aims to prove his arguments with "proofs from the Scriptures," since the Scriptures are "the ground and pillar of our faith." "When, however, they are confuted from the Scriptures," he adds of his opponents, "they turn around and accuse these same Scriptures, as if they were not correct, nor of authority and [assert] that they are ambiguous, and that the truth cannot be extracted from them by those who are ignorant of tradition."[20]

Even when we take contextual considerations into account, classical Protestants will have difficulty in their discussions with Orthodox theologians from the very start. The two begin with different theological methods (prolegomena), and this becomes apparent in every later debate throughout the loci. For confessional evangelicals, Orthodoxy is no more successful than Rome in explaining (1) how Scripture justifies extracanonical norms and (2) how such a practice obviates the difficulties of interpretive multiplicity. Councils contradict councils even in the patristic

---

[19]Daniel B. Clendenin, *Eastern Orthodox Christianity: A Western Perspective* (Grand Rapids: Baker, 1994). "In the early centuries of Christianity, the church struggled with attempts by Gnostic and Arian heretics to use the Scripture to their own ends. Vincent of Lerins, for example, complains in his Commonitorium that all the heretics claim scriptural support for their positions. In response, the early church developed notions of tradition, the rule or canon of Christian truth, in order to distinguish the true from false exegesis of the Word" (155–56).

[20]Irenaeus, "Against Heresies," in *The Ante-Nicene Fathers*, vol. 1, ed. Alexander Roberts and James Donaldson (Edinburgh: T & T Clark, 1899), 414–15.

period at certain points, and it is highly suspect that the great Fathers themselves regarded their conclusions as binding for any other reason than that they were based on the direct or inferential evidence of apostolic testimony deposited in Scripture. Having an infallible tradition to interpret an infallible text only leaves us with deeper difficulties. Who interprets the infallible tradition? Diversity does exist in Orthodoxy; is the church clearer in interpreting Scripture than Scripture is in interpreting itself?

According to Reformation theology, drawing on patristic sources, Scripture judges the church, not vice versa. Jesus judged "the tradition of the elders" because it contradicted the clear teaching of Scripture (Matt. 15:2, 6). Paul offers a similar rebuke in Colossians 2:8. The Apostle to the Gentiles does, of course, refer to tradition positively as well. He warns the Thessalonians to withdraw from everyone who walks "not according to the tradition which he received from us" (2 Thess. 3:6 NKJV). "Therefore, brethren, stand fast and hold the traditions which you were taught, whether by word or our epistle" (2 Thess. 2:15 NKJV).

But these verses suggest the opposite of Orthodoxy's contention. The traditions in question were limited to those taught "by word or our epistle" from the apostles themselves on good authority, not by a living tradition that was passed down through apostolic succession. Even at a time when the canon was not available, Paul restricted authoritative tradition to the teaching of the apostles that we now possess in the very form to which Paul referred: "our epistle." The only other time Paul refers to tradition is in Galatians 1:14, where he confesses that he persecuted the church beyond his peers—being "extremely zealous for the traditions of my fathers." His argument in this opening chapter to a church in danger of forfeiting the reality of the gospel for the shadows of the law is that the revelation of God to his prophets and apostles stands over and sometimes against the traditions of the fathers.

The heart of our differences emerges over the material principle: justification by grace alone through faith alone because of Christ alone. And here the cleavage becomes more obvious between our communions.

Sin and Free Will

Anselm's famous retort to his imaginary friend Boso, "You have not yet considered how great your sin is," applies to all of our communions, especially in this day of optimism about human capabilities. Despite agreements noted above, the Christian East, in our view, possesses an inadequate view of sin. This becomes apparent in its treatment of original sin, excluding inherited guilt from the picture and embracing a synergistic view of regeneration as well as a medicinal view of justifying grace.

To do justice to the Orthodox view, we must again recall that the reigning paradigm is relational and transformative. Humanity is on a pilgrimage—from innocence to mortality to immortality. It is a movement from image to likeness, from natural goodness to moral goodness. Father Palachovsky explains:

> We have been made in His image through Creation, but we must become like Him by ourselves, through our own free will. To be the image of God belongs to us by our primordial destination, but to become like God depends upon our will. . . .
>
> Human nature has not remained intact, as some theologians teach, but has become corrupt. Nevertheless, this corruption does not go so far as the Protestant theologians teach.[21]

We must appreciate the categories of Orthodox thought on this issue, since the context of early patristic development was Gnosticism, Manichaeism, and their kindred heresies in which creation and redemption were set in opposition. Matter was inherently evil because it was intrinsically temporal rather than eternal, changing rather than static, physical rather than spiritual, and so forth. Sin was accounted for in a cosmic fatalism grounded in ontological dualism. It would only make sense that the church fathers would confront this pagan determinism and dualism with an emphasis on human responsibility and freedom, as well as on the goodness of the Creator God (and therefore of every *natura* he creates).[22] There are some passages in Augustine, particularly in his description of the origin of sin, that come perilously close to viewing nature qua nature as sinful.[23] This, as we have seen, is thoroughly rejected by the Reformers and their successors.

---

[21]Palachovsky and Vogel, *Sin in the Orthodox Church and in the Protestant Churches*, 31, 35.

[22]Cf. Saint Augustine, *City of God*, trans. Gerald G. Walsh et al. (New York: Image Books, 1958), bk. 12, chaps. 3–5.

[23]Ibid., bk. 13, chaps. 13–16. See also Saint Augustine, *Confessions*, bk. 1, chap. 7; bk. 21, chap. 27.

Still, even granting this important point, Orthodoxy appears to deny clear biblical statements on this important question. Corruption and mortality are hardly the only categories in biblical teaching. Nevertheless, as Constantine N. Tsirpanlis writes in presenting the Orthodox view, "Now, Adam's sin was a personal choice and act, not a collective guilt nor a 'sin of nature.' Hence, inherited guilt is impossible.... In other words, the posterity of Adam inherited the consequences of his sin, i.e., physical death and mortality, sickness of corruption, and obscurity or distortion of God's image, but not his personal guilt."[24] John Meyendorff concurs that there is no place in Orthodox theology "for the concept of inherited guilt..., although it admits that human nature incurs the consequences of Adam's sin."[25] In fact, "There is indeed a consensus in Greek patristic and Byzantine traditions in identifying the inheritance of the Fall as an inheritance essentially of mortality rather than of sinfulness, sinfulness being merely the consequence of mortality."[26] "The opposition between the two Adams is seen in terms not of guilt and forgiveness but of death and life," he says, citing 1 Corinthians 15:47–48.[27]

First Corinthians 15:47–48 is a marvelous and much-overlooked side of the sin-and-grace message, as Reformed theologians such as Geerhardus Vos, Herman Ridderbos, and, more recently, Richard Gaffin, have argued.[28] Orthodoxy offers profound insight on this aspect, but in presenting half of the picture as if it were the whole, it ignores the obvious juridical elements and consequently leaves us not merely with an incomplete account but with an erroneous one. Can sinfulness be regarded as a consequence of mortality rather than vice versa, when Scripture so clearly states that "sin entered the world through one man, and death through sin, and in this way death came to all men, because all sinned" (Rom. 5:12)? "The wages of sin is death" (Rom. 6:23). Here in Romans 6, "wages" is a similarly legal category—a debt that is owed. The biblical testimony to the Savior's payment of a debt is so replete as not to require citations. The New Testament language for sin (e.g., condemnation of the law)

---

[24]Tsirpanlis, *Introduction to Eastern Patristic Thought and Orthodox Theology*, 52.

[25]Meyendorff, *Byzantine Theology*, 133.

[26]Ibid., 145.

[27]Ibid., 146.

[28]See Richard Gaffin, *Resurrection and Redemption* (Phillipsburg, N.J.: P & R Publishing, 1978).

and redemption (e.g., justification, imputation, reconciliation, acquittal) is unmistakably forensic as well as relational.

Even those who have not in their own persons committed exactly the same sin as Adam's are nevertheless guilty of that sin (Rom. 5:14). "The judgment followed one sin and brought condemnation" (v. 16), and "by the trespass of the one man, death reigned through that one man" (v. 17). "Consequently, just as the result of one trespass was condemnation for all men ..." (v. 18). I have purposely reserved the corollary of the second Adam for our discussion below. Paul repeats for effect, "through the disobedience of the one man the many were made sinners ..." (v. 19). Death comes through sin, inherited both in its power and in its guilt. Therefore the consequence is inherited. That is Paul's logic in this text.

The Orthodox view excludes original guilt, while the Western view admits both original guilt and original corruption/mortality. Despite Augustinian (and Roman Catholic) distortions of sin and nature, the confessional Protestant articulation of original sin is thus able to do greater justice to the fuller teaching of Scripture, even if it needs to give more attention to the emphasis on immortality in the second Adam.

Redemption

Neoorthodox theologies prepared the soil for a wide-scale reassessment of the Western tradition in terms of "relational" versus "legal" categories. From Harnack to Pinnock, Protestants have subjected what they have referred to as "Augustinian legalism" to relentless criticism. Perhaps partly because of the society in which many evangelical theologians now live, with its therapeutic culture in which justice must give way to love in every instance, the Pauline explanation for how God is, in Christ, both "just and the one who justifies those who have faith in Jesus" (Rom. 3:26) has lost its attraction for a growing number of those theologians. The difference between the two categories is the difference between a "courtroom" model and a "family room" model. The former is indisputably Roman, while the latter is thoroughly scriptural, it is suggested.

This is precisely the view expressed by modern Orthodox theologians such as Christos Yannaras:

A great misconception and distortion of the ecclesial truth about the abolition of death by the cross of Christ had already appeared in the West by the first centuries and progressively dominated the spiritual climate. Tertullian, Augustine, Anselm, and Thomas Aquinas are the great landmarks in the formation and imposition of this distortion which was finally proclaimed as an official teaching of the Western church at the Council of Trent (1545–1563). It is a matter of a legalistic interpretation of the biblical images of "ransom" which Christ paid with his death on the cross.... In the teaching of Luther and of Calvin later, it is not simply divine justice, but the wrath of God which must be appeased by the sacrifice of Christ on the cross.[29]

This account Yannaras can only regard as "sadistic," leading to "egocentric justification as well."[30] Individualistic and legalistic, this theology fails to recognize the ecclesial and cosmic redemption that comes from God as a passionate lover.

Orthodox theologians should attempt to understand the surprise of those who have seen in both Old and New Testaments a recurring emphasis on the cross of Christ as "payment," "propitiation," "sacrifice," "satisfaction," and the like. Acknowledging the important theme of *Christus Victor,* Reformation theology has nevertheless recognized the victory of Christ over Satan, mortality, evil, and the demonic as the consequence of his satisfaction of the Father's plan to propitiate God's wrath against sin. Even in one of the clearest *Christus Victor* passages, Paul apparently makes this very connection:

> When you were dead in your sins [a moral category, since his readers are still physically alive] and in the uncircumcision of your sinful nature, God made you alive with Christ. He forgave us all our sins, having canceled the written code, with its regulations, that was against us and that stood opposed to us; he took it away, nailing it to the cross. And having disarmed the powers and authorities, he made a public spectacle of them, triumphing over them by the cross.
>
> Colossians 2:13–15

---

[29]Christos Yannaras, *Elements of Faith: An Introduction to Orthodox Theology,* trans. Keith Schram (Edinburgh: T & T Clark, 1991), 111–13.

[30]Ibid., 113.

That last statement depends on that which precedes it. The power of Satan over us was chiefly God's own law, a recurring Pauline theme, but once this was satisfied by the substitution of Christ for sinners, the powers and authorities were disarmed. The "public spectacle" *is* a courtroom scene in which God judges his Son in our place.

Here, once again, this view accounts for both the *Christus Victor* motif and the substitutionary motif, while the Orthodox emphasis apparently cannot accept the very premise (i.e., God's wrath against sinners) that would provide a context for Christ's victory. Irenaeus, for one, incorporates both motifs in his thought. Not only by his incarnation but "by means of his passion" Jesus Christ has conquered death:

> For doing away with that disobedience of man which had taken place at the beginning by the occasion of a tree, "He became obedient unto death, even the death of the cross"; rectifying [a legal term] that disobedience which had occurred by reason of a tree, through that obedience which was [wrought out] upon the tree [of the cross]. . . . In the second Adam, however, we are reconciled, being made obedient even unto death. For we were debtors to none other but to him whose commandment we had transgressed at the beginning.[31]

Note that he says we were debtors to the commandment *we* had transgressed at the beginning—in Adam. Hence, human beings "are not justified of themselves, but the advent of the Lord."[32] There is, therefore, no basis for "trusting to works of righteousness."[33]

It is important to recognize that while certain affectations from Roman jurisprudence—or, more directly, medieval feudalism—appear in Western discussions (especially in Anselm's account), the Reformers explicitly criticized these tendencies while building on their labors. It is difficult to dismiss the Old Testament's legal character. In fact, as recent scholarship has underscored, much of the Old Testament may be read as a covenantal charter in the pattern of the ancient Near Eastern suzerainty treaty.[34] Without recognizing the legal character of

---

[31]Irenaeus, "Against Heresies," 544.

[32]Ibid., 499.

[33]Ibid., 550.

[34]Cf. Meredith G. Kline, *The Treaty of the Great King: The Covenant Structure of Deuteronomy* (Grand Rapids: Eerdmans, 1963).

the Mosaic economy, involving strict observance for remaining in the land and requiring the shedding of blood for remission of sins, and the anticipation in the prophets of a Servant who will bear the guilt of sinners, the Old Testament loses its plot and the New Testament loses its claim as the fulfillment of all types and shadows.

Justification

The parallel between the first and second Adams in Romans 5 draws together tightly the corollary of "double imputation": Adam's guilt and Christ's righteousness. Orthodoxy's apparent denial of original guilt and its reticence toward legal categories cannot help but lead to a denial of the imputation of Christ's righteousness, or "justification." Orthodox theologians frequently dismiss the entire discussion of justification as a Western debate, although it was the debate at the heart of Jesus' controversy with the Pharisees, of Paul's controversy with the Galatians, and of the writer of the book of Hebrews' controversy with the Judaizers who wanted to return to the shadows of Jewish temple ritual, including its sacrifices. "The righteousness that is by works" is set in opposition to "the righteousness that is by faith," not because works and faith are opposed in the least, but because the righteousness that God's justice requires is found only in Christ. It must be imputed, or credited—terms that are of Pauline, not Protestant, origin.

At this point, proof texts could be sent back and forth, but Orthodox theologians will not be likely to find ours appealing, since they do not accept the motif these texts assume. For instance, the gospel we find in Scripture (Luke 18:14) says that the believing tax collector (publican) went home justified once and for all rather than the Pharisee who had been trying to attain righteousness by his own efforts (perhaps even with the help of grace, since he does thank God that he is not like the tax collector). After demonstrating that the Old Testament saints were justified through faith alone, Paul announces, "But to him who does not work but believes on Him who justifies the ungodly, his faith is accounted for righteousness, just as David also describes the blessedness of the man to whom God imputes righteousness apart from works" (Rom. 4:5–6 NKJV). Paul says that a person is justified not when he ceases being ungodly but while he or she is ungodly, and that God imputes righteousness apart from works—not apart from works alone or through works that are performed in cooperation with God's grace, but by faith apart from works. We find the same construction earlier in Romans:

> But now the righteousness of God apart from the law is revealed, being witnessed by the Law and the Prophets, even the righteousness of God, which is through faith in Jesus Christ to all and on all who believe. For there is no difference: for all have sinned and fall short of the glory of God, being justified freely by His grace through the redemption that is in Christ Jesus, whom God set forth to be a propitiation by his blood, through faith. . . .
>
> Romans 3:21–25 NKJV

A denial of this point is no small thing for the apostles, as Paul relates in his distress:

> Brethren, my heart's desire and prayer to God for Israel is that they may be saved. For I bear them witness that they have a zeal for God, but not according to knowledge. For they being ignorant of God's righteousness, and seeking to establish their own righteousness, have not submitted to the righteousness of God. For Christ is the end of the law for righteousness to everyone who believes.
>
> Romans 10:1–4 NKJV

Just before, Paul had argued that salvation does not "depend on man's desire or effort, but on God's mercy" (Rom. 9:16), and later (chap. 11) he will warn Gentile Christians that they must not rely on their pedigree, since if the physical descendants of Abraham may be broken off to make room for believing Gentiles, God will certainly not fail to reject Gentiles who place the least confidence in their own cooperation with God.

Whether Orthodox, Roman Catholic, or Protestant, we must all take this to heart. It is trusting in Christ's merit alone, not in our cooperation with grace, that we are justified. It is by embracing the apostolic message, not tracing one's ministerial ancestry to the apostles, that a person or a church is approved by God.

Discerning in these New Testament lines of thought a clear distinction between law and gospel—that which commands without promise or assistance and that which gives without command or judgment—Reformation theology observes in Orthodox theology a serious confusion on this point. Despite the fact that the Orthodox use the Greek New Testament (as well as the Septuagint), Father Palachovsky cites Acts 2:38 in its erroneous Vulgate translation: "Do penance."[35] The Greek *metanoeō* (repent) is transformed into the Latin command "Do penance," and this leads to the same confusion of justification and penitential merit one finds in Roman Catholic soteriology. He distinguishes between *peccata leviora* and *peccata graviora*, the latter of which John apparently has in mind when he says, "Whosoever has been born of God does not sin" (1 John 3:9 NKJV).[36]

Even Father Callinicos's catechism asks, "On what basis will Christ judge the world?" The answer: "On the basis of His Gospel. Whosoever has believed in it and has acted in accordance with its dictates, will sit up on the right hand of the Judge. . . . Faith in Christ without good works is not enough to save us. Good works by themselves are also not sufficient. Our salvation will be the outcome of a virtuous life permeated and sealed by the inestimable blood of the Only-begotten Son of God."[37] Citing Augustine approvingly, Father Palachovsky says that daily sins "may be cleansed through: (1) the recitation of the Miserere, (2) almsgiving, and (3) fasting."[38]

Daniel Clendenin, who describes himself as an evangelical student of Eastern Orthodoxy, offers a sympathetic reading of this position:

> Orthodox theologians contend that in the West the doctrines of sin and salvation have been unduly dominated by legal, juridical, and forensic categories. These categories, they insist, are not only overly negative and alien to the spirit of Eastern Christianity, but, when allowed to dominate, are actual distortions of the biblical message. Ernst Benz suggests that this legal framework predominates in

---

[35]See Palachovsky and Vogel, *Sin in the Orthodox Church and in the Protestant Churches*, 14.

[36]Ibid., 16.

[37]Callinicos, *The Greek Orthodox Catechism*, 31.

[38]Palachovsky and Vogel, *Sin in the Orthodox Church and in the Protestant Churches*, 47.

Western thinking (both Catholic and Protestant). He notes how the apostle Paul [that great Western thinker!] frames his Epistle to the Romans in terms of divine law and justice, categories that are perhaps taken from Roman civil law, and that his idea of justification by faith answers the question of how guilty people can stand before a just God. Benz suggests that the Catholic church especially, with its doctrines of penance and indulgences, its concepts of the church, the role of the priest, and canon law, developed in this [Paul's?] legalistic direction. This accent on legal concepts, in contrast to the idea of mystical union perpetuated in the East, is seen by Orthodoxy as the "real issue that unites the West theologically and divides it from the East."[39]

Clendenin correctly notes that this is irreconcilable with the position of the Reformers:

In his *Institutes* Calvin described justification by faith as the "hinge on which all true religion turns," and in his precise definition of the doctrine he compares it to an acquittal in the courts of divine justice: "just as a man, deemed innocent by an impartial judge, is said to be justified, so a sinner is said to be justified by God when he asserts his righteousness." In the history of Orthodox theology, on the other hand, it is startling to observe the near total absence of any mention of the idea of justification by faith.[40]

Clendenin goes on to suggest that we need to balance Orthodoxy's emphasis on mystical union and Protestantism's forensic emphasis.[41] It is true that a genuinely Pauline theology will emphasize both mystical union and the "summing up" of all things in Christ on the one hand, and individual justification and reconciliation on the other. However, how one relates the two is all-important. Any view of union and recapitulation that denies that the sole basis for divine acceptance of sinners is the righteousness of Christ and that the sole means of receiving that righteousness is imputation through faith alone apart from works is a denial of the gospel. Calvin especially had a developed doctrine of mystical union with Christ, and it was in fact central to his thought, linking justification and sanctification in an inseparable bond, as both depended on Christ and all his benefits.

---

[39]Clendenin, *Eastern Orthodox Christianity*, 122.
[40]Ibid., 123.
[41]Ibid., 124.

I wonder what our Orthodox interlocutors would make of the following conclusion: From my perspective, both Orthodox and Roman Catholic theologies tend to collapse ontological and ethical categories—the East in a preference for good creation overwhelming sin, while the West tilted toward confusing sin with creation. It seems to me that the Pauline line of thought in particular presses us to distinguish ontological and ethical categories without either setting them in opposition or allowing one side to swallow the other whole. To be sure, God made the world and pronounced it good. Nothing evil can be attributed to nature as nature. And yet, Western theology is correct to recognize that sin has become an inherited part of human existence. By clearly distinguishing the ontological goodness of nature from the ethical depravity that makes the attainment of salvation impossible even for the most morally committed, one is able to uphold the integrity of creation and its consummation on one hand while doing justice to the imputation of guilt that leads to death on the other. In this way, both a subtle form of Manichaeism on one hand and a subtle form of Semi-Pelagianism on the other can be avoided.

Clendenin recognizes "a very clear synergism or cooperation between the grace of God and human effort" in *The Philokalia*.[42] But Clendenin simply takes this as a restatement of James: "Thus, faith without works and works without faith are equally rejected."[43] A further concession is made, one that could easily be made by an Arminian Protestant who shared the Orthodox understanding of synergism (i.e., regeneration as the fruit of free will's cooperation with grace): "The Orthodox emphasis on the importance of the human response toward the grace of God, which at the same time clearly rejects salvation by works, is a healthy synergistic antidote to any antinomian tendencies that might result from (distorted) juridical understandings of salvation."[44]

I include this because it seems to me that Clendenin's approach is typical of many evangelical responses to both

---

[42]Ibid., 135. *The Philokalia* is a collection of texts written between the fourth and fifteenth centuries by spiritual masters of the Orthodox Christian tradition. First published in Greek in 1782 and translated into Slavonic and later into Russian, *The Philokalia* has exercised a greater influence than any book other than the Bible in the recent history of the Orthodox Church.

[43]Ibid., 136.

[44]Ibid., 158.

Orthodoxy and Roman Catholicism. "Balance" would suggest neither Pelagian denial of grace nor what he calls an "antinomian" rejection of synergism. However, this seems to me to be wrong on two counts. First, it is simplistic. Reformation theology emphasizes "the importance of the human response toward the grace of God" just as vigorously as any, while denying what Clendenin regards as "a healthy synergistic antidote to any antinomian tendencies." Synergism, in our reading of Scripture, is never healthy, and as an antidote to antinomian tendencies it can only prove to be a cure worse than the disease. In fairness, Clendenin does encourage the Orthodox not to dismiss such biblical motifs as justification by faith as Augustinian corruptions.[45] However, to miss these biblical motifs is not merely to leave out a few pieces of the puzzle but is to make the puzzle into something else entirely. Orthodoxy has many healthy emphases, but its denial of the full seriousness of sin and its consequently high appreciation for the possibilities of free will keep it from recognizing the heart of the gospel.

Sanctification

If antinomianism is what one calls being freely justified (declared righteous, not made righteous) once and for all the moment one looks away from oneself to Christ and his merit as sufficient for all sins for all time, then I confess to being an antinomian. But, of course, classic Reformation teaching has always affirmed sanctification—the process of being conformed to Christ's likeness. Reformation theology has drunk deeply from the same wisdom as the Christian East on this reality of the new creation and the renewal that even now is taking believers "from glory to glory." But it has opposed every tendency to confuse justification and sanctification, rendering the former the goal of the latter rather than its basis.

John Meyendorff provides a helpful explanation of the Orthodox doctrine of *theosis* that, I would argue, can be understood in a manner consistent with evangelical theology:

> The man Jesus is God hypostatically, and, therefore, in Him there is a "communication" *(perichoresis—circumincessio)* of the "energies" divine and human. This "communication"

---
[45]Ibid.

> also reaches those who are "in Christ." But they, of course,
> are human hypostases, and are united to God not hypo-
> statically but only "by grace" or "by energy."[46]

In fact, Meyendorff clearly distinguishes the Orthodox view
from Pelagianism, but then he reiterates the synergistic perspective that remains at the heart of the debate between Reformation theology and its rivals: "It is not through his own activity
or 'energy' that man can be deified—this would be Pelagianism—but by divine 'energy,' to which his human activity is 'obedient'; between the two there is a 'synergy,' of which the relation
of the two energies in Christ is the ontological basis."[47]

In spite of his repudiation of Pelagianism, Meyendorff con-
firms our suspicion that Orthodoxy reflects a Semi-Pelagian consensus. Although it will sound like a gross oversimplification,
many of us will regard this as a difference—although an important one—of degree. To what extent can humans be said to contribute to their own salvation? Pelagians answer, "Entirely";
Semi-Pelagians say, "In part." Neither of these answers, from a
classical evangelical perspective, does justice to the biblical
account of sin; nor does either give the comfort that is held out to
us in "the good news."

Eschatology

We do not have the space to address, even briefly, other
areas of concern here. However, I would like to touch on one
issue that is closely linked to the preceding: the final state. While
many of Origen's ideas were condemned as too indebted to
paganism, Gregory of Nyssa's *De hominis opificio* and *Oratio
catechetica* emphasize the restorative nature of God's punishment. Once more it seems that the transformationist model of
theosis becomes a control-belief that shuts out the rest of biblical
teaching. Father Tsirpanlis describes the dominant Orthodox
perspective on this point:

> Present as well as future punishment, in the mind of
> Saint Gregory of Nyssa, is educational, just a way to help
> the soul return to God. . . . So, the punishment of the fall
> has medicinal effects. Gregory's view of Salvation is of a

---

[46]Meyendorff, *Byzantine Theology,* 164.
[47]Ibid.

process of catharsis of the soul from the spurious material alloy of the evil by a purgatorial fire and through the
divine force of God's very love for man. Saint Gregory
of Nyssa is certainly within the great Patristic Tradition
of the first four centuries in considering Christ's
Redemption a means to an end, that end being the reconsecration of the whole universe to God.[48]

At least this writer discerns more echoes of Plato than of
Paul. Even Satan is potentially saved by this saving work of
Christ, says Gregory, as part of the process of reconsecration.[49]
Given the definitive role of human obedience through free will,
the development of humanity into the likeness of God tends to
eclipse the divine irruptions in human history. One cannot help
but discern the similarity of this thinking not only to Origenist
but even to Cappadocian formulations and the ideas of Stoicism
and Neoplatonism. "Furthermore," Father Tsirpanlis argues,
"Universal Salvation is possible because man's free will inher-
its intrinsically good [sic] and is by nature good as the chief feature of rational soul which is herself the plenitude of every good,
since it is made in the Image of God."[50]

But what of those who, despite the goodness of their free
will and of their soul as the fountain of every good, do not cooperate sufficiently with God's purposes for creation? "Then, after
the Resurrection, the 'fire will be the more ardent the more it has
to consume.'"[51] In spite of the difficult passages concerning the
finality and severity of the last judgment, and the lack of any
scriptural warrant for purgatory, Orthodoxy's confidence in the
moral powers of human beings reduces the horizon to the theme
of cosmic transformation. The Orthodox use of *soteria* (salvation)
"is more inclusive and stronger than the Roman Catholic term
'redemption,' and 'reconciliation,' and the Protestant 'justification,'" Father Tsirpanlis tells us.[52] But is it more inclusive? Is it
not more likely that by identifying *soteria* with *theosis*, it has actually narrowed the range of what Orthodoxy can seriously incorporate from the whole biblical witness?

---

[48]Tsirpanlis, *Introduction to Eastern Patristic Thought and Orthodox Theology,* 69–70.
[49]Ibid., 70.
[50]Ibid., 74.
[51]Ibid., 75.
[52]Ibid., 13.

CONCLUSION

Orthodoxy gets things right from the perspective of creation but does not seem to go far enough with the fall. In other words, we agree with the Orthodox that had there been no fall, humanity would have, by continuing in obedience to the Creator's will, entered into the consummation—what the Orthodox call "apotheosis" or "deification," and what we call "glorification." (I think we mean essentially the same thing by our different terms once Western suspicions are set aside.) The trajectory would have been from creation to consummation. However, the fall introduced a break in this trajectory, whose radical character is not, we believe, taken seriously enough in the vast majority of Orthodox sources. According to Scripture, the image bearer could no longer realize his or her goal but was destitute of all righteousness before God and without hope of attaining the perfection enjoyed in creation. Now, therefore, the trajectory is from creation to fall to salvation to consummation.

We simply cannot conceive of redemption in terms of essentially getting back on the horse and riding on. While Western theology has often failed to give sufficient attention to creation and consummation, Eastern theology has often failed to account for the middle part of that series. What we need is a theology in which each moment in this series is given its due. It will no doubt require, among other things, greater attention to the integration of theological loci (especially creation and consummation, fall and common grace, justification and sanctification as well as glorification) and an eschatological perspective on these themes.

The New Testament epistles, even more than the Old Testament prophets, reveal just how quickly churches planted by the apostles themselves could be weakened by error. "I marvel that you are turning away *so soon* from Him who called you in the grace of Christ, to a different gospel, which is not another" (Gal. 1:6 NKJV, emphasis added). Orthodoxy's appeal to a direct line to the apostles is surely no greater ground for confidence than that which the Galatian churches could have claimed. Yet they were wrong. It is on the basis of the apostle's own rebukes that we know they were wrong, and their lofty place in the history of the church could not save them from the apostle's anathema.

The treasure that the church carries in earthen vessels is the gospel—the announcement that God has done for us in Christ that which we could never do for ourselves, even with his help. This is all we have at the end of the day, and without it our ancient pedigree and customs, liturgies and rites, ecclesiastical offices and powers, are worthless. Is it possible that Orthodoxy has, like the recipients of the epistle to the Hebrews, turned—even so soon—from the sufficiency of Christ and his eternal priesthood to return to the shadows of the law and its temporal priesthood that could never and can never take away sin?

We still have much to learn from each other, and I have enjoyed a deepening appreciation for the wisdom of the Christian East. As we continue the discussion, perhaps we evangelicals can also deepen our understanding of and appreciation for the clarity of the gospel of free grace.

A RESPONSE TO MICHAEL HORTON

Bradley Nassif

I have read Dr. Horton's comparative evaluation of Orthodoxy and evangelicalism with great interest. The open manner of his presentation, as well as its content, can only evoke a respectful and carefully measured response.

On the affirmative side, I wish to emphasize those areas we have agreed on as central to the common ground we share: the relationship between Scripture and tradition, the full humanity and divinity of Christ (including the Trinity, barring the *filioque*), created human nature and its relation to God's grace (with Dr. Horton giving us an uncommon interpretation of Calvin's and Augustine's theology of nature and grace that serves as a unifying bridge between the Orthodox and classical Protestant traditions), the close link of Christology and soteriology with creation and redemption and their relationship to our understandings of the church. These are no small areas of agreement because their consequences for Orthodox-evangelical compatibility are far-reaching, as we both have tried to explain from the perspectives our different traditions.

What appears to be lacking, however, is precisely the thesis I have tried to elaborate on in my previous essay. Dr. Horton himself states it very well under his treatment of "Incarnation and Redemption" (page 124):

> Orthodoxy has never separated the work of Christ from the person of Christ, as has often been done in the West. The incarnation is not merely a prerequisite for our redemption but is its beginning....

The close link of Christology and soteriology as well as creation and redemption is a helpful corrective to some of the reductionistic tendencies in Western formulations that miss the eschatological and cosmic dimensions of the incarnation and other saving events of Christ's work.... The position that Gustav Aulen would identify as the *Christus Victor* motif is an essential feature of biblical theology, and it has often been neglected in Western soteriology.

Herein lies the source and substance of our areas of agreement and disagreement. It has been my view that Orthodoxy's "christological maximalism" is what sets us apart from evangelicalism's "christological minimalism." I have already tried to explain the particulars of this in the main text and footnotes of my essay, so it is not necessary to go over it again here (see my treatment of original sin, grace, faith and works, justification, and substitutionary atonement).

Dr. Horton's chief criticism of Eastern Christian thought is that "the heart of our differences emerges over the material principle [of the Reformation]: justification by grace alone through faith alone because of Christ alone" (page 128). He claims that the Orthodox possess an inadequate view of sin because they exclude inherited guilt from the picture while adopting a medicinal view of justifying grace. And later he states, "Any view of union and recapitulation that denies that the sole basis for divine acceptance of sinners is the righteousness of Christ and that the sole means of receiving that righteousness is imputation through faith alone apart from works is a denial of the gospel" (page 137).

I have already addressed this topic (pages 137–40), stating that I do not believe this is or should be a church-dividing issue because the Orthodox and evangelical communities are in an imbalanced agreement on these points. It is an imbalanced agreement because the doctrine of justification is not always seen or properly emphasized by the Orthodox, but I do believe it is clearly there in a formal way in the Orthodox baptismal liturgy, sacraments, and patristic and ascetical literature of the church.

The Orthodox need to see in themselves what evangelicals have thought to be absent, while evangelicals need to see in their doctrine of justification the corollary of *theosis*. The Orthodox and evangelicals concur that justification and *theosis* are linked in an inseparable bond, for both depend on Christ and all his benefits. The two emphases are compatible because they are two expressions of the doctrine of salvation that exist in a state of sufficient harmony so as to allow reciprocal acquisition in their respective theological views (to use Edward Rommen's definition of compatibility; see page 235), even though neither side has as yet made this explicitly so. I gather from Dr. Horton's treatment of this issue and others related to the doctrine of the Trinity that he is not aware of the ecumenical dialogues that have taken place in Europe over the past decade between the Orthodox Church and the Reformed Churches of Scotland, which see far greater compatibility between Orthodoxy and Calvin than he himself has seen.

I have concerns about other parts of Dr. Horton's analysis that I do not feel compelled to address at length but shall note as simply mistaken. For example, in his opening statement he says that Orthodoxy regards "the first five centuries as definitive" (page 117); but this is not so, because "tradition" is never a static periodization of history but a dynamic, living reality in the ongoing life of the church, then and now. Also, when early on he invokes Calvin's perspective on the relation between Scripture and tradition as compatible with Orthodoxy (with which I agree), he later seems to contradict himself by elaborating on how he believes Orthodoxy and confessional Protestantism conflict in this vital area (see my treatment on the relation between Scripture and tradition, pages 61–67). Finally, he invites an Orthodox response to his conclusion (page 138) that both Orthodox and Catholic theologies tend to collapse ontological and ethical categories, thereby allowing a good creation to overwhelm the effects of sin (the Orthodox) or confusing sin with creation (Catholics). While it is true that certain forms of Catholicism do confuse sin with creation, it is not true that the Orthodox allow the goodness of creation to overwhelm the effects of sin, as is manifest in the major feast day of Theophany (Epiphany), which proclaims Christ's purification of the *fallen* creation.

Despite the concerns I have expressed here, it is important to recognize how valuable a service Dr. Horton has rendered to the Orthodox-evangelical dialogue. His section titled "Range of Agreements" is quite excellent and should be taken very seriously by both of our communities as further grounds for Orthodox-evangelical compatibility.

In the end, what Dr. Horton perhaps did not anticipate was his contribution to the inner life of the Orthodox Church itself.

By pointing out areas of our theology he deemed absent, he underscored our need for greater awareness of the evangelical character of our own theology. In this way, Dr. Horton was inadvertently prophetic: Unless Orthodox leaders (ordained and unordained alike) make a concerted effort to recover the evangelical character of the church's theology and place it at the very center of the liturgical and practical life of their local churches, the Orthodox Church will prove initially attractive to evangelicals but, tragically, end up as a revolving door for future converts, as has already been quietly taking place.

Until the Orthodox Church learns to recover its own evangelical tradition by focusing on the importance of preaching personal salvation through faith in Christ and the need for personal Bible study and personal piety—all within the communal context of the life of the church and its understanding of creation and deification—there will be many who will leave Orthodoxy to join the ranks of evangelicalism. There is something wrong in Orthodoxy when so many cradle and convert Orthodox in recent years have been led to leave the church in exchange for a life-giving community of fellow believers in various evangelical denominations. It will take more than rhetoric to convince Orthodox parishioners that these features of the gospel have indeed become a central "living tradition" in the everyday life of the Orthodox Church.

A RESPONSE TO MICHAEL HORTON

Vladimir Berzonsky

Michael Horton writes from the perspective of an evangelical Christian evaluating Orthodox Christianity. He argues that considerable accord has come about from dialogue between the communions; however, he regrets that this has not brought about visible ecclesiastical communion. Too many disagreements are yet to be resolved.

After reading his treatise I came away with the feeling that he has no real comprehension of Orthodox Christianity, mainly because he approaches the church from a jaundiced viewpoint. As a Western Christian, he seems unable to separate himself from the classic dialogue between Roman Catholicism and Protestantism. He searches in vain for "teeming citations" for "guilt, Pelagius, forgiveness, reconciliation, and propitiation" (pages 117–18).

My response is twofold: (1) The heresy of Pelagius, along with the problem of guilt that shapes and nearly consumes Western theology, is a matter more in keeping with the Augustinian definition of nature, which I will take up below. (2) Who has ever attended any of the various worship services in an Orthodox Church and not come away with the ongoing refrain "Lord, have mercy!" echoing through his or her ears? Why would we plead for mercy and beg forgiveness and ask for reconciliation that comes only with the grace of Christ Jesus transmitted via the Holy Spirit—if we were not convicted of our sins? For this writer Orthodoxy is little more than an Oriental version of Catholicism. Being Orthodox is then like being a husband to a widow whose every reference is inevitably to her first spouse.

Orthodoxy has no stake in the Reformation and Counter-Reformation polemics.[1] To present Calvin as a student of the church fathers means little when Calvin and most other Reformers returned to Augustine and reaffirmed the same premises upheld by Roman Catholics. Turning to the Bible for aid, we look at Romans 5:12. Here is the famous phrase concerning Paul's understanding of sin and death: "Therefore, just as sin entered the world through one man, and death through sin, and in this way death came to all men, *because all sinned [eph hō pantes hemarton]*" (emphasis added).

These four Greek words had been translated in Latin as *in quo omnes peccaverunt* (in [Adam] all have sinned). In the West this is taken to mean that the guilt of Adam had been transmitted to all his descendants. But the Greek does not justify this. *Eph hō* is better translated "because." Paul, therefore, means that death is the wages of sin (Rom. 6:23). The act of disobedience is universal, but not one that conveys guilt to his progeny, unless of course they sin as he did.[2]

Here is not the place to do more than allude to a basic difference from Western theology in general and Protestantism in particular, and lift up a plea to look at Orthodoxy and evaluate it for what it is. Essentially the Orthodox Christian theology calls for a cooperation with the Holy Trinity for our salvation. Indeed, it is a symbiotic action, lopsided though it may be. The gift is the *imago Dei* (the image of God), while the human being is called on to grow into the likeness of God. We have no reason to paralyze the potential of the human being from being all that she can be as made in God's image and open to rising, with the gift of the Holy Spirit that comes through the life, death, and resurrection of Jesus Christ, to become like God in all ways except in essence.

This is why not only the nativity of Jesus Christ but the annunciation to the holy *Theotokos* (Birthgiver of God) and the transfiguration, as well as Pentecost, are significant events in human history. Was it not the case that even God the heavenly Father would not put his plan for our salvation into effect without the affirmation of humanity in the person of the young virgin named Mary—"May it be to me as you have said" (Luke 1:38)? Again, near the end of our Lord's mission here on earth, he thought it time to share a vision of the world as it might be

---

[1]For a Roman Catholic reaction to Reformation theology, see Louis Bouyer, *The Spirit and Forms of Protestantism*, 2d ed. (New York: Scepter, 1964).

[2]John Meyendorff, *Byzantine Theology: Historical Trends and Doctrinal Themes* (London: Mowbrays, 1974), 144.

and should be, if the Father's will would be operative, when Jesus laments over Jerusalem and the fate that will befall the city but could have been avoided (Matt. 23:37; Luke 13:34). Have we not a glimmer of what humans are capable of grasping, even for an instant—an insight concerning heavenly things, holiness for those on their way to holiness?

Dr. Horton observes that "Orthodoxy holds views of the priesthood that must be rejected on the same grounds as criticism of Roman Catholic dogma" (page 125). However, he never explains what those views are, so we can only speculate: Triumphalism? Hardly, if we speak of the Orthodox. Bishops in the early church were celibate in order that they not leave behind a family if they should be martyred, or have a family to leave a legacy of material goods to after they died. All three orders—bishop, priest, and deacon—are duties of service. That bishops and priests be given the privilege of consecrating the Eucharist is, of course, different from evangelicalism, since there is an apparent difference in the nature of the body and blood of Christ blessed and distributed at the table of the Lord.

The writer takes offense at the prevalence of prayers for the dead (page 118). But the dead are alive in Christ. Surely the Scriptures will verify that, especially the book of Revelation. Again I sense the anti-Roman Catholic polemic, that is, assuming that these are prayers that would supposedly release souls from purgatory. No such an idea comes to the Orthodox Christian who prays not only for but also with his beloved who have fallen asleep in the Lord. In Christ they are more alive than we who are on our way to the grave.

Finally, on the matter of lifting up the sacred Scriptures as the ultimate source of reference, surely it need not be mentioned that the Bible requires hermeneutics, an interpretation that is basic theology. When we speak of church, we inevitably come to some form of tradition; otherwise we end up in the quandary of Protestantism, where unity of tradition comes from persuasion. Despite its flaws and weaknesses historically, the Orthodox Church can swim upstream from the present to the age of the apostles, having navigated another channel that avoided Scholasticism, Reformation, and Counter-Reformation, with all that these things brought to Western Christianity. This church has a right to be explored, investigated, and, of course, challenged from outside—but as the entity that it is and always has been.

A RESPONSE TO MICHAEL HORTON

George Hancock-Stefan

Evangelical scholar D. A. Carson has noted that many evangelicals have read comments on original works without bothering to read the originals.[1] Among Orthodox, on the other hand, Archimandrite Chrysostomos, in reviewing Seraphim Rose's book on Saint Augustine, remarks that Father Seraphim is one of the few Orthodox theologians who indeed have read Augustine and did not write a book on what others have said about him.[2] One of the great deficiencies among evangelicals (which is slowly changing) is the fact that many of us haven't read the original works of the church fathers—Eastern and Western. Michael Horton seems to be in the small minority who are the exceptions. He has read his original sources and interacts well with them.

I appreciated Horton's willingness to look at a subject from all possible angles. He wants to be fair to the conclusions of the Fathers by reminding us of their philosophical context, and he wants to be fair to Daniel Clendenin, who Horton believes is at times going in the wrong direction.

Horton's opening paragraph is pivotal for theological exchanges between the Orthodox and evangelicals. Is it possible that Orthodox theology stopped developing too early so that it has not reached some of the theological conclusions so central

---

[1]D. A. Carson, "Training the Next Generation of Evangelical Scholars," lecture, annual meeting of the Evangelical Theological Society, Orlando, Fla., November 1998.

[2]Archimandrite Chrysostomos, review of *The Place of Blessed Augustine in the Orthodox Church*, by Seraphim Rose, *Greek Orthodox Theological Review* 28, no. 1 (1983): 3842–44.

to evangelicals? Has Orthodoxy closed its theological doors too soon? On the other hand, is it possible that the Reformers have gone too far—or even gone astray?

In the three sections in which evangelicals are in qualified agreement with the Orthodox, even Baptists, who are considered to have weak ecclesiology, have to admit that they, while refusing to be labeled creedal, have left a plethora of confessional statements. In these confessional statements, we center our positions in the Scriptures, but with an acute awareness of what other people have said before us. No one does the proverbial jump from John the Baptist to the First Baptist Church of London!

I agree with Horton that the Reformers were well versed in the patristic writers but never placed any patristic Father (or tradition) at the same level as the Scriptures. Incidentally, I have done a systematic study of Calvin's *Institutes* and found that he scarcely ever mentions John of Damascus, who synthesized Orthodox theology. If one is to choose Calvin's favorite Eastern Orthodox Father, or the one to whom he refers most often, it has to be John Chrysostom.

In the subjects in which there seems to be agreement between evangelicals and Orthodox, one has to raise the question: Who speaks for the Orthodox Church? Is Palachovsky speaking for the Orthodox Church?[3] Is Callinicos's *Catechism* in the same category with other catechisms that functioned regionally, only to be dismissed at a later date for leaning toward the Reformers and Latinists and deviating from true Orthodoxy?

The strength of Horton's presentation is his vast textual exegesis. This exegesis provided two ironies: It was ironic (1) to see someone who is in the Greek church rely on a faulty Latin Vulgate manuscript in order to prove his point, and (2) to see that vast biblical texts have been dismissed because of a patristic interpretation that has invalidated the correct interpretation of the text.

It seems that there is a negative commonality between some evangelicals and Orthodox—the absence of seriousness with regard to sin. For many evangelicals this absence is cultural—the culture in which we live is not willing to hear how awful sin is. The Orthodox, theologically, have not allowed the awfulness of sin to be defined scripturally. It is this absence of scriptural

---

[3]See V. Palachovsky and C. Vogel, *Sin in the Orthodox Church and in the Protestant Churches* (New York: Desclee, 1966).

definition that has atrophied the Orthodox positions of redemption and eschatology. While in the days of Calvin, many of his church members were not sure of their salvation because they recognized how sinful they were, in Orthodox theology and in market-driven evangelicalism, universalism is slowly creeping in. If sin is not understood to be as awful as it really is, if sin is not described in scriptural terms, then Christ's death on the cross loses much of its importance.

Michael Horton presents a crystallizing perspective. He reminds us that we need one another in order to increase our knowledge and our faithfulness but that we should not sacrifice clarity in our quest to get together.

A RESPONSE TO MICHAEL HORTON

Edward Rommen

As an Orthodox believer I was deeply moved by Michael Horton's obviously genuine commitment to the authority of the Holy Scriptures and his infectious gratitude for God's salvific grace. Yet, this positive perception was disturbed by a strange dissonance. Every time I found myself saying "Yes, I agree" or "Yes, I believe that," he seemed to counter with a "No, you don't." For example, I agree that the Holy Scriptures judge the church, and not vice versa. It has always been the teaching of the Orthodox Church that the Bible is the inspired Word of God and, as such, is without error and the sole authority against which all questions of life and faith are to be measured.[1] Yet, Horton counters that the East "has generally accepted at least certain post-apostolic traditions as equal in authority to Scripture" (page 126).

In the area of soteriology, I encountered a similar dissonance. The Orthodox, taking the gravity of sin seriously, regularly emphasize themes such as sacrifice,[2] atonement, propitiation, and justification.[3] Our acceptance of these themes is not limited to theological statements but are, as can be seen from the footnotes, anchored in the liturgical practice of the church. We have set

---

[1]See Georges Florovsky, *Collected Works of Georges Florovsky*, vol. 1, *Bible, Church, Tradition: An Eastern Orthodox View* (Belmont, Mass.: Nordland, 1972).

[2]"Sacrificed is the Lamb of God, who taketh away the sin of the world for the life and salvation of the world" (prayer said by the priest during the preparation for every liturgy).

[3]"You are justified. You are illumined. You are sanctified. You are washed: in the Name of our Lord, Jesus Christ, and by the Spirit of our God" (spoken by the priest after the sprinkling of the one being baptized).

aside the fifth Sunday before the beginning of Great Lent for the commemoration of the Pharisee and publican, who was "justified" (Luke 18:14).[4] Yet, Horton writes that the Orthodox deny these soteriological motifs as well as the "full seriousness of sin" (page 139).

How is it that my evangelical colleague refuses to accept my expression of commitment to these biblical themes? We may simply be emphasizing different aspects of the same truth, as may be the case with the doctrines of sanctification and *theosis.* Are we separated by disparate definition of terms we both use, such as "tradition"? Or could it be that the evangelical widens the gap between us by imposing his own misreading[5] of Orthodox theology on the Orthodox, as when he speaks of *infallible* tradition and extracanonical norms. Can his commitment to the individual's right to interpret the Scriptures apart from the context of the church be so strong that he cannot see the difference between the diverse work of the Fathers and the councils, which defeated heretics and preserved the unity of the church for centuries, and the schismatic aftermath of the Reformation, which dissolved into countless theological interest groups?

Maybe the commitment to a particular system of theology requires the evangelical to make certain adjustments to the Scriptures, such as adding the words "once and for all" to our Lord's pronouncement of the publican's justification. Does the evangelical's hyperrational approach blind him to the mystery expected and accepted by the Orthodox, as may be the case in our discussion of the role of icons?

While these questions may help us explain some of the difficulties, the divergence is probably of a more fundamental nature. The Orthodox contributors to this book have suggested that many of the theological truths treasured by evangelicals are deeply embedded in Orthodox doctrine—Nassif spoke of concentric circles (pages 183–84), and I spoke of set and subset (page 105). Horton suggested that the Orthodox have lost some of the pieces to the theological puzzle and have thereby created an

---

[4]"O Lord, Thou has condemned the Pharisee who justified himself by boasting of his works, and Thou has justified the Publican who humbled himself and with cries of sorrow begged for mercy" (from the stichera of the Praises of Matins on the Sunday of the Publican and Pharisee).

[5]See Harold Bloom, *A Map of Misreading,* 2d ed. (New York: Oxford Univ. Press, 2003).

altogether different picture (page 139). Perhaps it would be more accurate to say that all of the pieces are available to Orthodox and evangelicals alike. But because evangelicals have focused so much effort on a few segments, which they mistakenly think constitute the whole puzzle, they tend to misunderstand or disallow the broader terminology, definitions, and categories used by the Orthodox, who have tried to grasp the overall panorama.

CONCLUSION

Michael Horton

Let me begin my concluding remarks by expressing appreciation to the general editor and to those who have contributed to this discussion and to my own understanding of Eastern Orthodoxy.

Father Berzonsky expresses the feeling often expressed by Orthodox brothers and sisters concerning the apparent impossibility—or at least great difficulty—of Western Christians to understand Eastern Christians. Or at least he has found my contribution in this volume to be "jaundiced" for not being able to analyze Orthodoxy on its own terms without viewing it through the lens of Western debates. I readily concede that although my effort has been to understand Orthodoxy through its primary sources—both the Greek fathers and their contemporary interpreters—I am certain that the Western tradition prejudices my reading.

At the same time, this charge is (I fear) often issued in these discussions as a way of circumventing a real conversation on the doctrine and practice at issue, saying, in essence, if you disagree with our position it is simply because you do not understand it—and probably cannot understand it because you are a Western Christian. While many of us as Christians in the West have attempted to discover convergences with the Greek fathers and the subsequent tradition, Father Berzonsky's consistent unwillingness to interact with the actual positions at issue, reducing the Reformation tradition to extreme caricature, represents a contradiction. Both traditions need to develop greater sympathy in getting each other right. Straw-man arguments merely reinforce the prejudices of the converted.

Despite Father Berzonsky's criticisms, my essay in no way implied (1) that Orthodox Christianity must be forced to choose whether to be Protestant or Roman Catholic or (2) that the cry for divine mercy is absent in Orthodoxy. Given my own agreement that Western Christianity needs to be corrected at certain points by Orthodox emphases, it is uncharitable to conclude, "For this writer Orthodoxy is little more than an Oriental version of Catholicism" (page 149).

Orthodoxy may not have a stake in the Reformation/ Counter-Reformation polemics per se, but it must have a stake in the exegetical questions and answers raised by that momentous debate. If Orthodoxy has no stake in interpreting such scriptural themes as union with Christ, justification, sanctification, and related aspects of Christian teaching, then it is hardly Christian. However, as Father Berzonsky himself recognizes, Orthodoxy *is* interested in these questions and provides its own answers. Instead of pretending to remain aloof, Orthodox, Roman Catholic, and Protestant interpreters should attempt in good faith to understand each other's distinct paradigms without dismissing them. Otherwise, the claim to be catholic/ecumenical is nothing more than a sectarian notion to which only our particular ecclesial community has proper title.

Father Berzonsky cites Romans 5:12 as evidence that Scripture denies what the West has identified as "original sin." Accordingly, far from asserting that death spread because all are in Adam, Paul writes, "Therefore, just as sin entered the world through one man, and death through sin, and in this way death came to all men, because all sinned [*eph hō pantes hēmarton*]" (emphasis in original). *Eph hō*, Father Berzonsky thinks, is better translated "because" than, as in the Latin, "in [Adam] all have sinned" *(in quo omnes peccaverunt)*. The point here, as the Pelagians taught in the West, is that no one is condemned for Adam's sin but only for their own. Sin is universal, but guilt is not inherited, Father Berzonsky argues from this verse. I will not quibble with Father Berzonsky's insistence on *eph hō* as "because." In fact, I think it strengthens the case for a strong covenantal understanding of our union with Adam in sin. Yet, Father Berzonsky fails to point out that there is a break in the sentence here. Lifted out of its context, verse 12 could be taken in the way he intends, but the verse begins a thought and breaks off, leaving verses 13 and 14 to complete it. So what do verses 13 and 14 tell us?

—for before the law was given, sin was in the world. But sin is not taken into account where there is no law. Nevertheless, death reigned from the time of Adam to the time of Moses, even over those who did not sin by breaking a command, as did Adam, who was a pattern of the one to come.

In other words, verse 12 introduces the origin (Adam) and extent (all people) of sin, and verses 13 and 14 explain how this occurred. Because of Adam's sin, death reigns "even over those who did not sin by breaking a command, as did Adam." But why? How can I be a victim of death's reign even if I did not commit exactly the same sin as Adam, the very conclusion that Father Berzonsky is unwilling to reach?

Paul's answer seems to be that I was there with Adam covenantally—"in his loins," as it were. Even though I was not personally present, I was representatively present in Adam. This is substantiated by the fact that Paul reiterates the view that Father Berzonsky here denies, namely, that "many died by the trespass of the one man" (v. 15); "the judgment followed one sin and brought condemnation" (v. 16); "by the trespass of the one man, death reigned through that one man" (v. 17); "the result of one trespass was condemnation for all men" (v. 18); "through the disobedience of the one man the many were made sinners" (v. 19) so that "sin reigned in death" (v. 21). This is how death reigns over all people, even though they have not necessarily committed the same sin as Adam personally.

If we do not grasp the representative, legal, covenantal nature of Paul's argument with reference to the imputation of original sin, we cannot comprehend the imputation of Christ's perfect obedience as the second Adam. That is to say, original sin and justification are bound up together as corollaries in this passage, and to misunderstand one is to misunderstand the other. Verse 12, then, rightly understood in the flow of the argument, tells us that every person participates in Adam's sin as truly as if they themselves were present in the garden. If each person "falls" on his own (with Satan's help), then each person can recover with the help of the Holy Spirit, but if each of us is under sin, condemnation, and death "in Adam," we can only be justified by inheriting Christ's obedience, justification, and immortality.

Is there a possibility of reaching common ground on this point by avoiding Augustine's sometimes speculative explanations and instead focusing on the potential convergence of the categories of covenant and recapitulation? Orthodox writers, it seems to me, need to do more than dismiss the Pelagian controversy as alien to Eastern categories; they need to show how their interpretation at specific points such as these (e.g., the exegesis of Romans 5) does not *amount to* the same Pelagian conclusions.

Those who see Orthodoxy on its own terms, Father Berzonsky insists, will recognize that it teaches "a cooperation with the Holy Trinity for our salvation" (page 150). But this *is* largely what the Reformation and Counter-Reformation polemics were all about. I, for one, do not dispute that this is the teaching of Orthodoxy. I just think that it is wrong, and not because I am using a Western paradigm for my thinking, but because of the grammatical sense of the Greek in the very passage he cites, which could also be supplemented by numerous other passages. I am convinced that if I were capable of adopting a Greek rather than Latin orientation, I would still affirm monergistic grace. It was, after all, in large measure the humanists' return to the Greek New Testament as a corrective to the Latin Vulgate that gave rise to the Reformers' exegetical questioning.

While the evangelical (i.e., Reformation) position must beware of simply identifying Orthodox and Roman Catholic soteriologies, the fact remains that the tie that binds both (namely, synergism) is rejected by our theology. We do not deny that we cooperate with God's grace and, by receiving the means of grace (Word and sacrament), grow into maturity in Christ, but we do deny that we can cooperate in our own regeneration (i.e., awakening to God) and justification (i.e., acceptance by God), our will being enslaved to sin until God graciously frees it to embrace Christ and all his benefits. We are not declared righteous *because* we have cooperated with God's grace; we are justified "freely by his grace" (Rom. 3:24) *so that we can.* To say that justification is "once and for all" is not to say that there is no progressive sanctification, any more than to say that justification as a legal declaration based on the righteousness of a representative entails the denial that grace also renews, heals, and finally glorifies the believer as part of God's new creation.

Finally, Father Berzonsky takes exception to my rejection of Orthodox ecclesiology and asks if this is a reference to "triumphalism" (page 151). And yet I do not know what else to call the sort of view expressed in his conclusion: "Despite its flaws and weaknesses historically, the Orthodox Church can swim upstream from the present age to the age of the apostles, having navigated another channel that avoided Scholasticism, Reformation, and Counter-Reformation, with all that these things brought to Western Christianity" (page 151).

What of the previous lines about every believer coming to the Scriptures out of a certain tradition, a view that I heartily endorsed in my own essay? The view expressed here at least seems to ignore the fact that Orthodoxy itself expressed its faith in the categories of Greek thought, the fact of which (as we have seen) representatives such as Father Berzonsky remind us frequently. I must confess that while I find the Greek fathers edifying, I also cannot help but be surprised at times at the degree to which concessions are made to Platonic and neo-Platonic habits of thought. Its view of the body as inherently corrupt, for example, expressed so frequently in the prayers and ascetic literature of the East as well as the West, seems at far remove from the purity of apostolic expression—or even from the affirmation of nature qua nature that the East rightly wishes to preserve against gnosticizing tendencies. To be sure, we all come to Scripture with our own prejudices and assumptions. And yet, to the extent that we all have access to the same Scripture and the same Spirit, we all have access to the apostolic faith. And this is the best hope for any genuine revival of the ecumenical spirit.

Dr. Hancock-Stefan's comments are encouraging, and I can only reaffirm my appreciation for the areas of our agreement. Despite our differences owing to different evangelical traditions, we share a fundamental commitment to the seriousness of sin and the utter graciousness of God's salvific action.

After offering generous remarks, Dr. Rommen provides constructive criticism concerning what he regards as my misunderstanding concerning the relation of Scripture and tradition in Orthodoxy. I will have to read Georges Florovsky on the topic more closely, and I appreciate the footnote provided. He further reminds us that themes such as sacrifice, atonement, propitiation, and justification are found in the liturgy, citing examples (mostly taken from Scripture directly). I do not deny this point, and it is one of the reasons we must beware of reading only a tradition's theological treatises while ignoring its liturgy, especially with respect to a tradition that both grounds and reflects so much of its theology in its liturgy. However, if the liturgical expressions are understood in the ways that at least some of the East's more representative exponents describe—particularly in the tendency to contrast Western "legal" with Eastern "relational" approaches—the presence of the words does not mean the presence of their proper sense.

While one can only applaud the pre-Lenten commemoration of the justified publican, I still cannot withdraw my concern that Orthodoxy downplays (and in some cases denies) certain emphases that evangelicals have regarded as central. It is no secret between us that the Eastern church has traditionally denied original sin, the view of the atonement as penal substitution, and justification as a strictly forensic declaration "apart from works" (Rom. 4:6), and has emphasized *instead* (not just *alongside* the above) a view of salvation as moral transformation (restoring the original likeness) through cooperation with the Holy Spirit.[1] While we may find more agreement in our actual practice (i.e., liturgy)—and this is a potential area of convergence worth pursuing—at least in our more elaborate theological formulations we are still quite far apart. From an Orthodox perspective, we may be seen as hopelessly pessimistic about human moral capacities after the fall, but evangelical Christianity can only see Orthodox theology as needing to more fully appreciate "the full seriousness of sin and its consequences."

Although he is generally evenhanded and constructive in his review, Dr. Rommen still wonders if my critique of the Orthodox view of tradition may be due to the (alleged) fact that my "commitment to the individual's right to interpret the Scriptures apart from the context of the church" is "so strong" (page 156). This despite my repeated agreement with criticisms of the radical individualism that permeates so much of modern evangelicalism in sharp contrast to its Reformation forms. Isn't it possible that, even though we share such critiques, we still simply *disagree* on the proper conclusion?

Dr. Rommen invites, "Does the evangelical's hyperrational approach blind him to the mystery expected and accepted by the

---

[1]It may be worth noting that, despite refusals to be drawn in to the Augustinian-Pelagian controversy, the East was not entirely aloof during the period in question. In fact, Pelagius's followers were frequently given shelter in the East when their views were proscribed by Rome.

Orthodox, as may be the case in our discussion of the role of icons?" (page 156). Perhaps it is hyperrationalism, but *must* it be so? The arguments that the Reformed have typically used are not at least overtly philosophical (rationalist or otherwise) but are rather similar to those employed in the history of Orthodoxy itself by the iconoclasts against the iconodules. Does Dr. Rommen deny that the earliest form of Orthodoxy held exactly the same position as the Reformed, appealing to precisely the same exegetical arguments? Whether the ancient Fathers or Reformed confessions were correct to identify such practice as idolatry, they were appealing to a deeply biblical antipathy toward visible representations of God (rooted in the Decalogue itself). Isn't it possible that we simply disagree over what is prohibited in the command that we not make any image or likeness of God?

More "puzzling" still is Dr. Rommen's comment concerning my puzzle analogy. Resisting the assertion that the Orthodox have lost some pieces to the theological puzzle, he suggests that "perhaps it would be more accurate to say that all of the pieces are available to Orthodox and evangelicals alike. But because evangelicals have focused so much effort on a few segments, which they mistakenly think constitute the whole puzzle, they tend to misunderstand or disallow the broader terminology, definitions, and categories used by the Orthodox, who have tried to grasp the overall panorama" (page 157). This, of course, is an ever-present danger we do not sufficiently avoid. However, it is essential to restate, perhaps more clearly and succinctly, my own position in this regard. I have recognized that categories such as *theosis* are often misunderstood by Protestants. With certain caveats, I would even be willing to endorse that concept, and in my essay I suggested some areas where I thought real convergence was not only possible but enriching.

If Dr. Rommen's criticism here is going to stick, Orthodox theologians must demonstrate where evangelical theology *denies* that the fall and redemption are cosmic as well as individual realities; that the Holy Trinity works through physical means; that the likeness to God lost in Adam is restored in Christ; that the incarnation, as well as the cross and resurrection, is redemptive; that the *Christus Victor* as well as the substitutionary motifs are essential, and that salvation includes both justification *and* sanctification *and* glorification (the last two I take to be included in the package called *theosis*); and that perseverance in faith to the end is necessary to the final enjoyment of the consummation. A great example of the complementary nature of the *Christus Victor* and substitutionary motifs is found in Colossians 2, where the apostle explains that *because* God has nailed the judicial record of our transgressions to Christ's cross, he has "made a public spectacle" of the powers and triumphed over Satan.

It is Orthodoxy that denies key elements of the evangelical interpretation on these matters. Reformed theology has so emphasized eschatological union with Christ as the overarching reality embracing both judicial acceptance and ethical transformation that it can hardly be justifiably charged with ignoring (much less denying) one or the other. But Orthodoxy does, in fact, deny the judicial aspect of inherited guilt (original sin) and imputed righteousness (justification) that we find clearly taught, for example, in the "two Adams" motif of Romans 5 and 1 Corinthians 15. For these reasons, among others, I find it difficult to understand how Orthodoxy can represent itself as providing a broad enough framework for doing justice to the panorama of biblical teaching.

Dr. Nassif's comments are particularly illuminating and deal directly with the key theological issues. Given his own background, it is not surprising that he is able to view evangelical concerns sympathetically, while being careful to correct evangelical misapprehensions and misunderstandings. Regarding justification in particular, he speaks of an "imbalanced agreement" between our traditions (page 146). I am in wholehearted agreement with his assessment (contra his Orthodox colleagues in this volume, who seem to think that evangelical theology reserves no place for sanctification and glorification) that "the Orthodox and evangelicals concur that justification and *theosis* are linked in an inseparable bond, for both depend on Christ and all his benefits" (page 146). In fact, this comment is so suggestive that I was disappointed he did not explore it more fully. Perhaps he will in the future—I'll keep my eyes peeled.

Since Dr. Nassif concludes by encouraging his own tradition to take evangelical concerns more seriously, I am spurred by his good example to do the same. I do not believe that we evangelical (yes, even Reformed!) Christians have a corner on the truth as it is in Christ. While facile contrasts between East and West must be avoided, there are emphases particularly in Irenaeus, Athanasius, and the Cappadocians that are insufficiently appreciated and developed in our own theology. At the same time, these lines have at least been more fully developed in the past than in the last century of evangelical systematic theology and particularly in evangelical church practice.

Too often, we see especially in modern American evangelicalism an individualistic and, frankly, gnostic piety that abstracts the soul from the body, the person from the church, and the church from the world. Despite our official theology (I speak here again as a Reformed Christian), in practice we have often downplayed ecclesiology (including the sacraments) in the interest of a one-sidedly inward, subjective piety that not only ignores the objectivity of Christ and his saving work but divorces the Spirit from the Father and the Son. The Reformers, I believe, would have found most of this entirely foreign or would have identified it with the "enthusiasts" against whom they wrote so many treatises.

Furthermore, while Reformation theology celebrates the glory of God in his sovereignty and holiness as well as in his condescension and mercy *(soli Deo gloria)*, many of our churches have replaced the liturgy with pop culture, the sacraments with "small groups," and the intergenerational tradition of the saints with the niche marketing of consumers. Our churches increasingly look more like malls or theaters than houses of worship where one might expect to encounter a holy God before whom all the earth must keep silence.

Just as Dr. Nassif notes that many Orthodox find greener pastures in evangelicalism, the highway clearly has traffic moving in both directions. Many young people, seeking a profound relationship with God beyond clichés and superficiality, are drawn to the transcendence and mystery of Eastern Orthodoxy. We, too, need to take a step back and ask ourselves some important questions about what is lacking in our own faith and practice that encourages so much dissatisfaction with the status quo. Perhaps as we do this, in conversation with writers like Dr. Nassif, we will rediscover our own deposit of "the faith that was once for all entrusted to the saints" (Jude 3) under our very own nose and find, ironically, more to talk about and share in common with brothers and sisters in other traditions.

Chapter Three

ARE EASTERN ORTHODOXY AND EVANGELICALISM COMPATIBLE? NO

An Orthodox Perspective

Vladimir Berzonsky

ARE EASTERN ORTHODOXY AND EVANGELICALISM COMPATIBLE? NO

An Orthodox Perspective

Vladimir Berzonsky

BARRIERS TO UNITY BETWEEN ORTHODOX AND EVANGELICAL CHRISTIANS

> I do not pray for these alone, but also for those who will believe in Me through their word; that they all may be one, as You, Father, are in Me, and I in You; that they may also be one in Us, that the world may believe that You sent Me.
>
> John 17:20–21 NKJV

The wish, the prayer, and the expectation of our Lord and Savior Jesus Christ for "those who will believe in Me" embraces evangelicals and Orthodox Christians. What would it take to fulfill his prayer? I write as an Orthodox Christian expressing my understanding of evangelicals, meaning mostly the contemporary use of the term to describe those theologically conservative Protestants who preach against secular humanism and challenge liberal Christianity in all its forms among Protestants and others. I am quite aware that the term is also used by many Christian believers who have a conservative Bible-based approach to their faith and practice, who have had a religious conversion commonly called being "born again," and who witness to their faith to others in society.

Evangelicalism is the most visible face Christianity presents to America. The great numbers of Roman Catholic and mainline Protestant churches cannot match the high profile currently enjoyed by evangelicals in our nation. To their credit they dominate the religious expressions in the media. Evidently their witness to the gospel appeals to the nation's masses, whose first, and often only, Christian experience is that of a preacher expounding the Word of God on television. One cannot have lived in America the past fifty years and not be familiar with Billy Graham, who for a half century has visited various parts of the nation and the world, bringing his famous crusades to societies everywhere. We rush to add that the recent interest in evangelicalism is not caused by any one leader or several leaders but rather by many subcultures representing other subcultures. The evangelicals influence mainline Protestant denominations, but they would prefer to remain apart from those bodies for a variety of reasons.

No one explanation will suffice to provide the cause of their success in recent decades. Any explanation would have to take into account the weariness of the nation with an expression of the Christian faith reduced to social welfare and to political causes passing themselves off as theology. A reaction—diffuse and uncoordinated, basically random and amorphous—came to a coalition around the 1973 Supreme Court decision in *Roe v. Wade*, making abortions legal in the United States. Not only Protestant evangelicals, but Jews, Orthodox, and Catholics have continued to come together in response to that outrage against the gift of life given humanity by God. All of us have been raised on the history of our nation. We have imbibed the pride of having spoken to Pharaoh—in our case, the British monarch—demanding freedom from perceived oppression and tyranny. How is it, then, that Orthodox Christians, conservative by definition and conviction, cannot unite with evangelicals? Or can they?

ROOTS

Resisting the American propensity for disregarding or forgetting history, Orthodox Christianity is about the history of salvation and the transcendence of time. To appreciate evangelicals, we must know all about them. We must discover their roots.

They are part of the Protestant Reformation of the sixteenth century, and they termed themselves evangelicals rather than Roman Catholics. They set themselves apart from what they believed was a sacramental system based on doctrines made by humans, not by God. An evangelical was someone who had rediscovered the true faith of the early church within the context of the New Testament. Rather than considering themselves an aberrant innovation, American evangelicals feel they are rooted and grounded in an ancient tradition. The characteristic feature— protesting against all historical and man-made accretions, paring away the superfluous and ambiguous—opens onto the rationale of iconoclasm by logical deduction. They believe what all classical Protestants believe, following the Reformers such as Luther and Calvin: *sola fides* (only faith saves), *sola gratia* (only by grace).

Here is a religion of the Spirit setting itself in opposition to all authority. Not accidentally emerging in the era of the Age of Reason and the Age of Enlightenment, it announces and champions the rights of the individual to know and accept what he or she believes, without help from outside. Søren Kierkegaard epitomizes the spirit of individualism best summed up by William R. Inge, former dean of London's Saint Paul's Cathedral: "One cannot be religious by proxy."[1] All rituals are suspect, since they involve group participation and affirmation by the community, which can lead to the evasion of personal decision. A Protestant would find that the Pharisee in the temple congratulating himself before the Lord missed the opportunity to offer God a prayer from the heart (Luke 18:11).[2]

The human is saved by grace alone—the gift of God and the action, or work, of God. The human being is capable of doing nothing for himself or herself, nor is it possible for one to add anything to the process of salvation, according to Martin Luther. The genuine Christian is the one who renounces everything human so that he or she will find his or her sole support in God alone. This is the faith that achieves salvation. It is not a mere abstract theory but the core of Protestantism. If any value can be

---

[1]Cited in Louis Bouyer, *The Spirit and Forms of Protestantism*, 2d ed. (New York, Scepter, 1964), 98.

[2]Interestingly, the Orthodox Church places supreme value on the prayer of the publican, the renowned "Jesus Prayer," which is the basis for the *hesychast* style of worship.

found in sacrifice or worship, it would be on behalf of the individual's relation to God. The focus of salvation is within the interior life of the person. Grace comes from God alone, not via anything earthly or man-made. There is nothing a person can do to accomplish his salvation. Even to say that he or she cooperates with the grace that saves is to be in error. God's power is manifested in human weakness.

To understand that relationship in this way, namely, that God is Judge and the Christian is a forgiven sinner who has done nothing to deserve the grace that saves him or her, is from the Orthodox Church's point of view to limit both God and the human, the One as little more than Judge, the other as no more than a sinner. The Orthodox Church knows God to be a Trinity of persons in a single essence, One of whom, having consented to become human in all ways—with the exception of sin—has broken down the three barriers that separate deity from humanity: (1) by becoming a man, Jesus Christ, the God-Man, united human nature to divinity, (2) by overcoming sin in himself, Jesus triumphed over the power in which sin held us fast, and (3) by accepting death, Jesus brought us through death and on to everlasting life. Judgment is his, given to him by the Father (John 5:19–24).

When Scripture says that Jesus Christ, the Son of God, took on human nature in the incarnation, it means that all human beings are given the possibility to receive the very uncreated energy of God by opening themselves to union with the Holy Trinity through incorporation into the God-Man, Christ. Here we find the meaning of the mysteries of baptism and Eucharist. Here we grasp the sense of Jesus' claim: "I am the vine; you are the branches. . . . If anyone does not remain in me, he is like a branch that is thrown away and withers" (John 15:5–6).

He replaces Israel and forms his church. Salvation is achieved through and in the church. All the various and disparate persons who come to him through baptism he will make into one body, his church. Adam was to have united the entire world to God; now the second Adam has come to earth to complete the recapitulation. Human nature discovers itself joined to the nature, or hypostasis, of Christ. This is the specific and unique work of the God-Man. He who shares the essence of deity with the Father and the Holy Spirit, being one of the three persons, or hypostases, of divinity, joins himself with human nature in order that a vast multitude of human persons can be united with him—and through him with the Father and the Holy Spirit.

As Orthodox theologian Vladimir Lossky points out, the outpouring of the Holy Spirit following Christ's resurrection comes twice.[3] When the Lord appeared among his apostles in the upper room (John 20:22–23), he breathed on them, conferring the Holy Spirit, giving them power to bind and set free the sins of humans. This is the gift of the Spirit to the church as the body of Christ. There is nothing personal in the sense of authority of any individual—all who minister do so not in their own names but as agents of Christ. He alone is the head of the community of the saved, and all who serve do so in his name by the Holy Spirit.

The second gift of the Holy Spirit is from the Father on Pentecost (Acts 2). Here is grace poured out on persons—not any arbitrary men but on the college of apostles. They are, of course, individuals with their unique gifts that contribute to the whole church. As Saint Paul prioritizes the variety of gifts from the same Spirit in 1 Corinthians 12 and 14, precedence is given to those who best serve the entire church.

When an evangelical and an Orthodox Christian use the term "person," a clarification is in order. The evangelical Christian is, as stated earlier, an individual who makes a personal, conscious, and free agreement to accept Jesus Christ as his or her Savior. Others may have done so before, but this is his or her special bond of fellowship with the Lord Jesus. This personal decision makes the individual different from all those who are not like him, separating the man or woman from the ecclesiastical body and setting him or her free and apart from all external symbols or features associated with the church. This personal awareness offers an objective way of looking at everything in light of the new and unique relationship with Christ. Infant baptism can have little interest for those who are better prepared at the start of adult life to accept Christ's grace through faith. Sacraments offered by the institutional church cannot bear the weight of grace, because they can be accepted without conscious awareness of the transforming power of the Holy Spirit. More, any

---

[3]Vladimir Lossky, *The Mystical Theology of the Eastern Church* (Crestwood, N.Y.: St. Vladimir's Seminary Press, 1976), chap. 8.

hope in their efficacy, any trust that they can act as vehicles of grace, are impediments to the true gift of the Spirit; besides, sacraments can promote pride if they are understood as taking part in the process of God's act. In the startling explanation of Luther, while everything comes from God and all depends on him for salvation, grace embraces the human like the envelope containing a letter; yet the human is not essentially changed in the process.

For the Orthodox Christian it is quite different. The whole person is an individual, but much more. He or she is not a face in the crowd, part of the hoi polloi, one without the ability to think and act for himself or herself. But that person is far more than that. He or she is set free not only in having been liberated from all impediments to autonomy, that is, set free from an enslavement to sin, to pedantry, to the limits of one's society. Beyond that, when such a person has, through great struggles with the old self, arrived at a second stage of freedom—arbitrary freedom, or the ability to choose without impediments—he or she then goes on to the third stage of freedom, which is a surrender of one's arbitrary and subjective freedom conditioned by the vagaries of human nature to a complete submission to the will of God. That person working out his or her own salvation "with fear and trembling" (Phil. 2:12) does so in the church, utilizing all the instruments of salvation, including prayer, fasting, contemplation, and the sacred mysteries provided by Christ through the church.

AUTHORITY OF SACRED SCRIPTURE

The question of authority as experienced within the Orthodox Church is not simple to grasp for Western Christians. Both Roman Catholics and Protestants cling to the need for something external, some infallible last word, to confirm the teachings and doctrines of the ecclesiastical community. For the former it is found in the person of the pope; for the latter it is the Bible itself. Neither can be considered the ultimate source of truth for the Orthodox Church. This is the basic principle securing truth within freedom, an insight of unity with liberty, yet a stumbling block for Roman Catholics and simply ridiculous for Protestants. Roman Catholics often point to the lack of papacy as the cause of Orthodox cohesiveness. Protestants hold in greatest esteem the personal quest for truth. Unfathomable to them is the need for submitting their own subjective comprehension of truth to the objectivity of the church.[4] To test one's private opinion by the wisdom of the Holy Spirit at work through the body of Christ does not compute. The doctrine of the church is for them a matter of personal opinion—or perhaps an accord with others of a common persuasion.

To point out the obvious, namely, that the church came before the New Testament, may not by itself be convincing. The fact that the creation of scriptural canon had been a matter of selection and rejection of various writings, the criteria having been established by the church and its leading thinkers, is not necessarily persuasive; nevertheless, the Bible requires interpretation. Saint Hilary wrote, *Scriptura est non in legendo, sed in intelligendo* (Scripture is not in the reading but in the understanding). Orthodox Christians agree that the God who acts in history saves us and that witnesses to his mighty deeds are found in the Bible. His Word is revealed in Jesus Christ, who is himself the living Word of God. We hear and obey that Word by means of grace that comes to us from the Holy Spirit. These fundamental tenets of belief Orthodox share with evangelicals. Yet we diverge when it comes to the method of interpreting what it is that the Word is telling us. Protestants themselves are selective with regard to the contents of the Bible, which Martin Luther demonstrated by rejecting as a "book of straw" the epistle of James, a challenge to his insistence on *sola fides*. This selectivity proves that the Bible is neither self-sufficient nor self-evident, while affirming that it has no defects and lacks nothing, nor is it in any way flawed.

The Bible is, in Orthodox terms, an image, or icon, of truth, but it is not truth itself in the same way Christ is truth. To say it is so is to limit Christ to the Bible and deprive the church of his continuing presence in history. To set the Bible as an abstract criterion of truth is to harness the freedom of the church to utilize its wisdom garnered from centuries of witnessing the gospel through countless thousands of Christians. To liberate the individual consciousness from the experience and demands of the consciousness of the church is to violate and even to destroy the corporate consciousness of God's people. This is what makes the

---

[4]See Sergius Bulgakov, *A Bulgakov Anthology*, ed. James Pain and Nicolas Zemov (Philadelphia: Westminster, 1976), 129.

results of the Reformation nothing less than sinful—sin being literally "missing the target."

Hear the word again of Dean Inge concerning the Reformers: "Their creed has been described as a return to the Gospel in the spirit of the Koran."[5] These are strong words, not kind or irenic; nevertheless, to proclaim the Bible to be self-sufficient is to open it to subjective, arbitrary interpretation. To say, on the other hand, that tradition is the historical memory of the church is not to consign interpretation to the past. The church had an oral tradition before the gospels were written. Christ was alive in the church, just as he reveals himself and continues to do so within his body, which is the church, and in the sacred Eucharist. It has been said that the church's experience provides us not with a system but with a key to the kingdom of God.

In contrast to the propensity of evangelicals, along with all Protestants, to uphold the individual's relationship with Christ as the means of salvation, the Orthodox offer the concept of *sobornost*. The term, which is difficult to define, means "assembly" or "togetherness"—"catholicity," in the literal meaning of "belonging to the whole." Each member of the church lives in constant unity with the whole church. It is felt especially when Christians share the celebration of the Holy Eucharist, all gathered around the banquet table of the Lord—the obvious assembly of the local community, in touch through the Holy Spirit with the universal church throughout the world, whether gathered in liturgy or in remote cells, as the anchorites apart from humanity yet not alone. Further, the church is also comprised of the people of God gone before us to their rest, the saints of all ages.

TEMPLE AND TENT

Imagine if Orthodox Christians and evangelicals were seriously interested in bonding together in unity and fulfilling the Lord's Prayer "that they may be one just as We are one (John 17:22 NKJV). Where would we meet? Both, or rather all, are pilgrims on "the Way," as the first community was called (Acts 9:2). Orthodox Christians are comfortable anywhere on God's earth when

---

[5]William Ralph Inge, *The Platonic Tradition in English Religious Thought* (London: Longmans, Green, 1926), 27.

they are themselves evangelizing to those in search of salvation, and of course evangelicals would affirm that statement.

However, when the Orthodox Christians come together to experience the joy of Eucharist, only the best will do. Church as building becomes a temple, set apart to be made holy—prelude and paradigm of the world become church. The structure is cruciform—using the Hagia Sophia as a model—where the four corners of the earth are crowned with the heaven above, the meeting between the Bridegroom and the bride he has come to claim. Within, the walls surround worshipers with the images of the saints of the past in company with angels and remind them of the saving events of sacred history. All the senses share in the earnest of the heavenly banquet feast breaking into a moment of time: the aroma of incense, the icons of the grace-filled saints, the sounds of chanted psalms and hymns, the ecstatic awareness of elevation beyond the mundane, and finally the invitation to taste and see how good the Lord is (Ps. 34:8).

What could the above mean to an evangelical Christian? He or she might accept it out of indulgence, patronizing his or her hosts; nevertheless, if he is true to himself, he will be uncomfortable. Is this not idolatry, a violation of the second commandment of the Decalogue? Explain to him, using words similar to that of Saint John Damascene, who in an attempt to enlighten the Muslim sultan, said that the admonition against making an idol had been in effect until the incarnation of the God-Man Jesus Christ.[6] When our Lord took on human flesh, matter was blessed as the bearer of holiness. Through him all matter is potentially restored to its status before the fall of Adam.

In simple terms we are confronted with the centuries-old differences between iconodules and iconoclasts. How would evangelicals respond to Orthodox Christians who bow in prostration before the cross of Christ and the icons of the saints—all this before the first words of prayer are uttered? And when prayers begin, they are addressed to the Holy Spirit, demonstrating the Trinitarian nature of Orthodox worship. The first prayer in this scene from the Divine Liturgy of the Orthodox Church is an invocation of the Holy Spirit—the prayer for the

---

[6]Saint John of Damascus, an ardent defender of icons, served as a high official in the court of the caliph (see "John of Damascus, St.," in *The Oxford Dictionary of the Christian Church*, F. L. Cross and E. A. Livingstone, eds. [Oxford: Oxford Univ. Press, 1997], 891).

Holy Spirit to come upon all the people and to show the bread and wine offered in remembrance of Christ to be the very body and blood of the Lord. The Orthodox acknowledge that all three persons of the Holy Trinity have a role in the Eucharist.

Conservative evangelicals in general affirm the great creeds of Christendom;[7] however, those in Western Christian communities assume the Nicene Creed includes the *filioque* term—that the Holy Spirit proceeds from both Father and Son—which is an unacceptable innovation renounced by the Orthodox Church.

Vladimir Lossky pointed out that when the great church fathers such as Saint Basil or Saint Augustine are studied, the way they will be understood is colored by the reader's background and mind-set. Easterners and Westerners comprehend in accordance with the traditions that nurture and nourish their points of view.[8] To properly understand the Orthodox approach to the Fathers, one must first of all understand the mystical characteristic of Orthodox theology and the tradition of the apophatic approach to an understanding—if "understanding" is indeed the proper word—of what the hidden God in Trinity reveals to us. This needs to be combined with the insight that what is incomprehensible to our reason inspires us to rise above every attempt at philosophical limitation and to reach for an experience beyond the limits of the intellect. The experience of God is a transcendence born from union with the divine—*henosis* (oneness with God) being the ultimate goal of existence. This makes the requirement for gaining of true knowledge (*gnosis*) the abandoning of all hope of the conventional subject-object approach to discovery. It requires setting aside the dead ends of Scholasticism, nominalism, and the limits set by such Kantian paradigms as *noumena/ phenomena*. One must return to, or better yet, find in one's heart (or *nous*, the soul's eye) union with the Holy Trinity, which has never been lost in the Orthodox Church.

God is approached not just by the intellectual ways that raise us to him but also by descending to where we are. One

---

[7]It is heartening to note evangelical understanding of creedal significance: "We have already argued that the ontological quest of the early church arose from an Old Testament view of God. In the same way, the need to express this reality of the incarnate Christ arose from, and was governed by, New Testament requirements. Chalcedon did not adopt philosophy; it took some basic philosophical words and forged a theology based on Scripture" (G. E. Bray, "Can We Dispense with Chalcedon?" *Themelios* 3 [January 1978]: 2–9).

[8]See Lossky, *The Mystical Theology of the Eastern Church,* 238.

finds in patristic and mystic writers such quotes as the following by Saint Gregory of Nyssa:

> We affirm that love for man is the reason why God accepts communion with him. Since it is impossible for what is small by nature to elevate itself over its own measure and attain to a height of nature which surpasses it, He Himself, humbling His philanthropic power toward our weakness that it might be possible for us to receive it, distributes the grace and benefit which come from Him.[9]

Such union with the Holy Trinity requires a wholesale transformation of the person. This spiritual heart operation comes through repentance *(metanoia)*, as one becomes aware of standing before the living, unknown God who yearns to share his being with us. Not, we hasten to add, with God's essence but with his uncreated energy. It comes about through the blend of grace and total freedom of the human being. The key to this experience is the Holy Spirit. The Spirit guides us without ever violating our integrity or free choice in becoming who we are.

We have been sealed with the indelible gift of the *imago Dei*. It takes at least a lifetime, however, to conform to God's likeness, which we find in Christ Jesus. Rather than simply accepting the grace of God through an act of faith, we go on from there to cooperate with the ongoing action of the Holy Spirit. The same Spirit "everywhere present and filling all things"[10] prevents the doctrines of the church from being mere abstractions. It is the Spirit who teaches us to love and appreciate the canons and external authorities that otherwise would be mere law that we would acknowledge with a blind faith.

It is the Spirit who helps us contemplate the inconceivable truth, so eloquently presented to the church by Saint Gregory Palamas, that monastics and others in the vein of *hesychia* (watchful, inner stillness in prayer) are not self-deluded or impostors. They can indeed bond with the uncreated energies of the living Lord. The incomprehensible, unfathomable God in Trinity reaches out to those who yearn to be united with him, and the Holy Spirit achieves this.

---

[9]Cited in Basil Krivocheine, "Simplicity of the Divine Nature and the Distinctions in God, according to St. Gregory of Nyssa," *St. Vladimir's Theological Quarterly* 21 (1977): 77–78.

[10]Part of the prayer that opens every council and liturgy.

It is the Holy Spirit who provides us with eyes to see Christ. And this is done in the church. Through the Spirit we come to know Jesus Christ. The gospel of John brings this out more clearly than the other evangelists. Christ appears in all his glory, radiant and triumphant, in the fullness of the Godhead—even on the cross and in the tomb. In all our worship and teaching, we strive to resonate with the vision of that grand evangelist: "We have seen his glory" (John 1:14).

The doctrine of the kenotic Son of God (Phil. 2:6–11) offers insight into the greatness of God's love. Even when Christ placed his life into the hands of his enemies, enduring all that their rage and cruelty expended on him, even dead and buried he remained ever the Master, the Vanquisher of the enemy. What followed? Descent into Hades, appearance among the disciples, ascension to heaven, being seated at the side of the Father—always Christ is One of the Holy Trinity. He is in all ways unique—with the Trinity, and on earth among humans. One never finds the Orthodox Christian imitating Christ. That would imply a limitation of one's own uniqueness. Rather, one opens himself or herself to the work of the Holy Spirit within the heart. By repentance, *penthos* (grief), prayer, contemplation, and sharing the mysteries of the church, a person opens the heart to an inner illumination—the uncreated grace of the Holy Spirit. Here is the reason why the transfiguration, an event so frequently ignored or misunderstood in most Western commentaries, has been so rich a mine of spirituality for the Orthodox Christian.

The Holy Trinity is so much a part of Orthodox Christian theology that we begin each liturgy by mentioning each person of the Trinity, for each has had a special role in our salvation.

Continuing the metaphor of our attempt to share our prayers, the Orthodox Church has a fixed outline for its worship that all everywhere proclaim. The prayers of evangelical Christians are generally impromptu, spontaneous expressions of faith. Except for the homily, specifically intended to bring forth the implications and truths hidden within the holy Gospels, nothing individual or idiosyncratic is uttered in the Orthodox Church.

If we Christians have inherited from Israel synagogue worship and temple sacrifice, it may be considered that evangelical Christians have adapted the synagogue style, while the Orthodox

Church unites both aspects. The Nicene Creed is the gate separating the two elements of this worship format.

Returning to the question of whether it is possible for Orthodox and evangelical Christians to unite, while "everything is possible for him who believes" (Mark 9:23), unity is impossible without *metanoia* (repentance). Evangelical theology, as I understand it, celebrates Christianity *semper reformanda* (always being reformed). The reforms are considered liberations and, as such, progress through the centuries. As stated above, this approach to theology may be quite in keeping with conventional American expectations; nevertheless, Orthodox Christianity is radically different. Instead, the Orthodox Church cherishes the "treasure hidden in a field" (Matt. 13:44) and the pearl "of great value" (v. 46) and more precious than all other jewels—the faith nourished, cherished, defended, and protected throughout the ages. That "good seed" (v. 37) given by the Son of Man to the heart of his worshipers takes everything within the bearer to cultivate.

A RESPONSE TO VLADIMIR BERZONSKY

Bradley Nassif

Father Berzonsky's article demonstrates a much deeper grasp of evangelical history and theology than most Orthodox interpreters of the movement have shown. He understands the role of evangelicalism in American society, the reasons for its popularity, and its key leaders and pivotal theological concepts. The roots of evangelicalism are articulated with a high degree of precision, which prepares the soil for a fruitful comparison with Orthodoxy.

I concur with much of what Father Berzonsky has said about the identity of evangelicalism, so I need not repeat his many points here. My only concerns are these: First, his statement that Orthodox and evangelicals use the term "person" in different ways (page 173) reflects, I believe, a slightly skewed analysis. He is correct to say that popular forms of evangelicalism often confine the term "person" to the individual; however, evangelical theologians such as Miroslav Volf, Colin Gunton, James Torrance, and others have drawn on Cappadocian Trinitarian thought to encourage reform in a more patristic direction by defining "person" not just in terms of the individual but also in the communal terms *(sobornost)* of social and family life, thus emphasizing the relational aspects of the word. If the popular forms of evangelicalism will integrate that perspective more thoroughly in their church life, it will surely narrow the gap in that regard between our two traditions.

A second concern I have is Father Berzonsky's assertion that the Bible is not a criterion of truth (page 175). I was not completely clear about what he meant, so I may be mistaken in my reaction to it. If he means that the Orthodox Church does not regard the Bible as truthful, I sharply disagree on all theological grounds that have made Orthodoxy, Orthodoxy. If, however, he means to say that the Bible is indeed truthful, but it is not the "final authority" in matters of faith and practice, then I believe he needs to explain himself more thoroughly than he has done here. It is true that Protestants and Catholics have two differing external authorities, the former the Bible and the latter the pope. The Orthodox position, as I explained in my essay, is that the Bible is indeed the final authority but not the only authority. The life of the Holy Spirit in the tradition of the church makes biblical interpretation not simply an exercise in individual interpretation but also a testing of one's interpretations by the Spirit-filled mind of the church.

Finally, Father Berzonsky's comment that "One never finds the Orthodox Christian imitating Christ" (page 180) is probably more an overreaction to medieval Catholic spirituality than it is a faithful rendering of Eastern Orthodox spirituality. Clearly Saint Paul exhorted his followers to be imitators of him as he, in turn, was imitating Christ (1 Cor. 4:16; 11:1; Eph. 5:1; 1 Thess. 1:6). *The Philokalia*—a classic collection of monastic spiritual texts of the Christian East—also contains numerous exhortations to imitate Christ by following the Christlike example of the spiritual father or mother.

Aside from these concerns, I believe that Father Berzonsky has done a fine job articulating a number of distinctive themes that contribute to Orthodox-evangelical *in*compatibility. I especially appreciated his treatment of Trinitarian and christological themes and how they have impacted the differing liturgical styles that distinguish Orthodox from evangelical forms of worship. I believe that a statement in his last paragraph encapsulates the final task that must accompany our spiritual efforts to achieve Christian unity: "unity is impossible without *metanoia* (repentance)" (page 181)!

A RESPONSE TO VLADIMIR BERZONSKY

Michael Horton

From his introduction on, Father Berzonsky's account of evangelical roots raises an important question of clarification: Are we talking about the empirical reality of contemporary American evangelicalism, which is in many ways rather different from the trajectory leading from the magisterial Reformation? For instance, the author lumps a disregard for tradition with the latter: "Here is a religion of the Spirit setting itself in opposition to all authority" (page 171). Since the author goes on to explain this in the light of the Enlightenment, perhaps we are to take this as a description of modern Protestantism in contrast to confessional Protestantism. "All rituals are suspect," he says concerning the target of his criticism (page 171). No credible historian of the Reformation, whether of the Lutheran or Reformed variety, would support these sweeping generalizations, although they were the common stuff of polemical Counter-Reformation tracts and appear nowadays in the writings from the pens of Stanley Hauerwas and evangelicals on the trail to Rome or Constantinople.

In reality, the author is more aptly describing radical Anabaptism, which is arguably the true precursor to the Enlightenment and modernity. (*That* thesis has considerable historical support!) The evangelicalism described by the author substitutes "personal decision" for "all rituals," but since those in the confessional Protestant traditions (Lutheran, Anglican, Presbyterian, and Reformed) relate fairly critically to revivalism and emphatically insist that the sacraments (which count as rituals) are "means of grace," this hardly works as a description of the evangelicalism that hails from the magisterial Reformation. This tradition maintains a churchly (i.e., covenantal) rather than a conversion-istic paradigm. In these confessional communities, the ecumenical creeds and evangelical confessions and catechisms have binding secondary status under Scripture.

Still, just after attaching some of these errant views to Martin Luther, the author charges, "The focus of salvation is within the interior life of the person. Grace comes from God alone, not via anything earthly or man-made" (page 172). This leads me to conclude that perhaps the Reformation and its successors are involved in this caricature. While it may describe certain strains of contemporary evangelical piety, it certainly bears no resem-blance to the views of the Reformers, whose whole passion was to call introspective souls agonizing over their spiritual condi-tion out of themselves and to look outward to Christ. "The gospel lies entirely outside of you!" Luther declared in some impatience to a temperamentally introspective Melanchthon. It was Luther's introspective piety, developed in the monastery, that led him to the very crisis through which the Holy Spirit drew him out through the external word of the gospel. The Reformed empha-sis on the unfolding drama of redemption in the historical covenant of grace (i.e., its so-called "redemptive-historical" hermeneutic) resists charges of introspective individualism.

As for the charge that in Reformation theology "Grace comes from God alone, not via anything earthly or man-made," the author is grossly misinformed. Martin Luther and John Calvin spilled a great deal of ink against this spiritualist error of the radical Anabaptists. For the Reformers, God uses ordinary earthly means to deliver his grace. In the sacraments, says Calvin, "our merciful Lord ... condescends to lead us to himself even by these earthly elements, and to set before us in the flesh a mirror of spiritual blessings."[1] God's use of earthly elements as means of grace is a major emphasis of the Reformers. While differences remain between Eastern Orthodox and magisterial Protestant views on the sacraments, it does not advance the con-versation to insert specious contrasts.

In Father Berzonsky's subsequent description of the Orthodox approach I find much to appreciate. As I've mentioned before, a close reading of Calvin and Irenaeus reveals striking parallels. While subsequent Eastern Orthodox reflection appears to under-

---

[1]John Calvin, *Institutes of the Christian Religion*, ed. John T. McNeill, trans. Ford Lewis Battles (Philadelphia: Westminster, 1960), 4.14.3., 1278.

value essential legal-covenantal motifs that one finds, for instance, in Irenaeus's *Adversus Haereses* (Against Heresies), Reformed theology has emphasized as well the organic union motif that is summarized as "recapitulation." In my estimation, evangelical theology has not fully appropriated the shared Reformed-Orthodox concern for this essential side of Paul's theology in which eschatology and ontology converge in a cosmic redemption. Reformed and evangelical theologies can only be enriched by this conversation with the Eastern fathers and Orthodoxy.

But just when this conversation looks promising, the author again adduces an evangelical interlocutor with whom confessional evangelicals would have little in common. The evangelical Christian, he says, is committed to a decisionism that separates "the man or woman from the ecclesiastical body and set[s] him or her free and apart from all external symbols or features associated with the church.... Infant baptism can have little interest for those who are better prepared at the start of adult life to accept Christ's grace through faith. Sacraments offered by the institutional church cannot bear the weight of grace, because they can be accepted without conscious awareness of the transforming power of the Holy Spirit. More, any hope in their efficacy, any trust that they can act as vehicles of grace, are impediments to the true gift of the Spirit" (pages 173–74). And again, astonishingly, he refers in this context to Luther, although he, like Calvin, offers sharp criticisms of this very view among the radical Anabaptists.

Citing examples from the Reformers, the confessions, and representative systems would require more space than we have to refute this serious misunderstanding. As for the first claim (tearing the individual away from the church and all ecclesiastical symbols), Calvin adduces Chrysostom for support against the Anabaptists on this very point, rejecting "all who, under the pretense of the Spirit, lead us away from the simple doctrine of the gospel" and the church.[2] Willem Balke makes this observation:

> For Calvin, redemption had cosmic dimensions. Asceticism did not involve world-flight, but demanded a positive redirection.... The church, as a sanctified fellowship, was created by God through His Word and Spirit.... Calvin felt that the social order could be changed only

---

[2]Cited in Willem Balke, *Calvin and the Anabaptist Radicals* (Grand Rapids: Eerdmans, 1981), 140.

through the renewal of the church, which is the *foyer actif* for the restoration of humanity.[3]

"'For what God has joined together, it is not lawful to put asunder'..., so that, for those to whom he is Father the church may also be Mother," Calvin wrote, invoking Cyprian's familiar maxim: "You cannot have God for your Father unless you have the church for your Mother."[4] Calvin also wrote, "Furthermore, away from her [the church's] bosom one cannot hope for any forgiveness of sins or any salvation, as Isaiah [Isa. 37:32] and Joel [Joel 2:32] testify," invoking another of Cyprian's sayings: *"Extra ecclesiam nulla salus"* [outside the church no one can be saved].[5]

As for the claim that confessional evangelicalism somehow denies infant baptism, the reader will recognize once again that Father Berzonsky has reduced all of evangelical Protestantism to radical Anabaptism and modern Baptist practice. Denial of the sacraments as efficacious "vehicles of grace" is condemned by every Lutheran and Reformed confession. The church may have many errors, said Calvin, yet "wherever we see the Word of God purely preached and heard, and *the sacraments administered* according to Christ's institution, there, it is not to be doubted, a church of God exists [cf. Eph. 2:20]."[6] It may be that the author is judging magisterial Protestantism and subsequent evangelicalism by his own experience with various contemporary evangelical groups, especially Baptists, but surely we are better off interacting with the actual theological positions and confessions of the churches we include in that general camp called "evangelical."

It is true, of course, that the Reformers did not regard the sacraments as occasions of synergistic cooperation leading to justification. It is precisely because they are *God's* acts that they are means of *grace* and not means of human moral endeavor. To suggest that, in the Lutheran and Reformed view, "the human is not essentially changed in the process" (page 174), is wide of the mark, as many citations could attest. The author's explanation of the almost exclusively moral role of the sacraments, however,

---

[3]Ibid., 267.

[4]John Calvin, *Institutes of the Christian Religion,* ed. John T. McNeill, trans. Ford Lewis Battles (Philadelphia: Westminster, 1960), 4.1.1., 1012.

[5]Ibid., 4.1.4., 1016.

[6]Ibid., 4.1.9., 1023 (emphasis added).

does seem to render them means of works-righteousness rather than means of grace. This does reflect a major cleavage between the two views of the sacraments.

Next, Father Berzonsky discusses the authority of Scripture. First, his reflections on Western experience of authority could be illuminating if they were not so stereotyped in terms of a pristine Eastern mentality and a corrupt Western orientation. Cultural captivity is apparently a Western phenomenon in this account. Once more he misstates at least the confessional Protestant view: "Unfathomable to them is the need for submitting their own subjective comprehension of truth to the objectivity of the church" (page 175). Not only is this fathomable, it is the common practice of confessional Protestants. (That is what it means to *be* confessional!) I am hardly unique in having to join my fellow ministers in a regular public act at synod, classis, and consistory (ecclesiastical assemblies), vowing to teach and confess the entire confession and catechism without reservation. And on that basis, I may be disciplined by the broader assembly and, ultimately, have my ordination withdrawn. All members of our churches similarly subscribe to these symbols in their entirety and are catechized in them from their youth and in catechetical sermons. To suggest that, for us, "To test one's private opinion by the wisdom of the Holy Spirit at work through the body of Christ does not compute" (page 175) reveals more than a lack of sympathy; it discloses a lack of concern for actually engaging in a real conversation with historic Protestants.

Father Berzonsky presents the traditional argument adduced by Roman Catholicism and Orthodoxy, namely, that the church precedes the canon, leading to the conclusion that "the Bible is neither self-sufficient nor self-evident" (page 175). We would reply at least in part by saying that, although it is undeniable that the church preceded the completed canon of Old and New Testaments, the material that composes the canon both precedes and in fact creates the church throughout history. There is a difference between saying that the church created the Bible and saying that the church recognized the undeniable marks of apostolic origin and authenticity of the written Scripture. In this the church had no choice but to be obedient to the Word of God written.

It is, of course, true that the church must interpret Scripture, but it can only do this because Scripture interprets itself. It is not a closed, dark, contradictory, or inscrutable Word that God has left his people. Allowing the fact that not all parts are "alike plain in themselves, nor alike clear to all," we nevertheless hold that "those things which are necessary to be known, believed, and observed for salvation, are so clearly propounded and opened in some place of Scripture or other, that not only the learned, but the unlearned, in due use of the ordinary means, may attain unto a sufficient understanding of them" (Westminster Confession 1.7).[7] If Scripture cannot interpret itself, surely the church cannot interpret itself more easily. Given the conflicting councils and decisions subsequent to the ecumenical creeds, it is only with considerable difficulty that one can have greater confidence in the church's interpretations than in Scripture's own witness to itself.

To be sure, God has given his church ministers. They are expected to be well trained in the biblical languages, biblical studies, theology, church history, pastoral ministry, and liturgics to lead their people in their understanding of Scripture. They are assisted in this by the creeds, confessions, and catechisms. This is not because Scripture cannot interpret itself, but because individuals and churches are fallible and, in fact, sinful. They require the checks and balances of wise Christian reflection over the ages. This is why the Reformers and their heirs give so much attention and weight to the church fathers. But all of this is subject to the final authority of God's Word, which Father Rommen, in his essay, appears to take more seriously than this author.

If by "self-sufficient" Father Berzonsky imputes to us the belief that our reading and hearing of Scripture is divorced from these helps, he misunderstands the notion of *sola Scriptura.* Those who place so much weight on the assistance of the communion of saints in interpreting Scripture cannot be accused of teaching that one can sit in a corner and read the Bible by oneself. That would not be "Scripture alone" as the final authority, but "myself alone" as the final authority. Scripture is self-sufficient, but we are not—which is why we need to read Scripture together with the faithful church in all ages. But because Scripture is itself the "unnormed norm," it always judges the church and is the criterion of its faithfulness in interpreting its message. One wonders,

---

[7]Can be viewed on the Web at www.cresourceei.org/creedwestminster.html.

given both the theory and practice of church history, whether Eastern Orthodoxy, like Rome, is capable of being addressed and undone by God's Word in Scripture.

Is it really helpful to appropriate the caricature of a liberal Protestant like Dean Inge concerning the Reformers that "Their creed has been described as a return to the Gospel in the spirit of the Koran" (page 176)?—especially when, as Dr. Hancock-Stefan has reminded us, evangelicals have, from the Reformation to the present time, expressed an eagerness for dialogue while Orthodoxy enforces nothing short of political repression of evangelical churches wherever it is dominant? This is undoubtedly a dead end for any meaningful exchange between our traditions.

In my reply to Father Rommen, I suggested the possibility that Orthodoxy tends toward an underrealized eschatology with respect to its liturgical assumptions (page 256). Could it perhaps be the case that in its view of the church, Orthodoxy is also hampered by an overrealized eschatology? Christ's indwelling of his church is indeed a great mystery and the source of all the church's joy. Yet, he cannot be simply equated with the church. He is her living Head, not only raised bodily from the dead to die no more but glorified in heaven at God's right hand. He is the forerunner of the church, the firstfruits of the harvest. But the church is still a pilgrim society, nourished by his life but still at war against the world, the flesh, and the Devil. This theology of the cross and resurrection is opposed to a theology of glory, which claims more for the present than is actually realized.

Father Berzonsky is surely correct to underscore the communal nature of the eucharistic community in his concluding thoughts concerning ecclesiology. He is, however, once again mistaken in contrasting this with the position of the magisterial Reformation. The Belgic Confession (Articles 27 and 28) reads as follows:

> We believe and confess one single catholic or universal church, ... awaiting their entire salvation in Jesus Christ being washed by his blood, and sanctified and sealed by the Holy Spirit. ...
>
> We believe that, since this holy assembly and congregation is the gathering of those who are saved and there is no salvation apart from it, no one ought to withdraw

from it, content to be by himself, regardless of his status or condition.

But all people are obliged to join and unite with it, keeping the unity of the church by submitting to its instruction and discipline, by bending their necks under the yoke of Jesus Christ, and by serving to build up one another, according to the gifts God has given them as members of each other in the same body.

Finally, under the section titled "Temple and Tent," Father Berzonsky returns to our Savior's prayer in John 17. What will be necessary for this to be fulfilled with respect to evangelicals and the Orthodox? It will be necessary, he says, for us to become Orthodox. "Church as building becomes a temple.... The structure is cruciform—using the Hagia Sophia as a model—where the four corners of the earth are crowned with the heaven above" (page 177). Some may reply, Well, that is interesting, and it would be worth talking further to understand the rationale. Others, such as myself, however, would in addition want to inquire, once again, as to whether Orthodoxy refuses to move on from the types and shadows of Moses to the reality that has arrived in Christ.

This is not a brief for ugly buildings but for the New Testament ecclesiology that clearly represents the people of God as his temple. There was a time for the temple, as Jesus told the Samaritan woman who wondered whether the true one was in Samaria or Jerusalem. The true one was in Jerusalem:

> Jesus declared, "Believe me, woman, a time is coming when you will worship the Father neither on this mountain nor in Jerusalem.... Yet a time is coming and has now come when the true worshipers will worship the Father in spirit and truth, for they are the kind of worshipers the Father seeks."
>
> John 4:21, 23

Jesus Christ is the true Temple not made with hands but born of the blessed Virgin. And he has made his people—not Hagia Sophia (now a Muslim mosque)—"living stones" who "are being built into a spiritual house to be a holy priesthood, offering spiritual sacrifices acceptable to God through Jesus Christ" (1 Pet. 2:5). This happens not by being able to "find in one's heart (or *nous*, the soul's eye) union with the Holy Trinity,

which has never been lost in the Orthodox Church" (page 178)—
the very epitome of the introspective piety challenged by Father
Berzonsky—but by "the word of faith we are proclaiming"
(Rom. 10:8). Here, where the gospel creates faith and a new creation *ex nihilo* once again, sinners are justified and lead the
creation in the birth pangs that will yield to the endless liberty
of the whole creation.

A RESPONSE TO VLADIMIR BERZONSKY

George Hancock-Stefan

The evangelicals in the Maybe category need to hear a clear and concise message like Dr. Berzonsky's in order to come to their full senses. He praises the evangelicals as the dominant group in media (I wish we were!) and tells us that we and the Orthodox Christians are conservative by definition and conviction. This is where the accolades end!

The section labeled "Roots" contains some major surprises. While it is true that the Reformation has hailed the priesthood of all believers and their rights to interpret Scripture, the idea of announcing and championing the rights of the individual sounds to me to be more from a secular history book than from the Reformers' convictions.

Foundational to Dr. Berzonsky's argument is his statement that "Salvation is achieved through and in the church" (page 172). While Dr. Horton argued that even Calvin referred approvingly to Cyprian's expression "Outside the church there is no salvation" and declared, "Furthermore, away from her [the church's] bosom one cannot hope for any forgiveness of sins or any salvation, as Isaiah [Isa. 37:32] and Joel [Joel 2:32] testify" (page 125), Calvin is clear that it is not the church that saves but Christ, who is in the church. The church cannot save us because the church did not die for our salvation.[1]

It is after this foundational statement that Berzonsky quotes Vladimir Lossky's interpretation of the Holy Spirit, then clearly

---

[1]See Mark R. Saucy, "Evangelicals, Catholics, and Orthodox Together: Is the Church the Extension of the Incarnation?" audiocassette of lecture presented at the meeting of the Evangelical Theological Society (Orlando, Fla., November 1998).

outlines the difference between the ways evangelicals and Orthodox define a person. Arguing earlier that the Reformed position is reductionistic both of humans and of God, he is uneasy with Luther's position on the freedom of the will. Yet the three stages that, Berzonsky argues, a person in the Orthodox Church passes through are also available in Reformed thinking, though not before the person is saved, or becomes a part of the kingdom of God.

It seems to me that the most threatening part for Father Berzonsky is that the Reformation has done away with the sacerdotal authority. For the Orthodox, the authority over Scripture in its canonization and in its teachings rests squarely in the church. According to Berzonsky, by lifting the Bible from the church and distributing it to the people, the Reformation has committed a sinful act. In the Orthodox Church and Catholic Church, the teaching of the church can never be wrong, because it is this *sobornost* (togetherness) that is connected with the Head, who is Christ. Yet, one has to face the historical reality and agree that the Roman Catholic Church, Eastern Orthodox Church, and Protestant churches have made mistakes.

Father Berzonsky writes, "The prayers of evangelical Christians are generally impromptu, spontaneous expressions of faith. Except for the homily, specifically intended to bring forth the implications and truths hidden within the holy Gospels, nothing individual or idiosyncratic is uttered in the Orthodox Church" (page 180). The fixed outlines and prayers that the Orthodox are reciting were new at one time, including some of the well-known liturgies. Is it possible that God inspired Chrysostom to create something new that was not in contradiction to the revealed scriptural text, but if such a creation is happening in 2004, it is contradictory? Is the Holy Spirit—who gives new life, who changes darkness to light—not able to give to individuals new revelation that will not be idiosyncratic? This concept lifts up the past but is threatened by the present, as though we do not serve the same God who illumined and who was revered and worshiped by the church fathers.

If one had progressive liberations, then in order to return to the Orthodox Church one has to repent—and not only of personal liberations but of the entire Reformation movement. Thus Father Berzonsky has spoken: We cannot return unless we repent of being evangelicals.

A RESPONSE TO VLADIMIR BERZONSKY

Edward Rommen

Throughout the course of this project we have collectively explored a wide range of theological issues. At times, our search for understanding has been thwarted by an exasperating misreading of our position. Having the intended meaning of our theological statements altered by our discussion partners, who forcibly insert them into the narrow categories of their own systems, transforms every divergence into an apparently insurmountable obstacle and leaves us with the feeling that if we could only get them to understand us on our own terms, we might be able to make some progress. But Vladimir Berzonsky has focused our attention on one issue, which may well be a truly insurmountable barrier, namely, our respective understandings of human nature and personhood.

Berzonsky suggests that the theological activity of the Reformation was driven by the Enlightenment's "opposition to all authority" (page 171), facilitated by its celebration of emancipated human reason and centered on the rights of the absolutely autonomous individual. It may be something of an overstatement to insist that the results of the Reformation are "nothing less than sinful" (page 176). Yet, as Berzonsky states, "to liberate the individual consciousness from the experience and demands of the consciousness of the church is to violate and even to destroy the corporate consciousness of God's people" (page 175). It is this "liberation" of human reason—overlooking the damage done to the divine image by sin—that rejects the need for an ecclesial context and insists on every individual's right and ability to interpret the Holy Scriptures without help and as they see fit.

It is this celebration of human *ratio* (reason) that leads to blind acceptance of the notion that the sin-damaged image can actually understand and with logical consistency explain every aspect of divine revelation and action. At the same time, it is the denial of human contingency, so dear to the "emancipated," that fuels the arrogant refusal to accept the responsibilities of the divine gift of free will by absolutizing sin's effect on the divine image and rejecting our own responsibility on the path of salvation.

While I am not quite as pessimistic as Father Berzonsky, it does seem that this anthropological divide between East and West will be very difficult to overcome. For that reason, we would do well to begin our discussions with an exploration of personhood and human nature. For it is a proper understanding of creation and the image of God in us that leads to full recognition of the seriousness of sin, comprehension of the truly cosmic scope of human salvation, wonder at the unmerited grace and atoning love of God, and acknowledgment of that treasury of salvation, namely, the church—"God's most supreme, most holy, most good, most wise and necessary establishment on earth."[1]

---

[1]Saint John of Kronstadt, "The Church: The Treasury of Salvation," *Orthodox Life* (July-August 1970), 14–29; can be viewed on the Web at www.orthodoxinfo.com/inquirers/krons_church.htm.

CONCLUSION

Vladimir Berzonsky

We have explored our divisions and have outlined the causes, each from his own point of view. The reader is able to realize that evangelical and Orthodox Christians stand on opposite shores of the theological Jordan River. He or she can bear witness to the ways we understand our approaches to the gospel and to the kingdom of God. Through the filter of self-awareness and self-justification it would appear futile to consider unity, indeed, even hopeless—if indeed a Christian can be at the same time in Christ and bereft of hope. If we are, in fact, baptized into Christ, and nothing that any one of us has written denies our legitimacy as siblings of our Lord God and Savior, then the symbolic river Jordan that parts us also joins us and indicts us for ignoring the tragedy of our separation. Are we to go on like this until Christ's second coming, and not let it trouble us? Even if we are not discomforted by his prayer, wish, and command—"that they may be one just as We are one" (John 17:22 NKJV)—then the practical purpose of possibly sharing the great mission of evangelization to the non-Christian and to the so-called post-Christian world ought to concern us.

For our part, the Orthodox Church has accepted an active role in serious attempts to seek ways to achieve a greater unity with Western Christians. This has not met with unanimous approval among our fellow Orthodox. At great risk of offending many of our brethren, most of the ancient patriarchies have given their blessings to those who would bear witness for the Orthodox Church in normal bilateral dialogues, as well as to accept membership in the World Council of Churches and the

National Council of the Churches of Christ in the United States of America. The concerns regarding membership in these bodies are profound and legitimate—nevertheless, some of our best theologians and renowned hierarchs have made their witness known by their presence at such dialogues and gatherings.

More than a tragedy, our divisions are nothing less than a scandal for all Christians who are bent on taking the gospel to people who do not know Christ. The simplest aborigines in any part of the world soon grasp the competition among Christian missionaries and ask which Christ they should embrace.

Our God is a unity of three persons in one essence. Beginning from that mystical and profound awareness of the Godhead, we ought likewise to be concerned with unity. As the great Orthodox theologian Georges Florovsky always insisted, unity belongs to the very essence of Christianity. How, then, can we be content to remain complacent toward one another? While we linger, taking as the norm our divisions, real people's lives are suffering because they don't know and accept Jesus Christ. It's not enough to express our points of view, criticize others, and go on blithely as though unity were a vague aspiration of little interest to us in comparison to the real work of the gospel. We respond with Cain-like cynicism to the Father's question: "Where is your brother?" (Genesis 4:9). Cain's absence, though we didn't kill him, is of little concern to us. The Orthodox theologian Paul Evdokimov said that the more Christian question is to Abel: "Where is your brother Cain?"[1] Those who stand on firm moral and doctrinal ground have a greater responsibility to all others. Here is a sobering meditation for all of us.

We have a glorious tradition as Orthodox Christians. Therefore, we have a responsibility to share our magnificent spiritual treasures with those who are unfamiliar with them. And we must do so without pomp, affectation, or paternalism, realizing that "we have this treasure in earthen vessels" (2 Corinthians 4:7 NKJV). And we realize that many others do not respect these traditions, which is a major cause of our divisions. In spite of this, serious Orthodox Christians take up the challenge of searching for ways of reconciliation without sacrificing the great truths of the faith, which are our spiritual heritage.

---

[1]Paul Evdokimov, *Ages of the Spiritual Life* (Crestwood, N.Y.: St. Vladimir's Seminary Press, 1998), 103.

In more recent centuries, from the age of the Reformation through the nineteenth century and into the twentieth, whatever earlier visions of oneness there were among the fragmented Christian bodies gave way to the intransigence, exclusivity, and proselytism that are still with us in the twenty-first century. The twentieth century was the age of the ecumenical movement, and it may have lost its earlier zeal. In the beginning it had the effect of leading the Christian communions on a journey beyond themselves. In the words of Patriarch of Constantinople Bartholomew: "Out of their self-sufficiency and isolation in search of each other, they were obeying the Spirit of God in a spirit of repentance, pardon, reconciliation, and Christian love."[2]

Will such a quest for unity characterize serious theologians from both evangelical and Orthodox communions and lead the way to formulating bonds of unity in the future? Will the distortions and caricatures that many Western Christians hold of the Orthodox Church—that we are exotic, decadent, stultified, intransigent, embedded in the past—be overcome by meeting together as evangelical and Orthodox Christians and exploring our common faith in Jesus Christ?

A salient question for us to explore together is this: What is the nature of the unity we seek? If it is friendship, fellowship, and dialogue, we do not have far to go. Indeed, we may have already arrived. Respecting one another's spiritual communities—choosing not to proselytize but rather to aid and encourage the members of a church to reassess the communion in which they had been baptized before incorporating them into one's own congregation—would be yet another goodwill expression of fellowship. Is this realistic and even possible, given the fact that we each claim to be bearers of the whole truth of the gospel of Jesus Christ?

If we are able to overcome the above difficulty, will we then proceed to a more intimate expression of union in the body of Christ—the convergence of all the elements of doctrine pertaining to divinity, ecclesiology, and all the rest? For example, using a phrase from the familiar Christmas carol, we will ask, "Do you see what I see?" When we say *church*, we affirm all those united in oneness of teaching and expression of faith globally, including

---

[2]Cited in Thomas FitzGerald, "Orthodox Theology and Ecumenical Witness," *St. Vladimir's Theological Quarterly* 42, no. 3–4 (1998): 344.

those who have gone before us to their rest. We Orthodox recognize angels and saints, the first saint being the mother of our Lord God and Savior, and thus in that awareness we say that she is the mother of the Son of God who is in all respects God. Will we be able to worship together with evangelicals in all sincerity, expressing the sacred Scriptures in our liturgy? The church's year, and even the daily cycle, recapitulates the history of salvation from the creation and the fall and through the various covenants made by God for humanity, then Christ's birth, life, death, resurrection, ascension, and return to the Father, followed by the Pentecost event and the work of the Holy Spirit—not only through the apostles but in the church through the ages and centuries.

All of the above would of necessity be explored and affirmed with any persons or communions that might wish to partake of the eucharistic meal, the ultimate act of union with the Orthodox Church.

Chapter Four

ARE EASTERN ORTHODOXY AND EVANGELICALISM COMPATIBLE? MAYBE

An Evangelical Perspective

George Hancock-Stefan

ARE EASTERN ORTHODOXY AND EVANGELICALISM COMPATIBLE? MAYBE

An Evangelical Perspective

George Hancock-Stefan

BIOGRAPHICAL

Writing on a topic such as this one is not strictly an exercise in historical theology. For indeed, no matter how hard we try to be objective, the subjective aspects are forever with us. While by all definitions I am a Protestant evangelical by conviction, education, and practice, my life and thinking have been intersected by my interactions with the Eastern Orthodox Church. Most of the men on my father's side were blessed with a tenor voice, and all participated in the Orthodox liturgy as cantors. On my mother's side, the women were a part of the revival in the Orthodox Church called The Lord's Army. Yet, my mother and father became Baptists when I was seven years old—which, indeed, has led to a great transformation in our family. It was through my parents that I met the Lord Jesus Christ, and, thanks to them, I grew up in a family where we recognized the presence of the Holy Spirit with joy and thanksgiving.

As a result of my parents' decision to become Baptists, however, I felt marginalized during my childhood and throughout my teenage years. The Communists persecuted us because we were Christians, and they told us we had no opportunity to advance because we were retrograde and dangerous. The Orthodox Church told us we were not Christians because we were not

Orthodox; moreover, we were not Romanians because Romanians are Orthodox. In spite of all these declarations, I knew I was a Christian, I knew I was Romanian, and I knew I was not retrograde or dangerous. I continued to attend regularly the local Baptist church, and during major holidays and family festivities, I would go with my relatives to the Orthodox church.

During my seminary studies, I wrote papers on Eastern Orthodoxy ("Calvin and the Use of the Patristic Fathers"; "Lukaris and the Reformation"), concluding with my doctoral dissertation (Ph.D. diss., Trinity International University, 1997) on "The Impact of Reformation on the Romanian People: 1517–1645 (Wittenberg to Iasi)." Wittenberg is the city in Germany where the Reformation began, and Iasi is the place in Romania where the Orthodox Church, like the Roman Catholic Church at the Council of Trent, anathematized the Reformation.[1]

EVANGELICAL DIFFICULTIES

In addressing the participants at the Society of the Study of Eastern Orthodoxy and Evangelicalism meeting in Irvine, California, in September 1999, J. I. Packer identified the first difficulty, namely, how one goes about speaking on behalf of the evangelical community.[2] The evangelical community in the English-speaking world includes Anglicans like J. I. Packer, Baptists like Jerry Falwell, Pentecostals like Jack Hayford, and Methodists like Lyle Schaller. While they all claim to be evangelicals, their ability and willingness to dialogue with the Orthodox, or even to consider the question of a dialogue, vary to the degree to which they hold other

---

[1]This is the synod held in Iasi in 1645, not the more famous Synod of Iasi, better known in the West as the Synod of Jassy (1642), which anathematized the very theologically Reformed confession of Cyril Lucar, who had been the patriarch of Constantinople (Istanbul), and confirmed the very Roman Catholic confession of Peter Mogila. See "Jassy, Synod of (1642)," in *The Oxford Dictionary of the Christian Church,* F. L. Cross and E. A. Livingstone, eds. (Oxford: Oxford Univ. Press, 1997), 864. For more on the significance of the 1645 synod, see my doctoral dissertation (unpublished Ph.D. dissertation, Trinity Evangelical Divinity School, 1997; copies are available from University Microfilms).

[2]James Packer, "A Stunted Ecclesiology? The Theory and Practice of Evangelical Churchliness" (presented at the September 1999 meeting of the Society of the Study of Eastern Orthodoxy and Evangelicalism). Dr. Packer's speech was published under the same title in *Touchstone* (December 2002), 37–41; can be viewed on the Web at www.touchstonemag.com/docs/issues/15.10docs/15-10pg37.html.

important doctrinal positions with regard to believers' baptism and the spectacular gifts of the Holy Spirit. Meanwhile, within the last twenty-five years, dialogues with the Orthodox and many other denominational groups have taken place. It seems as though every major denomination held at least an initial meeting.[3]

The second difficulty was identified by Romanian pastor Josef Tson at a 1990 meeting in Wheaton, Illinois.[4] He mentioned that the dialogue between the evangelicals and the Orthodox is taking place primarily in the United States, where the Eastern Orthodox Church is seeking a place at the table. Will Herberg, in his book *Protestant, Catholic, Jew,* observed that the Orthodox were not noticed until the second half of the twentieth century.[5] In the countries where the Eastern Orthodox Church is the dominant church, the evangelicals are never invited to the table. Whenever non-Orthodox are invited, the Orthodox and secular publications mention only the name of the Orthodox patriarch. The names of all other important denominational leaders are included in that amorphous noun "others."

Likewise, in the Orthodox countries, evangelicals often encounter difficulties if they want to evangelize, while in the Western countries, the Orthodox justifiably feel that they have an equal right to invite all to come and join the Eastern Orthodox Church. Yet, I wonder what the reaction of the Orthodox would have been if, in the second part of the twentieth century, a Protestant leader had publicly expressed a view similar to the one the patriarch of Moscow expressed about not needing evangelicals to evangelize Russia: *We are a Christian country here in America; we do not need the Orthodox to evangelize us!*

DEALING WITH EXISTING REALITIES

The first reality is that within the last quarter of the twentieth century some evangelicals have become Orthodox. American evangelicals were much more aware of evangelicals such

---

[3]See Daniel B. Clendenin, *Eastern Orthodox Christianity: A Western Perspective* (Grand Rapids: Baker, 1994), 23–24.

[4]Comments made in "Roundtable Conclusions" by Josef Tson at the conference "Glasnost and the Church," sponsored by the Institute of East-West Studies, at Wheaton College in 1990.

[5]See Will Herberg, *Protestant, Catholic, Jew: An Essay in American Religious Sociology* (Garden City, N.Y.: Doubleday, 1955).

as Thomas Howard and Richard Neuhaus becoming Catholics; during this same time, however, Baptists, Pentecostals, Methodists, and Presbyterians have made Eastern Orthodoxy their home. Some, such as Peter Gillquist and Carnegie Calian, have written extensively about their pilgrimage,[6] while others, such as Jaroslav Pelikan, the eminent Lutheran church historian, converted quietly.[7]

Those of us who work near various ethnic Eastern Orthodox churches have seen a minuscule percentage of our evangelical friends become Orthodox. The conversations I and others have had with our friends who became Orthodox reveal that the majority did not do so because they were convinced of the Eastern Orthodox theology. They felt a spiritual drought in their previous church and were magnetized by the Eastern Orthodox liturgy and all the accompanying pomp. The local evangelical church did not provide for them the aesthetic and spiritual expression they claim to find in the Orthodox church. In this regard, Daniel Clendenin quotes English professor and novelist Thomas Doulis, who says that "beauty was always the conversion factor in Orthodoxy from Tsar Vladimir to our days."[8]

The second reality is that, in international ecumenical encounters, evangelicals are finding they have more in common with the Eastern Orthodox than with the liberal segments of Protestantism that have gone so far that there are almost no boundaries. A colleague of mine remarked that it was the Orthodox, not the evangelicals, who, in Canberra, Australia, staged a walkout at worship services that seemed pagan beyond question.[9] This courageous stand created a camaraderie among evangelicals and the Eastern Orthodox. Christians unite in protest when, in ecclesiastical gatherings, the triune God is no longer the sole recipient of our worship.

---

[6]See Peter Gillquist, *Becoming Orthodox: A Journey to the Ancient Christian Faith* (Brentwood, Tenn.: Wolgemuth & Hyatt, 1989); Carnegie Samuel Calian, *Icon and Pulpit: The Protestant-Orthodox Encounter* (Philadelphia: Westminster, 1968).

[7]See Dimitra DeFotis, "Finding Faith in Orthodoxy: An Increasing Number of People in the U.S. Are Converting to Orthodoxy," *Chicago Tribune* (April 19, 1998); can be viewed on the Web at www.holytrinity-la.org/engl/pages/bltn298/artcl4.html.

[8]Cited in Clendenin, *Eastern Orthodox Christianity*, 74.

[9]See Willmar Thorkelson, "Will Orthodox Exit the WCC?" *Christianity Today* 35 (April 8, 1991): 66–67; "Evangelicals Find Inroads, Remain Cautious," *Christianity Today* 35 (April 8, 1991): 67–68.

The third reality is that the Holy Scriptures in the Orthodox Church occupy a high position. It is always the Word of God as Scripture speaking to us. While Scripture is a closed, unknown book for the majority of the Orthodox, there is enough reverence that the Orthodox believer stands at attention whenever the Word is read. Evangelical familiarity with the Bible has tended to create an absence of awe when the Word of God is spoken. Therefore, when the evangelicals see the Orthodox stand for the reading of the Scriptures, they greatly admire them for this act of reverence.

The fourth reality is that many evangelicals who studied with such Orthodox theologians as Georges Florovsky and John Meyendorff were impressed with their erudition and with their holy lives. Their specialty was patristics, an area totally foreign to many evangelicals. This mentoring relationship whetted their appetite for that period of church history.

The fifth reality is missiological effectiveness. Many of the large evangelical parachurch groups, especially those that work on university campuses, have sought and found direct contact with members of the Eastern Orthodox Church for the purposes of evangelization of nominal Orthodox. Their valid argument in defense of this approach is that it is more effective to present their message to the Orthodox students, overlooking some of the Reformation specifics, than to persuade the Orthodox students to become evangelicals. They argue that they have found the Orthodox very willing to expand their knowledge of the Christian faith and to accept evangelicals as a part of their community. Another colleague of mine argues that the witness of one evangelical Orthodox working within the Orthodox Church is more numerically effective than ten outside evangelicals in introducing nominal Orthodox (in evangelical terms) to a relationship with Jesus.

Therefore, Paul's admonition to the Philippians has become the motto for many evangelicals with regard to accepting the Orthodox: "And if on some point you think differently, that too God will make clear to you. Only let us live up to what we have already attained" (Phil. 3:15–16). The assumption is that we agree on the majority of the essential Christian beliefs. However, a clear reading of this assumed agreement reveals that the evangelicals are leaping over vast areas of disagreement.

DEFINING THE EVANGELICAL AND
ORTHODOX POSITIONS

The majority of evangelicals consider the Reformation extremely important for their teachings. The affinity with the Reformation among evangelicals differs according to what segment of the Reformation one identifies with—the magisterial or the radical Reformation. Nevertheless, all evangelicals consider the Reformation a vital part of church history. All evangelicals agree on the supreme importance of the three *solas*—*sola fide, sola gratia,* and *sola Scriptura.* The Reformers did not seek another church,[10] but were convinced that these conclusions were central to the true church. While the Reformers appreciated the church fathers, they did not hesitate to criticize them when they felt they contradicted the Scriptures.[11]

The majority of Orthodox historians and theologians see the Reformation as resulting (theologically) from a faulty Augustinian interpretation of Romans or (historically) as representing God's punishment on the Roman Catholic Church for breaking fellowship with the Eastern Orthodox Church.[12] No Eastern Orthodox sees any major significance in the Protestant Reformation for the Orthodox Church. One gets the sense that the final words of the patriarch of Constantinople's reply to the Lutheran scholars is still accepted by the Orthodox: *Unless you change there is nothing we can discuss.*[13]

The Eastern Orthodox Church calls itself "the church of the seven ecumenical councils." They celebrate the Seventh Council (Nicea, AD 747) as the Sunday of Orthodoxy. This council proclaimed the victory of the iconodules over iconoclasts. On this Sunday, all who are iconoclasts are anathematized with regularity.[14]

---

[10]See John Calvin, *Institutes of the Christian Religion,* ed. John T. McNeill, trans. Ford Lewis Battles (Philadelphia: Westminster, 1960), 9–31.

[11]See George Hancock-Stefan, "Calvin and the Use of the Patristic Fathers" (unpublished paper, Princeton Theological Seminary, 1994).

[12]See George Hancock-Stefan, "The Impact of Reformation on the Romanian People: 1517–1645 (Wittenberg to Iasi)" (Ph.D. diss., Trinity International University, 1997), 30–35.

[13]Ibid., 40–43.

[14]See Timothy (Kallistos) Ware, *The Orthodox Church* (London: Penguin, 1964), 39; Ernst Benz, *The Eastern Orthodox Church* (New York: Doubleday, 1952), 3; Clendenin, *Eastern Orthodox Christianity,* 80.

The Reformers and contemporary evangelical historians and theologians, while exhibiting a great appreciation for the creedal conclusions of the Nicene and Chalcedonian ecumenical councils,[15] stay away from embracing the conclusions of the Seventh Council.[16] They are aware that icons were initially supposed to be the gospel for the unlearned, for those who could not read. In view of that necessity, icons should have been removed a long time ago, since very few Orthodox claim illiteracy. They are also aware that the distinction made by theologians between worship and veneration is very blurry for ordinary worshipers. They are also aware of the Sunday of Orthodoxy when they get anathematized and declared non-Christians.[17]

CONFRONTING THE HURDLES

In addition to these theological differences, three major hurdles stand in the way of genuine Orthodox-evangelical dialogue:

Ethnicity and Orthodoxy

The first major hurdle is the equal sign between ethnicity and Orthodoxy. The Orthodox churches in Eastern Europe, Russia, and Greece all claim that to be Romanian (or Russian, Bulgarian, Greek) is to be Orthodox. Every Orthodox patriarch has argued that his country is Christian, but by Christian he means Orthodox. This inclusive/exclusive concept is a manipulative one. It excludes evangelicals who are Trinitarians (and therefore a part of the current ecumenical discussions—where the Orthodox participate in dialogue) from having any part in the history of the nation or being considered as existing in the present formation of the nation. The parliaments of Russia, Romania, Greece, and Bulgaria all introduced legislation where the Orthodox patriarch sought sole recognition as the state church. It was interesting to see how this legislation was resisted and defeated

---

[15]See Mark Noll, *Turning Points: Decisive Moments in the History of Christianity* (Grand Rapids: Baker, 1997), 47–82.

[16]See James R. Payton, "Calvin and the Legitimation of Icons: His Treatment of the Seventh Ecumenical Council," *Archive for Reformation History* 84 (1993): 222–41.

[17]See J. I. Packer, *Knowing God* (Downers Grove, Ill.: InterVarsity Press, 1973), 38–44. Some of the laypeople in my church removed all Sunday school pictures of Jesus after reading Packer's chapter on "The Only True God."

by a coalition of evangelicals, nonbelievers, and some Orthodox who were ostracized by the church.

Dr. Mircea Pacurariu, the most authoritative contemporary Romanian church historian, published a book in 1996 titled *Dictionary of Romanian Theologians*.[18] In this group there were only Orthodox theologians. The tragic fact was that, although the title of the book is not *Dictionary of Orthodox Theologians,* other theologians were ignored simply because they were not Orthodox. This concept was then carried into the national historical books written by secular historians who were afraid to deviate from this concept. History books written in the last ten years continue this dominant line of thinking: *ethnicity equals Orthodoxy.*[19]

Moreover, while carefully reading national histories, one discerns that the Reformers (whose paternity evangelicals are claiming) are treated with the same unkindness as the Islamic infidels—both groups were charged with tearing away at the unity of the Christian nations.[20]

Attitude of Orthodox toward Evangelicals

When listening to evangelicals who want to become Orthodox, I sometimes feel they operate within an ahistorical, a priori set of assumptions. I want to ask every evangelical to read the correspondence between Wittenberg Lutheran scholars and the patriarch of Constantinople, and see what conditions the patriarch established for the continuation of the dialogue.[21] Or if that reading is too distant historically, one should read about the reception given to Peter Gillquist and his evangelical brothers who wanted to join the Orthodox Church in Constantinople in the 1980s. With the exception of the patriarch of Antioch, no patriarch welcomed them home. Instead, the patriarch of Constantinople refused to see them.[22]

Moreover, the revival and renewal groups within the Orthodox Church are considered a nuisance by the bishops and the

---

[18]Mircea Pacurariu, *Dictionarul teologilor romani* (Bucharest: Ed. Univers Enciclopedic, 1996).

[19]See, e.g., Kurt Treptow, ed., *A History of Romania* (New York: Columbia Univ. Press, 1996).

[20]See Hancock-Stefan, "The Impact of Reformation on the Romanian People," 119–69.

[21]Ibid., 40–50.

[22]See Gillquist, *Becoming Orthodox*, 143–52.

patriarchs. The founder of The Lord's Army in Romania, Father Iosif Trifa, was defrocked and not allowed to be buried in his priestly clothes (Trifa was later rehabilitated), and recently some of the more innovative priests in Russia have been removed from Moscow because they were considered too evangelical.[23]

Concept of Salvation

The most difficult hurdle has to do with the concept of salvation in the Orthodox Church. This is the area where J. I. Packer, being Anglican, would be closer to the Orthodox Church than someone who is a Baptist like I am and who grew up in an Orthodox and Communist country. The reason for this affinity between the Orthodox and the Anglicans has to do with baptism and its significance and the time when it is applied.

During the 1980s I had a conversation with a Ph.D. candidate (who today is in the upper echelon of the Orthodox hierarchy) regarding the salvation of Nicolae Ceausescu, the cruel dictator of Romania. He assured me that Ceausescu was saved because he was baptized as an infant. Ceausescu was a true son of the Orthodox Church. Since my colleague was in this expansive theological mood, I asked him if he thought that I, as an evangelical, was also part of the redeemed. To my dismay he replied that he was not sure! According to this student, since Ceausescu was baptized in the church, with all the appropriate rites, it did not make any difference what he did when he grew up, nor did it matter that he kept saying he was an atheist and that he sought to destroy the church. However, since I was baptized outside the Eastern Orthodox Church at the age of seventeen, he could not tell me that I was a part of the redeemed people of God.[24]

In the Orthodox-evangelical dialogue, the conflicting issue often seems to be justification versus *theosis.* On a practical level among Orthodox, however, there is very little emphasis on *theosis* and the greatest reliance on baptism and chrismation. It is true that

---

[23]See Clendenin, *Eastern Orthodox Christianity,* 141, n. 3.

[24]A similar answer was given to Daniel Clendenin: "But whether or not a non-Orthodox person can even be saved is an open question in Orthodox ecclesiology. Over coffee one day, I asked an Orthodox priest whether I, as a Protestant theologian, might be considered a true Christian. His response: 'I don't know'" (Daniel B. Clendenin, "Why I'm Not Orthodox," *Christianity Today* 41 [January 6, 1997]: 36).

the Orthodox theology has a powerful emphasis on cosmic salvation—on Christ recapitulating the whole universe,[25] an emphasis
often lacking among the evangelicals. The weakness of the Orthodox concept of salvation is that the individual is lost. In the Orthodox Church, one can justifiably paraphrase the jailer's question
(Acts 16:30) from "What must I do to be saved?" to "What must
the church do in order for me to be saved?"[26]

Many of the Orthodox clergy and laity who became Baptists, Seventh-day Adventists, and Pentecostals confess that they
had no idea what it meant to be a child of God. The church
repeatedly assured them that they are, but they had no relation-

---

[25]See Dumitru Staniloae, *Theology and the Church* (Crestwood, N.Y.: St. Vladimir's
Seminary Press, 1980), 223, 225–26. This view is criticized by David Wells in his essay
"Reservations about Catholic Renewal in Evangelicalism," in *The Orthodox Evangeli-
cals,* ed. Robert Webber and Donald Bloesch (Nashville: Nelson, 1978), 220–24.

[26]In his unpublished article "Individualizing a Person's Relationship with God,"
Josef Tson summarizes his view of the major theological deficiencies of the Orthodox
Church with regard to salvation: (1) The church has introduced the dogma that salvation, which was purchased by the Son of God, is deposited in the church. Thus the
church has become the "deposit of grace." (2) The priest gives the saving grace through
the sacraments. (3) People are no longer called to come to Jesus to receive their salvation through him, and thus to enter into a personal relationship with God. The position of Jesus Christ as the only Mediator has tacitly, yet practically, totally disappeared.
(4) People now hear a different calling: "Come to our Mother Church." (5) The pre-
vailing dogma of our day is that the church saves the nation, which is why in Bucharest
they are building the Cathedral of the Nation's Salvation. (6) The personal relationship with God has disappeared. The only thing left is a personal relationship with the
church. In 1995, when the leading contemporary Romanian poet, Ioan Alexandru,
started to talk about a personal relationship with God, the Romanian Orthodox theologians attacked him publicly, stating with utmost clarity that there is no personal
relationship with God but only a personal relationship with the church. (7) If someone
no longer has a personal relationship with God, there is no longer a need to read the
Scriptures. The only place for the Scriptures is on the altar. (8) If there is no personal
relationship with God that must be maintained through holy living, and if the priest
is able to forgive all of the sins after a confession and to forgive the sins of the dead
after their death, then every reason for holy living has disappeared. (9) These are the
main reasons why the Orthodox Church does not have a credible message against the
current corruption of the country. (10) The abolishing of corruption can be accomplished only by bringing back in our society the importance of a personal relationship
with God. This is the reason for the existence of evangelicals in Orthodox countries
such as Romania: they are here to bring back the most important thing that the Son of
God brought to this planet, and that is a personal relationship with God. This treasure
was lost when we introduced the priesthood and the church, which became a state
problem and a national problem. The task of evangelicals is to bring this treasure into
the life of each individual, and through this, into the life of the nation.

ship with God because they had never committed their lives to God. In fact, if one asks an Orthodox if he or she is saved, the pious answer is "Only the good Lord knows."

THE "MAYBE" CATEGORY

As a "maybe" contributor, I'm reminded of Revelation 2:15–16 (my paraphrase): "I wish you were hot or cold. So because you are neither—hot nor cold—I will spit you out of my mouth." The categories of "yes" and "no" are much easier than "maybe."

At the same time, I am reminded of Paul's desire for his kinsmen to be saved (Rom. 10:1). I often ask myself (like Iosif Trifa, the founder of The Lord's Army did), *What can we do in order to make sure that the salvation of our kinsfolk is secure?* In my nearly forty years as a Baptist in both Europe and the United States, and specifically during my work among the Romanians, I have seen thousands of people baptized by immersion as adults—and the great majority came from the Orthodox Church. This throng all testified that they did not know Jesus Christ as their Savior, nor were they sure of their salvation until they gave their lives to Christ in a Baptist church. Yet, during these same years, I have known fewer than five people who left Baptist churches to become Orthodox.

CAN AN EVANGELICAL BECOME ORTHODOX?

When I ponder whether an evangelical can become Orthodox, here are some of the great positives.

First, like so many evangelicals, when I go to the Eastern Orthodox Church and listen to the whole liturgy, my soul is exalted, and at that moment I want to become a part of the Orthodox Church. When I go to the Easter service, I conclude that there is no other service in Christendom as powerful and demonstrative of the resurrection of Jesus Christ as the Eastern Orthodox service.

Second, when I listen to the readings of Scripture and see the reverence that the Orthodox people have toward the Holy Book, I want to applaud—and I want my evangelical brothers and sisters to have the same reverence.

Finally, when I read of the historical struggle of the Orthodox Church and see how it withstood the onslaught of the

Ottoman Empire by preserving the witness among the people, I want to feel a part of it. This is the church of my forefathers.

On the other hand, these are some of the difficulties I encounter when I think of the possibility of an evangelical becoming Orthodox:

First, when I participate in the liturgy and see the lack of response by the congregation, my return to the evangelical fold is quickened. During the centennial of the Romanian Bible, I went to a three-day national celebration in Cleveland, Ohio. On Saturday, in the presence of the Romanian Orthodox bishop Nathanael, I read a paper on the importance of the Bible for Romania. On Sunday I went to the Romanian cathedral with my Orthodox relatives. The cathedral was packed. I was elated because the bishop used some of my ideas in his homily! After the homily, he celebrated the Eucharist. From this vast congregation of over a thousand people, fewer than ten people went forward to receive the Eucharist. Suddenly the mood changed in the cathedral. Everyone could see that the bishop was highly disappointed. Out of his disappointment and grieved heart he began to preach again. He lamented the reasons so few people, on this day of national celebration, chose to partake of the body and the blood of the Lord. He knew there was unconfessed sin, and he knew their behavior did not reflect any degree of *theosis*. When I see, even on high holidays, that the people are not practicing their faith, I say no to evangelicals becoming Orthodox.

Second, when I read historical textbooks published by the Orthodox Church that blatantly deny the right of evangelicals to exist in traditionally Orthodox countries, I say no.

Third, when I see the persecution of the evangelicals by the Orthodox Church, the denial of permits to build and expand churches, and the exclusion of evangelicals from public television in some nations, I must say no.

Finally, when I read about the persecution of some revival groups within the Orthodox Church who wanted to stay a part of the Orthodox Church, I say no.

WHAT MIGHT IT TAKE FOR AN EVANGELICAL TO BECOME ORTHODOX?

Here are a few changes that could facilitate an evangelical's joining the Orthodox Church:

First, *undo some of the anathemas*. When one reads some of the anathemas hurled at the Protestants in the sixteenth and seventeenth centuries by the Eastern Orthodox Church, one is shocked at the vehemence of these pronouncements. When one reads some of the anathemas penned in the twentieth century against the so-called Neo-Protestants (Baptists and Pentecostals) equating them with the heretics of patristic times, one feels great pain.[27] When one sees that every Orthodox seminary has a course on sects in which atheists are lumped together with Moonies and Baptists, one is indeed grieved.[28]

Second, *take another look at what it means to be saved*. The vast majority of people who left the Orthodox Church did so over the issue of salvation as manifested in a changed life. Evangelical history is filled with priests and laity who have experienced their salvation in Jesus Christ after they left the Orthodox Church. Many of the revival groups within Orthodoxy started over this issue of salvation. There are books describing the conversion of evangelicals to Orthodoxy,[29] and I think it is high time for some evangelicals to write books on their conversion from Orthodoxy. At the same time, evangelicals must stop calling Orthodox countries lands of darkness (as though the gospel were being preached to them for the first time), and Orthodox bishops and patriarchs must stop calling evangelicals sheep stealers when these evangelicals are sincerely concerned for the salvation of those who are in doubt about their eternal destination.

Third, *appreciate other believers who sincerely and truthfully love the Lord*. While evangelicals are truly thankful that, in the history of the many Eastern Orthodox countries, we have never experienced something similar to the Roman Inquisition, persecution of Christian believers is plentiful. While the bishops are careful to present only the theological dangers of evangelicalism, the local priests and authorities are known to systematically persecute the non-Orthodox.

---

[27]See Ilie Cleopa, *Calauza in credinta ortodoxa* [A Guide in the Orthodox Faith] (Galati: Editura Episcopiei Dunarii de Jos, 1991).

[28]See P. I. David, *Calauza Crestina (Sectologie)* [A Christian Guidebook (Sectology)] (Curtea de Arges: Editura Episcopiei Argesului, 1994).

[29]See, e.g., Thomas Doulis, ed., *Journeys to Orthodoxy: A Collection of Essays by Converts to Orthodox Christianity* (Minneapolis: Light & Life, 1986).

In conclusion, one has to state that there is only a very slim possibility for someone who is a committed evangelical with an understanding of the Reformation to become Orthodox. Nevertheless, if one esteems the conclusions of the ecumenical councils (except the last one), treasures the position of the Bible in liturgy and ecumenical gatherings, and is willing to disseminate the knowledge of the Lord, one might decide to become an Orthodox. However, I do not know if someone with these convictions would be welcomed into the Orthodox flock. Thus, I conclude with the words spoken by Jesus regarding the conversion of the rich: as "through the eye of a needle."

A RESPONSE TO GEORGE
HANCOCK-STEFAN

Bradley Nassif

I first met Dr. Hancock-Stefan over ten years ago when he was a doctoral student at Trinity Evangelical Divinity School in Deerfield, Illinois. Then, as now, I appreciated the warm and humble attitude he displayed toward the Orthodox Church. It is important for readers to understand this side of his character, because some of the things he wrote in this essay might sound harsh to those who are unfamiliar with him. It is, in fact, his sincere humility that should cause Orthodox readers to attend even more intently to what he has written.

Like many other evangelicals living in Orthodox lands formerly dominated by Communist ideology, Dr. Hancock-Stefan has lived at the crossroads between the Romanian Orthodox Church and a Baptist denomination. He knows what it is like to be socially marginalized for his faith, even though he regularly attended an Orthodox church during major holidays and family festivities. I understand his criticisms of nominal Christianity among the Orthodox, the sinful equation of ethnicity with Christian faith, the injustices of exclusionary policies concerning religious freedom in Eastern Europe that give evangelicals a second-class socioreligious standing, the false grouping of cults with evangelical denominations, the former history of ecclesiastical opposition to Orthodox renewal groups such as The Lord's Army in Romania, and the closed-minded bigotry of some Orthodox churchmen toward the churches of the West. I understand his criticisms and must sadly agree that there is more truth to his concerns than we have been willing to admit. Those sins do indeed belong to us in varying degrees, and we do Christ and his church no service by denying it. Thus there can be no genuine unity between Orthodox and evangelicals unless there is also a genuine spirit of repentance on our part.

In addition to the practical issues Dr. Hancock-Stefan has raised, there are also theological issues that need to be addressed. He asserts that "No Eastern Orthodox sees any major significance in the Protestant Reformation for the Orthodox Church" (page 210). That is certainly not true of the present author, nor is it supported by the official ecumenical dialogues that have occurred between the Orthodox Church and the Reformed, Lutheran, and Anglican communities in the past twenty-five years. Dr. Hancock-Stefan also presents a truncated view of icons as being chiefly "the gospel for the unlearned" (page 211) and criticizes the Orthodox on that ground. But, in fact, the iconoclastic controversy was concerned far more with the christological foundations of iconography, the function of tradition in Christian images, and the role of the Bible in doctrinal debate. The specific theological issues Dr. Hancock-Stefan sees as separating the Orthodox and evangelical communities have been addressed in my own chapter, and thus, I hope, need no further comment.

I was especially struck by one comment the author made about the Orthodox Church minimizing the personal side of salvation. He states, "In the Orthodox Church, one can justifiably paraphrase the jailer's question (Acts 16:30) from 'What must I do to be saved?' to 'What must the church do in order for me to be saved?' (page 214). As with Dr. Horton's essay, Dr. Hancock-Stefan actually helps the Orthodox Church by posing this question to us. Saint John Chrysostom and the liturgy itself repeatedly exhort us to affirm that the personal side of salvation must never be minimized or lost in the preaching of the gospel. Our priests do indeed often neglect the personal side of salvation by overemphasizing the ecclesiological resources of the faith. But in the end, the two must be kept in balance, with neither side excluding or overruling the other. We must remember that the personal question asked by the Philippian jailer was addressed to and answered by a communal member of the church, of which Christ is the head.

A RESPONSE TO GEORGE HANCOCK-STEFAN

Michael Horton

Dr. Hancock-Stefan's essay provides a very useful biographical and anecdotal context for his take on the question "Can an evangelical become Orthodox?" His experience being quite remote from my secondhand knowledge of Eastern Orthodoxy, the author brings theoretical discussions to the level of concrete performance, and this is helpful on both sides of the debate.

His examples reflect a general evangelical concern that Orthodoxy, not unlike Rome, is not very ecumenical after all. Cyprian and other church fathers insisted that when one bishop presumes primacy over all other pastors, he has committed schism. Even if there were no essential doctrinal differences, we would have reason to be suspicious of the claims of any part of Christ's visible church to be the only true church on the earth.

Once upon a time it really was the case that there was one true visible church and a host of sects. The Catholic Church, whether in the East or in the West (before the schism), was set over against the heretics (Gnostics, Monophysites, Nestorians, Arians, Sabellians, Donatists, and so on). The Protestant Reformers saw themselves as struggling for a reformed, evangelical, catholic Christianity in continuity with that ancient Catholic Church and against all heresies and schisms. But the new reality, which was occasioned in the West by the anathematization of the gospel itself, led to a considerably more confusing ecclesiastical landscape. On one hand, if the gospel is the essential mark of the true church, the Roman Church had compromised its catholicity—indeed, its claim to be part of the true church, much less the only true church. On the other hand, Protestantism itself splintered: first, between the Lutheran and Reformed, and then among the radical sects that proliferated and continue to do so. But while the Lutheran-Reformed schism may be unjustified, others are surely imposed on Protestantism from without, as in the condemnations of the Council of Trent and in the tragic success of theological modernism.

Reformation Christians will always find the true church wherever the Word is rightly preached and the sacraments rightly administered according to the Word of God, as the adage goes.[1] They track the "true church," not according to age or a particular genealogy of ordination, but according to the apostolic gospel and sacraments. If this makes Reformation Christians schismatic, they are at least in good company. All sorts of differences may be tolerated for the sake of the peace of Jerusalem. "But even if we or an angel from heaven should preach a gospel other than the one we preached to you, let him be eternally condemned!" (Gal. 1:8). The gospel is the measuring line, and if Paul places himself as an apostle under this criterion, surely no other standard can prevail for popes, patriarchs, or councils.

In line with the usual form of subscription in our circles, while I affirm that our Reformed and Presbyterian confessions embody the system of doctrine taught in the Holy Scriptures, I do not regard all non-Reformed churches as lacking the marks of the true church. Rome and Orthodoxy, however, do regard all those outside their respective communions as outside the true church, which would seem, on the face of it at least, to render them at least more schismatic. The anecdotal evidence provided by Dr. Hancock-Stefan is confirmed in my own experience with friends who have become Orthodox. There is a perceived arrogance that is hardly becoming of the shepherds of God's people.

The author is correct, I think, to suggest that the most difficult hurdle in ecumenical discussions with Orthodoxy touches soteriology. He remarks that J. I. Packer, an Anglican and Reformed conversation partner with the Orthodox, is closer to Orthodoxy than he is himself, given Packer's view of baptism (page 213). It is certainly true that there are important affinities between the Reformed and the Orthodox on the sacraments, as

---

[1]See the Belgic Confession, article 29.

I note in my response to Father Rommen (pages 262–64). However, heirs of the magisterial Reformation are undoubtedly closer to Dr. Hancock-Stefan because of their common confession of *sola gratia, sola fide.* While his criticism of *theosis* may be somewhat sharper than my own, he is correct to suggest that justification-versus-*theosis* is at the heart of this debate.

Dr. Hancock-Stefan also points up the danger of "culture Christianity," a threat one does not have to wander too far from Protestantism to find. Although a typical American mixture, I belong to a primarily Dutch-American denomination. I imagine that in some of our churches one could be put off by the confusion of ethnicity and creed about as much as in, say, Serbian Orthodoxy. Barth saw quite clearly the heretical dangers of *Kulturprotestantismus* in the so-called "German Christian" movement of his day. Doctrinal divisions are tragic but sometimes necessary. But there is no excuse for tolerating ethnic tribalism in the church. How often in the Epistles is the gospel explicitly linked to ethnic inclusiveness? To expect Gentiles to become Jews was to deny the gospel, Paul declared repeatedly (see especially Gal. 3:26–29). While it may be useful to recognize the differences in Eastern and Western modes of thinking, for instance, it is utterly unhelpful to raise these to the level of differences over substantial doctrinal matters. Eastern modes of thinking are no more inerrant than Western ways, and we must work hard to understand what each other is saying instead of lazily dismissing particular expressions and accounts.

On the positive side, I share the author's appreciation for the reverence one finds in Orthodox liturgy, in contrast to that which has become common in evangelicalism. Standing for the reading of Holy Scripture reveals at least an external respect for hearing God speak that does not find ready parallels in most evangelical services. This, in fact, is one of the most striking aspects I noticed when I joined a Presbyterian church, but it is increasingly difficult to find this in the Reformed tradition as well today, as the liturgy is stripped of anything weighty, transcendent, and vertical. But how proud can we be of "unchanging" liturgies if the people do not really know God's Word and the liberating assurance of being justified even while falling far short in this life of the *theosis* that God's righteousness requires for reconciliation and restoration?

A RESPONSE TO GEORGE
HANCOCK-STEFAN

Vladimir Berzonsky

It is difficult not to be touched in soul by the poignancy of Dr. Hancock-Stefan's essay. It well describes from a personal view the tragedy of separation between Orthodox and evangelical Christians, not academically only, but from a personal witness as well. Our Master himself prayed for his followers to be one and thus to demonstrate the reality of his mission and message, yet he also declared, "I did not come to bring peace, but a sword" (Matt. 10:34).

In the case of Dr. Hancock-Stefan, the spiritual sword of Jesus Christ has divided his heart in two—nostalgia for his former Orthodox persona while embracing his new evangelical self. He wants somehow to hold on to the traditions and celebrations that were so much a part of the Orthodox Church of his heritage and to do so as a Baptist minister. More, and precisely as a confessing Baptist, whenever he attends the services of the Orthodox Church, he judges the faith of the faithful and finds it wanting. He is annoyed that his message is neither welcome nor accepted. He yearns to "save" them, and in a naive way he appears not to understand why his vision of salvation is unwanted and, for the most part, ignored. He is stymied and frustrated by the cool reception he normally receives from Orthodox Christians to what he considers the "hot" news he brings of salvation (to follow his Laodicean imagery). For him, the Orthodox are lacking in zeal. They are uninspired. It would not do to suggest that other forms of spirituality might nurture the souls of his countrymen and countrywomen who are Ortho-dox. Why they go on century after century serving the Lord in the Orthodox fashion, even at times laying down their lives for their beliefs, completely escapes him.

Clearly Dr. Hancock-Stefan would not be open to an inner awareness of the spiritual activity of the Holy Trinity tran-scending the emotionalism of a Baptist revival or enthusiastic inspiration from a Bible preacher. Nor would I expect him to realize that, while he may attend the Divine Liturgy, his attitude is that of a guest at best, and more likely as a critic. The call at the midpoint of the sacred service to imitate the cherubim (that is, to rise to the transcendence of the highest rank of angels) and to lay aside all earthly cares is impossible for one who is held in bondage to his reason and immersed in negative thoughts of criticism and judgment.

Christianity, like Judaism, is a religion of revelation. It is God who acts, and he does so despite the limits of the human being's ability to comprehend what he is doing for the life of the world. This doesn't mean that faith is wrapped up in mystery. Nevertheless, Christianity is by definition transcendent. We all worship a God Unknown. Serious theologians understand that speaking of God is better done apophatically, that is, by telling what God is *not* rather than by trying to describe who he is. The God who revealed himself in Christ Jesus revealed his tran-scendence. We come to know the Unknowable One not by think-ing or by understanding but by progressive unions.

The Divine Liturgy, the normal Sunday morning service, divides into two basic parts. The first half includes the readings for the day taken from the epistles of the New Testament and followed by a fixed reading from one of the gospels. The pastor normally preaches a homily based on those readings. Here ends the service of learning, and in the early church a prayer was offered for catechumens, who then were dismissed. Following their dismissal one hears a deacon announcing, "The doors, the doors!" What ensues is for the initiated only. The call is made to shut out all unbelievers and, for those who remain, to invite them to open the doors of their souls and receive the grace that will come in Christ's very body and blood for those who are pre-pared to receive it. Nobody says to the cynic and doubter, "Friend, how did you get in here without wedding clothes?" (Matt. 22:12), but they should realize that they are strangers to the sacred mystery, which by judging and condemning they not only will not comprehend, but they will also fail to appreciate the celebration of life.

A scholar, now an Orthodox bishop, told Dr. Hancock-Stefan he wasn't certain if the writer was among the redeemed, which caused him to be dismayed (page 213); but the scholar merely responded with the wisdom of Mary, the Birthgiver of God: "May it be to me as you have said" (Luke 1:38). To say more would be impertinence.

The heresy of Anabaptism begins with rejecting all traditional authority, which is in the church, thus creating an artificial church, a purely human construction that results in enslavement to human reason.[1] The great twentieth-century Orthodox theologian Father Justin Popovich put it well: Man-God is substituted for the God-man.[2] The authority of the individual then becomes the unique authority on earth. His or her personal experiences become the one criterion of faith. When, therefore, the anathemas are read on Orthodoxy Sunday, so repulsive to Dr. Hancock-Stefan, is it any wonder that the Reformationists are included along with Arius and the others? I agree that these anathemas are not always read with love; yet, it is imperative to continue telling the truth (Eph. 4:15).

On the positive side, Dr. Hancock-Stefan notes that evangelical and Orthodox Christians have much in common as together they face the challenges of humanism. They stand together in confronting liberal expressions of Christianity that compromise the gospel and its implicit or explicit ethics, or in choosing to stay away from any worship services that appear pagan or that compromise the glorious gospel of the Lord.

Yet even in his compliments Dr. Hancock-Stefan cannot help but throw barbs. For example, he writes that evangelical Christians became Orthodox when they "felt a spiritual drought" and were "magnetized by the Eastern Orthodox liturgy and all the accompanying pomp" (page 208)! And while the Orthodox Church holds the Holy Scriptures in high position, "Scripture is a closed, unknown book for the majority of the Orthodox" (page 209). My experience is that many of the blessed elderly, simple

---

[1]See Louis Bouyer, *The Spirit and Forms of Protestantism,* 2d ed. (New York: Scepter, 1964), 212.

[2]Father Justin Popovich, *Orthodox Faith and Life in Christ* (Belmont, Mass.: Institute for Byzantine and Modern Greek Studies, 1994), 102.

people know more of the Sacred Scriptures than those who sit in high places and have degrees to commend them. They need only listen to the Bible chanted in the sacred services throughout the year. They may not be able to proof-text. They are uncomfortable when challenged by those who have been trained to expound on select passages from the Bible, building a thesis on those selections while ignoring whatever is in conflict with their fixed opinions. Yet they live for the Lord, they pray devoutly, they live by the Spirit of the Lord, and they die for their convictions, as they have proved in the past century.

A RESPONSE TO GEORGE
HANCOCK-STEFAN

Edward Rommen

George Hancock-Stefan's essay appears to be a primarily emotive response to volk-Orthodoxy based on regionally limited anecdotal evidence. While he does raise significant issues of history, ethnicity, and current affairs, he does very little to advance the theological discussion central to this book. The only section of the essay in which the author addresses what he calls "theological differences" deals with merely two issues, neither of which is dealt with theologically, fairly, or accurately.

The first issue is raised by simply stating the well-known fact that the Protestant Reformers were reacting to the inadequacies and abuses of medieval Roman Catholic theology and practice. That being the case, the distinctives of Reformation theology should be evaluated in terms of their historical context and the specific Roman doctrine they sought to redress. To universalize the Reformers' conclusions would seem to imply that the Orthodox Church was party to the Roman doctrines criticized by the Reformation. That was (and is) not the case. Thus, to suggest that "no Eastern Orthodox sees any major significance in the Protestant Reformation" (page 210) is misleading. The Orthodox recognize the significance of the Reformation but do not see themselves as being directly addressed by the concerns of the Reformers. Surely the communication between Patriarch Jeremiah II and the Lutheran theologians at Tübingen (1576–81)—as well as more recent discussions, e.g., the

Lutheran–Orthodox Dialogue (1985–89)—illustrates broad areas of agreement, the mutual respect, and the genuine desire for continued discussion that existed between the two. It should also be noted that the Tübingen-Constantinople discussions did not end with the "you change or we don't talk" arrogance insinuated by Dr. Hancock-Stefan but rather with a deep appreciation of the breadth of existing agreement, an agreement to disagree on other issues, and a desire for continued friendship.[1]

The second "theological" issue is nothing more than an emotive rejection of the teachings of the Seventh Council (page 211). Dispatching with mere "appreciation" the theological findings of the earlier councils, the author simply dismisses the teachings of the Seventh Council. He refers to, but does not discuss, the important and clearly understood distinction between the veneration of icons and worship, which is reserved for God alone. His reference to Orthodox literacy reveals a gross misunderstanding of the place of icons in Orthodox theology, worship, and piety. Surely, it must be known that icons are more than aids for the illiterate. He takes offense at the anathemas associated with the Seventh Council and fails to understand that the primary emphasis on the Sunday of Orthodoxy (first Sunday in Great Lent) is the celebration of the unity of the church and its victory over the forces of schism.

These criticisms notwithstanding, I can identify with many of the other issues raised in this essay, since I have made the journey from evangelicalism to Orthodoxy. As a local parish priest, I am keenly aware of the general lack of commitment that characterizes many Orthodox. As a theologian, I am deeply distressed by the widespread absence of a functional knowledge of the Holy Scriptures and the sometimes inaccurate understanding of the teaching of their own church. As a former missionary, I find the lack of missionary urgency a significant impediment to church planting. And I note with sadness the occasional difficulty the church has in integrating converts, myself included. Yet, all of these things (personal commitment, Bible study, missions) are firmly anchored in our doctrine, are expressed in our

---

[1]See George Mastrantonis, *Augsburg and Constantinople* (Brookline, Mass.: Holy Cross Orthodox Press, 1982), 288, 306.

rich history, and are being recovered. While it may be true that the present state of Orthodoxy does not always rise up to the standard of its own doctrine, yet one does not reject a church because of the inadequacies of its present members. Rather, one accepts it because of the soundness of its overall structure and teaching and because it provides a fertile environment for the spiritual life.

CONCLUSION

George Hancock-Stefan

Close to two decades ago, I was looking for a pastoral position—and the terminology of political correctness was not yet in place. A friend of mine sent me a list of requirements for the candidates. Among their wishes was that the new minister would not preach from the first three chapters of Revelation for at least three years, due to the fact that the last two pastors had started there. However, the oddest requirement was that the minister had to be one-handed—a requirement that came about because, whenever the congregation thought they understood their previous ministers, the ministers would suddenly say, "But on the other hand!"

Writing from a "maybe" position is definitely a handicap. The "yes" and "no" are so much easier to perceive. Dr. Nassif is able to articulate a position of "yes" in a splendid way. Dr. Horton and Father Berzonsky, with their clear-cut perspectives and their knowledge of their theology and their experiences, cannot imagine a point where there could be reciprocal exchanges between Orthodoxy and evangelicalism. No sooner have I precariously balanced myself on the "maybe" position than I am challenged to look again to see if my position is not simply a mirage.

I think the best way I can conclude this round is by quoting one of my favorite songs, written by Timothy Dwight in 1800:

I love thy kingdom, Lord, the house of Thine abode,
the Church our blest Redeemer saved with His own
    precious blood.

I love Thy Church, O God! Her walls before Thee stand,
dear as the apple of Thine eye, and graven on Thy hand.

I think that Bradley Nassif, Michael Horton, Vladimir Berzonsky, Edward Rommen, and I are driven by our shared love and passion for the Lord Jesus Christ, which finds expression in the love we have for his redeemed people and for the lost ones.

Together with John Calvin in his introduction to his *Institutes of the Christian Religion*, I argue that there is only one church—one holy, apostolic, and catholic church. We love this church, which is made up of Catholics, Orthodox, magisterial Reformers, and radical Reformers, and we hope we will be able to do what Timothy Dwight suggests:

For her my tears shall fall; for her my prayers ascend;
to her my cares and toils be given, till toils and cares
shall end.

Beyond my highest joy I prize her heavenly ways,
her sweet communion, solemn vows, her hymns of love
and praise.

My prayer is that Orthodox and evangelicals together will find ways to work with one another so that the church of Jesus Christ will benefit and prosper and the Lord Jesus Christ will be pleased and glorified through our work.

Chapter Five

ARE EASTERN ORTHODOXY AND EVANGELICALISM COMPATIBLE? MAYBE

An Orthodox Perspective

Edward Rommen

ARE EASTERN ORTHODOXY AND EVANGELICALISM COMPATIBLE? MAYBE

An Orthodox Perspective

Edward Rommen

The basic thesis of this essay is that under certain conditions some evangelical doctrines may be compatible with the teaching of the Orthodox Church. Compatibility, as used here, refers to the possibility of two expressions of a given doctrine being able to exist in a state of sufficient harmony so as to allow reciprocal acquisition in their respective systems with little or no modification. This does not necessarily imply an isomorphic match but rather comprehensibility and mutually acknowledged legitimacy.[1] Depending on the extent to which facilitating factors are affected by inhibiting forces, one might reasonably expect several degrees of concurrence.

FACTORS THAT FACILITATE COMPATIBILITY

There are several factors that make some level of Orthodox-evangelical doctrinal compatibility a distinct likelihood: Orthodox and evangelicals share the same biblical texts, are equally committed to the authority of those texts, and, to the extent they allow it, are guided by the same Holy Spirit.

---

[1]For example, there are within the evangelical world widely varying expressions of the doctrine of election. Nevertheless, I assume that the difference between the positions proffered by Calvinists and Arminians would not necessarily be construed as incompatibility.

Shared Biblical Texts

With the exception of the Hebrew text of the Old Testament,[2] as well as its apocryphal books, Orthodox and evangelical theologians derive doctrine from the same biblical sources. The evangelical emphasis on the biblical text is evidenced in the efforts of evangelicals to preserve, edit, publish, and study the biblical texts.[3] Similarly, Orthodox faithful "place heavy emphasis on the use of Scripture, preserving and studying the text liturgically and academically, as well as in private devotion."[4] Today most Orthodox parishes have Bible study groups. And what else would one expect in a church whose Fathers have for centuries urged the faithful to study the Holy Scriptures and to meditate on them day and night.[5] If the sources of our doctrines are the common biblical texts, and if, as can be assumed, the meaning of God's Word is generally comprehensible, it should not surprise us to find significant areas of agreement.

Shared Commitment to the Absolute Authority of the Holy Scriptures

It has always been the teaching of the Orthodox Church that the Bible is the inspired Word of God and as such is without error and the sole authority against which all questions of life and faith are to be measured.

I realize that some would question the Orthodox commitment to the authority of Scripture because the Orthodox Church does not accept the Reformation articulation of *sola Scriptura* and because it uses Holy Tradition as a guide to the interpretation of Scripture. However, it must be pointed out that the Reformers formulated that principle as a response to certain false teachings

---

[2]The Orthodox Church favors the text of the Septuagint.

[3]Note, for example, the Bible societies' work on the Greek New Testament editions.

[4]Father John Matusiak, "Orthodox Study of the Bible"; can be viewed on the Web at www.oca.org/pages/orth_chri/Q-and-A_OLD/Study-of-the-Bible.html.

[5]Of Saint John Chrysostom W. R. W. Stephens writes, "There is no topic on which he dwells more frequently and earnestly than on the duty of every Christian man and woman to study the Bible" (Philip Schaff and Henry Wace, eds., *Nicene and Post-Nicene Fathers* [Peabody, Mass.: Hendrickson, 1995], 9:21–22); cf. Chrysostom, "Homily II," in *Nicene and Post-Nicene Father*, 9:252.

of the Roman church, in particular those regarding the relationship between Scripture and Tradition. The Roman church had elevated Tradition (the teaching of the Fathers and canon law) to the normative level of Scripture. As a result, there existed two equally authoritative sources for doctrine. In an attempt to remedy the situation, the Reformers, while reestablishing Scripture in its rightful place, all but eliminated the role of Tradition—and in doing so abandoned one of the most valuable interpretive tools available to the church.

From an Orthodox perspective, biblical texts must be interpreted with the help of historical-grammatical exegesis and the rules of hermeneutics within the context of the church, i.e., in light of that which has been passed down from generation to generation from the apostles. The basic assumption here is that not everything our Lord and the apostles did and said is contained in the written canon (cf. John 21:25). In 2 Thessalonians 2:15 Saint Paul admonished the believers to preserve both written and oral traditions. Both of these are understood to be the instructions given by Christ and his apostles.

During the time before the New Testament was formally codified, these oral instructions and teachings were used to guide the church. Later, after the canon of the New Testament had been established, differences in interpretation caused by linguistic ambiguity were resolved in light of the apostolic tradition. This does not mean that Scripture is somehow subject to Tradition. If there is any obvious discrepancy between Tradition and Scripture, Scripture is the final authority. In other words, if on the basis of sound exegesis the meaning of Scripture and Tradition cannot be reconciled, Scripture is always favored over Tradition. So Tradition is viewed as the larger historical context within which Scripture was given. As such, Tradition does not have the authority of Scripture but is to be used as an aid to interpretation and as a source of instruction on matters not explicitly dealt with in Scripture.

If the sources of our doctrines are the common biblical texts, and if, as can be assumed, the meaning of God's Word is generally comprehensible, and if both Orthodox and evangelicals are committed to the binding authority of these texts properly interpreted, it should not surprise us to find significant areas of agreement.

Operation of the Holy Spirit

One of the most prominent features of Orthodox doctrine is its emphasis on the role of the third person of the Trinity—the Holy Spirit—in the life of the church. We are taught that the Holy Spirit participated in creation and spoke the Word of God through the prophets, and, in keeping with the promise of our Lord, the descent of the Spirit at Pentecost marks the beginning of the church. The Spirit enables the church by means of his special gifts (1 Cor. 12; Eph. 4:7–16), through his work in the sacraments,[6] and by bringing the faithful ever closer to God-likeness. The Spirit also guides us into the truth (John 16:13), reveals our own sinfulness (John 16:8–11), and in general draws men and women to God.

This divine activity is not necessarily limited to the visible realm of the canonical church.[7] Father Georges Florovsky distinguishes between the "canonical" boundaries and the "charismatic" boundaries of the church and suggests that they are neither contiguous nor coinciding. As he sees it, the canonical boundaries are precisely those "external" boundaries that are defined by dogma and canons, while the charismatic boundaries are circumscribed by the presence of Christ and the indwelling of the Holy Spirit, which always heals the infirm and completes what is lacking.[8]

Few could deny the evangelicals' desire for spiritual growth and piety. With such treasures as Philip Jacob Spener's *Pia Desideria*,[9] and given the whole history of the pietist and holiness movements, it is hard to imagine evangelicalism without a

---

[6]Consider the words spoken by the priest at the consecration of the bread and wine during the Divine Liturgy: "And make this bread the precious Body of thy Christ. And that which is in this cup the precious Blood of thy Christ. Changing them by thy Holy Spirit."

[7]"There may be members of the Church who are not visibly such, but whose membership is known to God alone. If anyone is saved, he must, in some sense, be a member of the Church, but in what sense, it is not always possible to say. The Spirit of God blows where it will, and as St. Irenaeus points out, where the Spirit is, there is the Church!" (St. Tikhon's Monastery, *These Truths We Hold* [South Canaan, Pa.: St. Tikhon's Seminary Press, 1986], xii).

[8]See Georges Florovsky, "The Limits of the Church," *Church Quarterly Review* 11 (October 1933): 117–31; can be viewed on the Web at www.wcc-coe.org/wcc/who/crete-01-e.html. Cf. Florovsky, "The Doctrine of the Church and the Ecumenical Problem," *The Ecumenical Review* 2 (1950): 152–61.

[9]Philip Jacob Spener, *Pia Desideria* (Philadelphia: Fortress, 1964).

sustained emphasis on the sanctifying work of the Holy Spirit. If then, there is a commitment to allowing the Spirit of God to lead and sanctify, and if the Spirit's activity is not completely limited to the church, then it seems reasonable to assume that the Spirit of truth will in fact lead to mutual recognition of truth.

FACTORS THAT MAKE COMPATIBILITY UNLIKELY

There are also several factors that militate against Orthodox-evangelical compatibility: (1) the culturally and historically based differences between Eastern and Western frames of reference can render their respective articulations of a given doctrine incompatible; (2) the personal investment in private convictions may blind some to the merest possibility of truth in another's position; and (3) the church has on occasion responded to the theological opinions of other groups in such a way as to declare those teachings incompatible with the doctrine of the church.

Culture Boundness: East versus West

One of the most difficult things about the discussion at hand is that we are dealing with two very distinct mind-sets, two cultures and conceptual frameworks, that are the result of different histories and cultural paths. Consider just a few of the resulting differences: (1) the East tends to be more interested in relationships, whereas the West concentrates on propositions; (2) the East emphasizes person; the West focuses on nature; (3) the East unites reality and symbolism, while the West tends to associate symbol with that which is not real.[10]

Each of these differences gives rise to areas of apparent disagreement: (1) when defining salvation the East is primarily interested in the "new life in Christ," whereas the West concentrates on our change in legal status—our justification; (2) when exploring the doctrine of God, the Eastern theologians emphasize the person of God, while in the West the focus is on the nature of God; (3) when venerating an icon, the Eastern believer has no difficulty relating the reality of an icon's prototype with

---

[10]Obviously this is an oversimplification. However, it does accurately indicate significant differences in conceptual frames of reference or thought paradigms; see Alexander Schmemann, *For the Life of the World* (Crestwood, N.Y.: St. Vladimir's Seminary Press, 1963), 135–51.

its symbolic representation, while Western believers have considerable difficulty.

Personal Convictions

There are, of course, some involved on both sides of this discussion who believe they have recognized some truth and, having articulated it, have developed what might be described as unassailable convictions.[11] Once such an individual position is adopted, learning ceases and is replaced by arrogance and deliberately sustained ignorance. In some cases, those who are so convinced cannot even allow for the possibility of truth in positions that differ from their own. Sadly, this often leads to a determined effort to discourage or even prevent opportunities for significant exchange. Occasionally, such convictions are even couched in terms usually reserved for one's worst enemies rather than for those with whom one supposedly wishes to explore the truth.

Personal convictions of this sort can actually blind one to the truth and lead to a steady stream of inaccurate, erroneous, and slanderous statements concerning that with which one disagrees. Perhaps Friedrich Nietzsche was right after all: "Convictions are a more dangerous enemy of truth than lies."[12]

Specific Teachings of the Church

Throughout its history the church has responded to theological issues, as well as to the teachings of other groups. If an issue or doctrine has been specifically addressed by the church, its faithful are bound to adhere to that position.

Take, for example, the issue of icons. Christian images have been used since the church's very inception—the cross, the church seen as an ark, Christ depicted as a lamb, and so on. Theologically the church's teaching on images is grounded in the doctrine of the incarnation. God himself gave us an icon of himself in Christ and thereby, at least in principle, sanctioned

---

[11]As distinguished from Saint Vincent of Lerins's statement: "We hold that Faith which has been believed everywhere, always, by all" (Saint Vincent of Lerins, 2d Commonitorium, chap. 29, a.).

[12]Friedrich Nietzsche, *The Portable Nietzsche,* trans. Walter Kaufman (New York: Penguin, 1954), 63.

the use of such imaging. The church's teaching was not formulated in detail until the great iconoclast controversy during the seventh and eighth centuries. Appealing to certain Old Testament injunctions against the use of idols, the iconoclasts declared all images idolatrous and with much bloodletting and violence sought to destroy not only the images themselves but also those who venerated them. The council that met at Nicea in 787 to resolve the issue reaffirmed the use of and the veneration of such images but was very explicit in distinguishing between veneration *(proskunasis)* and worship *(latreia)*, which was due God alone.[13] Since the time of that council, Orthodox faithful have used icons as practical aids for worship and personal piety. Because the church has specifically articulated its teaching on the issue, it is hard to imagine any liturgical act in the Orthodox Church without icons.[14]

At other times, the church has responded directly to the teachings of other groups. For example, Patriarch Dositheus of Jerusalem convened a synod (Jerusalem, 1672) in order to review the doctrines of the Reformers, in particular those of John Calvin. This was done "so that each of the Faithful may be able to compare, and judge of both, and easily know the Orthodoxy of the Eastern Church, and the falsehood of the heretics."[15] Dositheus did indeed reject some of Calvin's teaching as heresy. With reference to the doctrine of predestination, the synod, in its third decree, makes this statement:

> We believe the most good God to have from eternity predestinated unto glory those whom He hath chosen, and to have consigned unto condemnation those whom He hath rejected; but not so that He would justify the one, and consign and condemn the other without cause.... But since He foreknew the one would make a right use of their free-will, and the other a wrong, He predestinated the one, or condemned the other....

---

[13]See Philip Schaff and Henry Wace, eds., *Nicene and Post-Nicene Fathers* (Peabody, Mass.: Hendrickson, 1995), 14:550.

[14]See Leonid Ouspensky, *Theology of the Icon* (Crestwood, N.Y.: St. Vladimir's Seminary Press, 1992), 1:8.

[15]J. N. W. B. Robertson, trans., *The Acts and Decrees of the Synod of Jerusalem* (New York: AMS Press, 1969), 110.

> But to say, as the most wicked heretics do . . . that God, in predestinating, or condemning, had in no wise regard to the works of those predestinated, or condemned, we know to be profane and impious. . . .
>
> But than to affirm that the Divine Will is thus solely and without cause the author of their condemnation, what greater calumny can be fixed upon God? And what greater injury and blasphemy can be offered to the Most High?[16]

Whatever one might think of the particular statements issued by hierarchs and councils, it should be apparent that the possibility of compatibility is severely limited. In such cases, compatibility can only be conceived of as the degree to which a given position conforms to that which Christ specifically articulated. The Orthodox Church believes that, because it has faithfully preserved the teachings of Scripture and the apostolic tradition in unity for almost two millennia, it most closely expresses what Christ intended; it is the church. Saint Simeon of Thessalonica wrote this:

> With love, we pass on to you that which we have taken from the Fathers. For we offer nothing new, but only that which has been passed on to us, and we have changed nothing but we have retained everything, like a creed, in the state which it has been given to us. We worship exactly as Christ Himself did and as did the Apostles and the Fathers of the Church.[17]

DEGREES OF COMPATIBILITY

If doctrinal compatibility can be anticipated under certain conditions, what form or degree is it likely to take? Perhaps it would be best to speak of several types or levels of compatibility.

Actual Compatibility

One of the earliest attempts at Protestant-Orthodox dialogue came during the sixteenth century, when several Lutheran

---

[16]Ibid., 114, 115, 116.
[17]Cited in Ouspensky, *Theology of the Icon*, 1:22.

theologians at Tübingen entered into a theological exchange with Patriarch Jeremiah II.[18] In spite of the eventual collapse of the dialogue, it does indicate significant areas of agreement and compatibility, which was no doubt due to the fact that the Reformers had no intention of doctrinal innovation. "On the contrary," wrote Georges Florovsky, "they struggled to purify the church from all those 'innovations' and accretions which, in their opinion, had been accumulated in the course of ages, particularly in the West."[19] In doing so they appealed not only to the Holy Scriptures but also to the witness of the early church and seem to have urged the patriarch to believe that Lutherans were loyal to the teaching of the Scriptures and of the Fathers.[20]

As noted above, the common use of the Scriptures and the early Christian texts coupled with a commitment to the authority of Scripture does, in fact, facilitate doctrinal compatibility. Thus the participants in this early East-West dialogue discovered significant areas of agreement. Greek Orthodox cleric George Mastrantonis made this observation:

> Jeremiah and the theologians were in agreement, as a whole, on the following: the truth and inspiration of the Scriptures; God, Holy Trinity; ancestors' sin and its transmission to all men; evil as caused by creatures and not God; Christ's two natures in a single person; Jesus Christ as the head of the Church; second coming of Christ, last judgment, future life, endless reward, endless punishment; Eucharist, two species, bread and wine (the body and blood) given to the faithful; the rejection of indulgences . . ."[21]

---

[18]See George Mastrantonis, *Augsburg and Constantinople* (Brookline, Mass.: Holy Cross Orthodox Press, 1982). His Beatitude is responding to a Greek translation of the Augsburg Confession, which itself seems to have been an attempt to contextualize. According to Georges Florovsky, "The translators deliberately toned down the forensic or juridical tenor of the Augustana doctrine of redemption," and "There was an obvious desire to adjust the exposition to the traditional convictions of the Greek church." For example, writes Florovsky, "instead of the concept of justification, the dominant idea of the Greek version is that of healing" (Georges Florovsky, *Collected Works of Georges Florovsky,* vol. 2, *Christianity and Culture* [Belmont, Mass.: Nordland, 1974], 159).

[19]Florovsky, *Collected Works,* vol. 2, *Christianity and Culture,* 146.

[20]Ibid., 148.

[21]Mastrantonis, *Augsburg and Constantinople,* 22.

Limited Compatibility

Another type of compatibility exists where, in spite of claims to the contrary, there is, in fact, considerable doctrinal overlap. This may occur in cases where select elements of a doctrine, which can only be fully understood as part of a broad theological context, are emphasized outside of that context. One such doctrine is justification by faith. This doctrine is a vital element of the Orthodox understanding of salvation. Consider, for example, the statement of the already mentioned Synod of Jerusalem: "We believe no one to be saved without faith. And by faith we mean the right notion that is in us concerning God and divine things, which, working by love, that is to say, by [observing] the Divine commandments, justifieth us with Christ; and without this [faith] it is impossible to please God."[22]

In spite of such clear statements, many evangelicals misconstrue Orthodox soteriology by implying that it does not conform to the New Testament teaching on justification by faith. The source of this misperception is the different contexts in which a soteriology is developed. For most evangelical Protestants the doctrine of salvation is developed within a context limited by the concepts of sin and redemption (Rom. 3–6). From an Orthodox perspective, confining the development of soteriology to the individual sin/redemption axis makes it impossible to effectively relate these elements to the larger context of creation and the ultimate goal of humanity, namely, deification. While not denying the centrality of sin, faith, and redemption, Eastern Christian thought views them as parts of a wider context defined by creation and deification. Thus, it might be said that the evangelical doctrine is a subset of Orthodox soteriology.

In the beginning God created the heavens and the earth, and out of the dust of that earth he created the human frame and breathed life into it. Thus, the universe and humanity are irrevocably related in that they share a material nature. As Gregory of Nazianzus put it, "In my quality of earth, I am attached to life here below, but being also a divine particle, I bear in my breast the desire for a future life."[23]

---

[22]Robertson, *The Acts and Decrees of the Synod of Jerusalem*, 122.

[23]Cited in Vladimir Lossky, *Orthodox Theology* (Crestwood, N.Y.: St. Vladimir's Seminary Press, 1989), 70.

To creation, man is the hope of receiving God's grace and being united with him. But man also represents the danger of failure and fallenness. And so "'Creation anxiously awaits this revelation of the sons of God,' writes St. Paul. 'It is indeed to vanity that creation was made subject, not willingly, but because of him who subjected it; with, however, the hope that creation would also be liberated from the slavery of corruption to participate in the glorious liberty of the children of God' (Rom. 8:19–21). . . . And this anthropocosmic link is accomplished when that of the human image is accomplished, with God its prototype."[24] In other words, the universe can only be what it was intended to be if humanity is what it was intended to be. And that, in turn, depends on continual communion with the divine prototype.

What is this God-intended goal of humanity? Scripture teaches that God created man in his own image and in his own likeness (Gen. 1:26–27).[25] In Orthodox theology the terms "image" and "likeness" are considered to be distinct, and this distinction provides an important element of the context in which soteriology is developed. The image of God is that which reflects God's nature in man. It is that which all human beings have in common and that which constitutes human existence. It presupposes the divine prototype.

There have been many suggestions as to the exact nature of the image, such as man's intellect, his capacity for reproduction, and his free will.[26] This image is, writes theology professor

---

[24]Ibid., 71.

[25]Keil and Delitzsch, for example, state, "Modern commentators have correctly observed that there is no foundation for the distinction drawn by the Greek and after them by many Latin Fathers between *eikōn (imago)* and *homoiōsis (similitudo)*, the former of which they supposed to represent the physical aspect of the likeness to God, the latter the ethical; but that, on the contrary the older Lutheran theologians were correct in stating that the two words are synonymous and are merely combined to add intensity to the thought" (*Biblical Commentary on the Old Testament*, vol. 1, *The Pentateuch* [Grand Rapids: Eerdmans, 1956], 63). They go on to compare this word pair to certain German word pairs, such as *Bild* and *Abbild* and *Umriss* and *Abriss*. Two comments are in order. First, the physical/ethical distinction they read into the Fathers is inaccurate. Second, although the terms are similar there are subtle differences even in the German pairs, which translate into the English as "likeness" and "copy," and "outline" and "sketch."

[26]See Georgios I. Mantzaridis, *The Deification of Man* (Crestwood, N.Y.: St. Vladimir's Seminary Press, 1984), 16.

Georgios Mantzaridis, the "common property of all men."[27] Therefore, without this image, man could not be considered human.

Image is a static term and "signifies a realized state, which in the present context constitutes the starting point for the attainment of the 'likeness.'"[28] *Likeness*, though, is a dynamic term that points to a potential. "From the moment of his creation," writes Mantzaridis, "man strives to approach his archetype, God, and so to be deified. This movement of man from 'image' to archetype is generally expressed in the Fathers by the phrase from Scripture 'after his likeness.'"[29]

To become "in the likeness" depends on our will; it is acquired in accordance with our own activity. Mantzaridis observes, "Likeness to God, while it constitutes the goal of human existence, is not imposed on man, but is left to his own free will. By submitting himself freely to God's will and being constantly guided by His grace, man can cultivate and develop the gift of the 'image,' making it a possession individual, secure, and dynamic, and so coming to resemble God."[30]

This resemblance of God, then, is the other pole of the soteriological axis. Usually referred to as deification, it is defined as a union or communion with God that is so complete that it can be said of man that he is like God. Adam was not created perfect in an absolute sense. But he was created without sin and in communion with God—and therefore with the potential to achieve that for which he was created, namely, deification. Man, being created, could, of course, never acquire what the uncreated Trinity was by nature. But by God's grace it was possible for mankind to advance toward God-likeness.

However, that potential was squandered in disobedience and rebellion. Not only did man lose the potential, his very nature was corrupted, and generation by generation he drifted further and further away from God, the source of his life. The only hope of restoration was with God. Two things were needed: (1) human nature had to be healed of corruption and freed from death, and (2) the tainted human will needed to be cleansed and

---

[27]Ibid., 21.
[28]Ibid.
[29]Ibid.
[30]Ibid., 22.

forgiven of its manifold sins. Both were accomplished in the incarnation, death, and resurrection of Christ.

Rather than seeing the sacrifice as an attempt to assuage the offended honor of God or to silence his anger, the sacrifice is aimed at the root problem, which is the corruption of man's very nature and the inevitable result—death. Using the curse of death itself to defeat that which held humanity in its grip, Christ atones for our sins—but not by providing a payment of human debt owed to God but by assuming the consequence of our sin, namely, death itself. By doing so he canceled the certificate of debt, with its requirements, that was against us. And he took it away, having nailed it to the cross (Col. 2:14). The statement of offense normally nailed to the cross at the execution of a criminal contained in the case of Christ not his sins but ours. There is obviously a form of expiation (a canceling of sin) involved in what Christ did.[31] But there is so much more, for even death was not able to dissolve the divine-human union in Christ, and as a result his "incorrupt" death[32] "imparted life to death itself."[33] So the redemption achieved by Christ on the cross "was not just the forgiveness of sins, nor was it man's reconciliation with God."[34] It was the final victory over sin and death, the abolition of corruption and mortality in human nature.

How can salvation be appropriated? This, of course, depends on what one understands salvation to be. For most of the Protestant world, salvation is the immediate change in a person's status before the Judge of all things. Without Christ's sacrifice we are

---

[31]There is considerable debate as to the exact meaning of the Greek word group *(hilasmos)* to which such terms as expiation and propitiation belong. It has been noted that Greek usage outside the Scriptures involves an averting of wrath. However, some have argued for a specifically biblical (Septuagint and New Testament) usage in which "it denotes expiation (the cancellation of sin), not propitiation (the turning away of the wrath of God)" (Walter A. Elwell, ed., *Evangelical Dictionary of Theology* [Grand Rapids: Baker, 1984], 888).

[32]"In other words, though separated in death, the soul and the body remained still united through the Divinity of the Word, from which neither was ever estranged. This does not alter the ontological character of death, but changed its meaning. This was an 'incorrupt' death, and therefore corruption and death were overcome in it, and in it begins the resurrection. The very death of the incarnate reveals the resurrection of human nature" (Georges Florovsky, *Collected Works of Georges Florovsky,* vol. 3, *Creation and Redemption* (Belmont, Mass.: Nordland, 1976), 136.

[33]Jordan Bajis, *Common Ground: An Introduction to Eastern Christianity for the American Christian* (Minneapolis: Light & Life, 1996), 236.

[34]Florovsky, *Collected Works,* vol. 3, *Creation and Redemption,* 225.

said to remain in a state of unrighteousness. When personal, individual faith is placed in the Savior—that is, if one believes that God's just demands are satisfied by the death of Christ—then all sin is canceled and one's status is changed to justified. Due to the extremely individualistic approach and the judicial understanding of salvation, a person is either saved or not saved. There can be no other state, no progress, no spiritual journey, and no loss of that status.

However, the New Testament clearly speaks of salvation in the past, the present, and the future tenses, indicating that it is a process that has a clear beginning and a definite goal.[35] The Eastern church distinguishes between two aspects of salvation. On the one hand, there is the healing of human nature. And for this no human appropriation is required, since it has already been accomplished by Christ and since its concretization at the general resurrection will include all mankind. In the words of Father Florovsky, "Nature is healed and restored with a certain compulsion, by the mighty power of God's omnipotent and invincible grace. The wholeness is in a way forced upon human nature. For in Christ all human nature is fully and completely cured from unwholeness and mortality."[36]

On the other hand, there is the healing of the human will. In this case, healing comes only as a result of a genuine turning to God in lifelong repentance, faith, and love. Florovsky makes this observation:

> The will of man cannot be cured in the same invincible manner; for the whole meaning of the healing of the will is in its free conversion. Only by this spontaneous and free effort does man enter into that new and eternal life which is revealed in Christ Jesus. A spiritual regeneration can be only in perfect freedom, in an obedience of love, by a self-consecration and self-dedication to God.[37]

So we have been saved by the work of Christ into which we enter by faith and repentance, as expressed in baptism and chrismation. We are being saved as we journey through life in repentance

---

[35]Cf. E. M. B. Greene, *The Meaning of Salvation* (Philadelphia: Westminster, 1965).

[36]Florovsky, *Collected Works*, vol. 3, *Creation and Redemption*, 147.

[37]Ibid., 148.

and obedience. On this journey the church aids us through its sacraments, its teaching, and the communion of all the saints. And finally we will be saved when we are fully united with God and reach the final goal—deification.

Absence of Compatibility

Finally, it must be pointed out that there are areas of doctrine and practice in which it is not possible to expect compatibility. If the church has formally declared a particular teaching to be unorthodox, compatibility can only take the form of a willingness to abandon that false teaching and embrace the sound doctrine preserved by the church. Any further discussion becomes useless and counterproductive.[38]

One such doctrine is that of the Eucharist. Patriarch Jeremiah II, explicitly rejecting the teaching of the Augsburg Confession, states that "after the consecration the bread is changed by the Holy Spirit into the very body of Christ and the wine into [his] very blood." Then, alluding to the role of the priest, he reaffirms that, "having been changed and altered by the *epiklesis* and grace of the all-powerful Spirit, the source of consecration, through the holy petitions and words of the priest, the bread is the very body of our Lord and the wine is the very blood of the Lord."[39]

There is in these statements no room for discussion, no compatibility possible other than submission to the teaching of the church. From the Orthodox perspective, any understanding of the Eucharist that is at variance with this teaching, and any practice of the Eucharist not administered by a properly ordained Orthodox priest, is simply not the Eucharist.[40]

---

[38]Even Patriarch Jeremiah II "felt himself obliged to put an end to these deliberations which were obviously now of no promise. He suggested a termination of the hopeless theological dispute, but was quite prepared to continue friendly contacts" (Florovsky, *Collected Works,* vol. 2, *Christianity and Culture,* 154).

[39]Mastrantonis, *Augsburg and Constantinople,* 55.

[40]As stated by the Jerusalem Council: "Further, that this Mystery of the Sacred Eucharist can be performed by none other, except only by an Orthodox Priest, who hath received his priesthood from an Orthodox and Canonical Bishop in accordance with the teaching of the Eastern Church" (Robertson, *The Acts and Decrees of the Synod of Jerusalem,* 149–50).

CONCLUSION

It is my contention that if the Holy Spirit is allowed to guide us, we may, if using the Holy Scriptures—accepted as authoritative and properly interpreted with the help of early Christian tradition—find that some evangelical teachings are compatible with the teaching of the Orthodox Church. I thank God for such common ground and gladly participate in any discussions that strengthen our faith, clarify our beliefs, and bring honor to our God. At the same time, I must acknowledge that there are other areas of evangelical doctrine and practice that the church has formally rejected as unorthodox. In such cases, I submit to the teaching of the church and will seek to avoid encouraging pointless theological debates.

A RESPONSE TO EDWARD ROMMEN

Bradley Nassif

Of all the evangelical converts to Orthodoxy I have known over the years, Father Edward Rommen stands out as having the most intellectual credibility. His knowledge of evangelical theology is dependable and carefully nuanced, his cultural sensitivity to hermeneutical issues is wise, and his missiological skills at contextualizing the gospel are almost unparalleled in the Orthodox world today (even beyond Father Ioan Bria, the widely respected Romanian Orthodox missiologist, and in a close tie with Archbishop Anastasios Yannoulatos of Albania). I can only hope that Orthodox hierarchs will maximize his talents.

In the essay before us, Father Rommen provides a useful definition of compatibility by which we can measure our areas of agreement with evangelicals. I concur with his analysis of the "Factors That Facilitate Compatibility," with only one qualification: The Orthodox Church still needs to clarify its position on the text and boundaries of the Old Testament canon for doctrinal use (the Hebrew text versus the Greek Septuagint).[1] Without making a rigid separation between the two, we might view the Hebrew text as the final court of appeal for doctrine, while retaining the primary role of the Septuagint for worship and devotion. The late Father John Meyendorff, one of this century's greatest Orthodox scholars, seemed to take this approach. If it is so adopted, evangelical and Orthodox theologians will derive their doctrines from the same biblical sources.

---

[1]See Harold Scanlin, "The Old Testament Canon in the Orthodox Churches," in *New Perspectives on Historical Theology: Essays in Memory of John Meyendorff,* ed. Bradley Nassif (Grand Rapids: Eerdmans, 1996), 300–312.

Father Rommen's treatment of "Factors That Make Compatibility Unlikely" provides a convenient summary of the key differences in conceptual categories that give rise to areas of disagreement between Orthodox and evangelical Christians. My only regret is that his treatment was more skeletal than substantial, more descriptive than analytic, more prolegomena than actual analysis of the specific theological issues that divide us.

Father Rommen does an excellent job of discussing "Degrees of Compatibility" as well. His suggestion that we think in terms of "several types or levels of compatibility" (page 242) goes far in building a bridge between the Orthodox and evangelical communities. I especially appreciated his affirmation that "the common use of the Scriptures and the early Christian texts coupled with a commitment to the authority of Scripture does, in fact, facilitate doctrinal compatibility" (page 243). The doctrine of justification by faith also facilitates doctrinal compatibility, as Father Rommen and I have both affirmed in different ways in our respective essays. His treatment of the significance of the biblical expressions "in the image of God" and "in the likeness of God" was largely faithful to the Greek patristic tradition but appeared to be a rather forced reading of the Genesis account. One need not agree, however, with every point of doctrine in the early church fathers in order to be faithful to the church's vision of truth, since there were a variety of views on different theological topics. Like the Fathers themselves, we today can and should be open to new insights in linguistics and Hebrew rhetorical devices, but we don't need to feel compelled to repeat all aspects of the Fathers' theological anthropology.

I also disagree with Father Rommen's rejection of the interpretation of the death of Christ as a propitiatory sacrifice aimed at appeasing the wrath of God. He seems to simply repeat the views of other Orthodox theologians without critically assessing their validity in light of the biblical and patristic evidence. Also his assertion that "the New Testament clearly speaks of salvation in the past, the present, and the future tenses" (page 248) is affirmed by both Orthodox and evangelical theologians and actually serves as a unifying bridge to soteriology, not as a church-dividing issue, if these terms are properly explained in relation to each other.

In the section titled "Absence of Compatibility" Father Rommen illustrates how incompatible Orthodoxy and evangelicalism are by focusing on the presence of Christ in the Eucharist. He concludes that unless one accepts Patriarch Jeremiah's rejection of the Augsburg Confession, no compatibility is possible "other than submission to the teaching of the church," and that "any practice of the Eucharist not administered by a properly ordained Orthodox priest is simply not the Eucharist" (page 249). To be sure, the presence of Christ in the Eucharist is an undeniable reality for the Orthodox Church. But much progress has been made on the meaning of the Eucharist in recent ecumenical dialogues between Orthodox and Lutheran theologians in their official negotiations. Clearly, Father Rommen's rigorist views have also been rejected by church-sponsored theologians in recent Orthodox–Roman Catholic dialogue where each other's priests have been mutually recognized as celebrating legitimate Eucharists. I cannot go into all the details and nuances of these dialogues but must allude to them as an indication that the door is at least open for discussion concerning the ministerial validity of evangelical pastors.

I should also say in closing that a blunt appeal to church authority will not be very helpful to either Orthodox or evangelical readers. It only underscores the bigger problem, which is not addressed by Father Rommen, namely, how can we interpret the church's interpretations? That is, can we be confident of the church's interpretation any more certainly than we are of our own? I do indeed think we can, but unless we explain how this is so, we can easily leave the impression that to be Orthodox is to be mindless, and this is surely not what Father Rommen intended to say. On the contrary, his essay was so very thoughtful that I found it unnecessary to highlight the countless constructive points that comprise the vast majority of his illuminating analysis.

A RESPONSE TO EDWARD ROMMEN

Michael Horton

Despite the suspicions many evangelicals quite rightly have of modern ecumenism in general, concrete instances of such dialogue often yield a more hopeful assessment. This volume is surely an example of the latter. Where the conversation partners are unwilling to surrender their particularity to some noncontroversial consensus, not only do the others become better informed; often they discover that there is greater agreement than secondhand accounts seem to have suggested. Father Rommen's essay forced me to see more clearly our important agreements as well as disagreements.

On the plus side, the author affirms a shared authoritative text and the guidance of the Holy Spirit. To be sure, Orthodoxy does regard Tradition as in some sense supplemental to Scripture: "The basic assumption here is that not everything our Lord and the apostles did and said is contained in the written canon (cf. John 21:25). In 2 Thessalonians 2:15 Saint Paul admonished the believers to preserve both written and oral traditions" (page 237). And yet,

> This does not mean that Scripture is somehow subject to Tradition. If there is any obvious discrepancy between Tradition and Scripture, Scripture is the final authority.... So Tradition is viewed as the larger historical context within which Scripture was given. As such, Tradition does not have the authority of Scripture and is used as an aid to interpretation and as a source of instruction on matters not explicitly dealt with in Scripture (page 237).

I suspect we would soon discover important differences in our exegesis of John 21 and 2 Thessalonians 2. For instance, it does not appear to necessarily follow that, because Jesus and his apostles said and did many things left unrecorded in Scripture, there are extant records of these doings and sayings that stand up to historical scrutiny. Nor does it necessarily follow that such alleged records are required for the health of the church. The point of John 21:25, for example, seems to be that, although volumes could be filled, they need not be; that the evangelist's selection criteria were met. We have everything necessary for our salvation and restoration in Christ. Nevertheless, there is nothing in principle that Reformed theology would reject in the author's characterization of the relationship of tradition to Scripture in his clarifying statement.

We also share in the fact of the Holy Spirit's ministry to his people, even though, strictly speaking, Protestants are probably among those regarded as *extra ecclesiam*. Father Rommen mentions the pietist-holiness tradition as an example of a Protestant tradition that shares affinities with Orthodoxy's stress on growth in holiness, although he might have included some recognition of the remarkably high pneumatology in Reformed thought as well. With considerable justification Princeton Seminary professor B. B. Warfield characterized Calvin as "the theologian of the Holy Spirit." While these and other parallels we will explore below are often well known in the circles of Reformed theology and "Calvin studies," outside of our circles there seems to be the impression that the latter represents a dry intellectualism and an exclusively forensic cast. But more on this below.

On the minus side, according to Father Rommen, evangelical and Reformed theologies participate in the broader problems of the contrasting West-East paradigms that also separate Orthodoxy from Rome. The East conceptualizes its faith and practice in terms of relationships, persons, and the unity of reality and symbol, while the West is generally preoccupied with propositions, nature, and the opposition of sign and reality (page 239). For the West, it seems to the Orthodox, symbol and reality stand for "untrue" and "true." Again, more on this below.

Not only are there divergent conceptual paradigms; there are divergent emphases that follow: "new life" and "legal justification"; the person of God and the nature of God; and the role of icons (pages 239–40). Further, there are divergent personal convictions and, more importantly, differences over specific church teachings. On icons, for example, Father Rommen argues, "Christian images have been used since the church's very inception," and find their ground in the incarnation itself. "God himself gave us an icon of himself in Christ and thereby, at least in principle, sanctioned the use of such imaging" (pages 240–41). While, logically speaking, this conclusion may be valid, it certainly does not necessarily follow from the premise. Evangelical Protestants have pointed to both the *historical* arguments (e.g., the fact that icons and images were condemned by the earliest traditions of the church until the triumph of the iconodules in the eighth century) and the *theological* arguments.

At least Reformed theology has, in fact, appealed to the premise of the incarnation for precisely the opposite conclusion. Throughout Israel's history there was the danger of giving devotion to even the divinely given signs (e.g., the brass serpent), much less creating one's own "point of contact" with God (e.g., the golden calf). It is possible to worship the correct God (the first commandment) while worshiping him according to our own imagination (prohibited by the second commandment). All of the Old Testament prohibitions against idolatry were meant to preserve God's people from preempting the incarnation, from resting in the signs instead of in the reality to which they witness. "When the time had fully come," we read (Gal. 4:4), God sent his own Son, the icon *(eikōn)* of God. In him, and in him alone, sign and thing signified become one. He alone is God's univocal, if paradoxical, presence in flesh. The Reformed, therefore, are concerned that some Orthodox approaches to this question—and aspects of its liturgy that follow from them—reflect an underrealized eschatology, living in the types and shadows while the Reality has come. Our ecumenical conversation might be enriched by a common exposition of the book of Hebrews.

The author refers to the circumstances surrounding the sixteenth-century Patriarch Lucaris, whose embrace of Calvinism was subsequently repudiated by Patriarch Dositheus at a synod in Jerusalem (1672).[1] This synod condemned the doctrine of predestination as it had been taught not only by Calvin but by

---

[1]Cf. George A. Hadjiantoniou, *Protestant Patriarch: The Life of Cyril Lucaris (1572–1638), Patriarch of Constantinople* (Richmond, Va.: John Knox, 1961).

a number of church fathers (in the East and West), most notably Augustine, as well as by Aquinas, Gregory of Rimini, Archbishop Bradwardine, and Luther. The statement issued by that synod, cited by Father Rommen, represents Calvin's view in terms that neither Calvin nor subsequent Reformed dogmaticians would recognize—and, in fact, it was a view they countered repeatedly. The ensuing position of Orthodoxy, the author states, is a conditional election (i.e., election on the basis of foreseen cooperation). Because of this, he says, "the possibility of compatibility is severely limited" (page 242). We might point out, to the delight of some and the chagrin of others (including myself), that this would probably not constitute a real threat to compatibility, of course, for the majority of contemporary evangelicals.

Finally, Father Rommen urges the argument of antiquity: "The Orthodox Church believes that, because it has faithfully preserved the teachings of Scripture and the apostolic tradition in unity for almost two millennia, it most closely expresses what Christ intended; it is the church" (page 242). For many, including a number of evangelicals who have joined Eastern Orthodoxy, the claim to unbroken continuity is appealing. Evangelicals influenced by restorationist narratives of church history (i.e., "going back to Acts") and disillusioned with sectarian revivalism have found this argument convincing. Here is a church in which there is nothing new; nothing has changed. The author quotes Saint Simeon of Thessalonica: "We worship exactly as Christ Himself did and as did the apostles and the Fathers of the Church" (page 242). We would contest this claim on a number of fronts, but to do so would take us too far afield from more crucial questions. It appears at least to some of us that this claim does not adequately account for the substantial differences between ancient practice and Byzantine innovations and embraces an unrealistic ecclesiology.

Father Rommen offers a helpful scheme for analyzing more fully the convergences and divergences. With respect to the former, he refers to constructive conversations between Lutherans and Patriarch Jeremiah II in the sixteenth century. Here the author reveals greater awareness of the Reformation's objectives than is usually the case, even among some evangelical interpreters. Convergence was possible here and there in the sixteenth century, he says, "no doubt due to the fact that the

Reformers had no intention of doctrinal innovation" (page 243). Luther and Calvin represented the broad agreement of the magisterial Reformers—against the Anabaptists—concerning the catholicity of doctrine. It was Rome that had been given to innovation. Repeatedly both Luther and Calvin insist that their liturgical goal is to restore worship to its ancient practice, purging it of its medieval accretions.

The rock of offense in these discussions, however, was— and still remains—the doctrine of justification. This doctrine is "a vital element of the Orthodox understanding of salvation" (page 244). But it is also the case that Orthodoxy and evangelical Protestantism affirm two different conceptions: "And by faith we mean the right notion that is in us concerning God and divine things, which, working by love, that is to say, by [observing] the Divine commandments, justifieth us with Christ" (quoting from the Synod of Jerusalem, page 244). There is no salvation without faith and grace, but these are not sufficient, according to Orthodoxy. Furthermore, in the definition above, faith is reduced to assent *(assensus)*, just as it is in Roman Catholic theology, which therefore requires the addition of some animating element (namely, love) in order to render it justifying. Evangelical theology, Orthodoxy maintains, is too "limited by the concepts of sin and redemption (Rom. 3–6)," which leaves out creation and deification. "Thus it might be said that the evangelical doctrine is a subset of Orthodox soteriology" (page 244).

Whatever the merits of each case, however, Father Rommen is inconsistent on this point. If, as his definition above indicates, Orthodoxy denies the evangelical doctrine of justification (namely, that it is by grace alone through faith alone because of the imputation of Christ alone), it can hardly be a subset of Orthodox belief. It is not simply the case that evangelical Christianity merely reduces all of soteriology to justification but that it fundamentally misunderstands it. This is an essential point if we are to actually address our central differences.

Father Rommen offers a fine description of the Eastern doctrine of *theosis* ("divinization"). In my patristics course I find it necessary to emphasize that the Eastern fathers such as the Cappadocians must not be understood to be teaching what Western Christians typically hear in such terminology. As I will argue below, I regard the emphasis on recapitulation and the restoration of all things in Christ as a necessary, but often misunderstood and undervalued, aspect of Pauline eschatology. But we do find this side of biblical thought developed already in Martin Bucer, John Calvin, the federal theology of Johannes Cocceius, Abraham Kuyper, and Herman Bavinck. Recent Reformed explorations in biblical theology (Geerhardus Vos, Herman Ridderbos, Richard Gaffin, Meredith Kline, and others) have also underscored this. Furthermore, I think the Reformed tradition would be congenial to seeing Western theology chastened for a nature-oriented rather than person-oriented ontological paradigm. Fruitful explorations of this relationship should be encouraged in historical-theological scholarship.

But what I find troubling in Father Rommen's analysis is the apparent suspicion of what he regards as a too "Western" obsession with guilt and grace, involving an overly forensic approach to the atonement. After the fall, writes Father Rommen,

> Two things were needed: (1) human nature had to be healed of corruption and freed from death, and (2) the tainted human will needed to be cleansed and forgiven of its manifold sins. . . .
>
> Rather than seeing the sacrifice as an attempt to assuage the offended honor of God or to silence his anger, the sacrifice aimed at the root problem, a corruption of man's very nature and the inevitable result—death. . . . Christ atones for our sins—but not by providing a payment of human debt owed to God but by assuming the consequence of our sin, namely, death itself. By doing so he canceled the certificate of debt, with its requirements, that was against us. . . . There is obviously a form of expiation (a canceling of sin) involved in what Christ did. But there is so much more, for even death was not able to dissolve the divine-human union in Christ . . . (pages 246–47).

Not just expiation, then, but victory. Again, I suspect that the differences between us are more complicated than mere emphasis. Evangelical theology has hardly neglected the relational aspect; nor has it undervalued the theme of sanctification. Reformation theology, at least, has had a very high doctrine of creation and the restoration of the created world rather than escape from it, even if pietism, revivalism, and millennialism have retreated from this world-affirming emphasis.

The *Christus Victor* theme is hardly absent from Lutheran and Reformed dogmatics, but Christ's victory is adumbrated in different ways by Protestant and Orthodox interpreters. For the former, the Pauline passage to which Father Rommen refers clearly indicates that the cancellation of our debt constitutes the basis on which Christ's victory over the world, the flesh, and the devil is announced. It is for us quite opposed to the natural sense of this passage to say that Christ "atones for our sins—but not by providing a payment of human debt owed to God but by assuming the consequence of our sin, namely, death itself." After all, Paul refers explicitly to the canceled "certificate of debt." This is an example of the reductionism that seems to characterize aspects of this account. Reformation theology does not reduce salvation—or even the atonement—to a legal question. Nevertheless, it does certainly affirm the legal question as an essential, even central, aspect of atonement. Orthodoxy does not, as Father Rommen claims, incorporate the evangelical view into a more balanced account, but it rejects the evangelical view altogether. If we can establish that the evangelical view incorporates the legal and the relational—propitiatory sacrifice and victory over the powers—it will be seen that the evangelical view succeeds precisely where the Orthodox account fails.

Father Rommen's essay moves on then to the appropriation of Christ's saving work. Reflecting a chorus of opinion within contemporary evangelicalism as well as outside of it, Rommen claims that the Protestant view is individualistic and legal. Thus, "There can be no other state, no progress, no spiritual journey, and no loss of that status. However, the New Testament clearly speaks of salvation in the past, the present, and the future tenses, indicating that it is a process that has a clear beginning and a definite goal" (page 248). It is undoubtedly true that many evangelical accounts of the application of redemption are unduly individualistic, resting everything on the *ordo salutis* (individual rebirth, justification, sanctification, glorification), without giving serious thought to the cosmic proportions of God's redemptive plan *(historia salutis).*

This characteristic has been challenged within evangelical Protestantism no more insistently than by Reformed theologians. We have all heard of Luther's response to the question as to what he would do if he knew Christ were to return tomorrow: "I would plant a tree," he reportedly said. Calvin challenged

Cardinal Sadoleto for confining religion to individual striving for one's own salvation while neglecting the world.[2] Abraham Kuyper and B. B. Warfield reflect a striking emphasis on the restoration of all things in Christ and underscore the point that, while Roman Catholic theology tends to contrast nature and grace, Reformed theology affirms that grace restores nature. I suspect there would be much greater convergence on this aspect of biblical soteriology than Orthodoxy might initially suspect.

Orthodox theology, Father Rommen explains, distinguishes two stages in the application of redemption: healing the nature and healing the will. Again, while we hardly object to the good news that includes healing as well as propitiation and justification, is it not reductionistic to make healing the only metaphor for salvation? And in doing so, is Orthodoxy not doing exactly what it accuses evangelical theology of doing, namely, excluding other important aspects? If everything is reduced to healing, there is no conceptual space for the unmistakable legal, economic, and related metaphors for God's action in Christ by his Spirit. Furthermore, as Rommen's explanation indicates, Orthodoxy affirms the healing of nature as utterly gratuitous while the healing of the will requires human cooperation for its success. In fact, "The will of man cannot be cured in the same invincible manner [as the healing of the nature]; for the whole meaning of the healing of the will is in its free conversion. Only by this spontaneous and free effort does man enter into that new and eternal life which is revealed in Christ Jesus" (citing Florovsky, page 248).

In conclusion, Father Rommen turns to the category of "Absence of Compatibility"—the Eucharist. While there may be compatibility on issues where there is overlap, when it comes to this issue, we are told, we must simply submit. If Protestants will not submit to the Eastern Orthodox Church's view of the Eucharist, which includes reception of the sacrament only from Orthodox clergy, the conversation is apparently concluded: "From the Orthodox perspective, any understanding of the Eucharist that is at variance with this teaching, and any practice of the Eucharist not administered by a properly ordained Orthodox priest, is simply not the Eucharist" (page 249).

---

[2]John Calvin and Jacopo Sadoleto, *A Reformation Debate*, ed. John C. Olin (Grand Rapids: Baker, 1966), 58.

What are we to make of this claim as we summarize our response to Father Rommen's illuminating contribution? First, I think he is correct to schematize the discussion in terms of full, partial, and no compatibility. This, it seems to me, is more fruitful than following historical theology professor George Lindbeck's cultural-linguistic approach, in which doctrines are treated as grammatical rules that obtain in some contexts but not in others. Where I differ from Rommen's scheme is in his characterization of which doctrines go where. For instance, I would place the evangelical doctrine of justification where he places the Orthodox doctrine of the Eucharist. For a variety of reasons that cannot be explored in this space, I am fully persuaded that there is a great deal of overlap between Orthodox and Calvinian views of the Holy Supper. Furthermore, even on the nature of the relation of signs to the reality signified, Calvin seems more Orthodox and less Augustinian than, say, Zwingli. If Western theology is dogged by the opposition of *signum* (sign) and *res significata* (the thing signified), it is probably due more to Platonism than to any East-versus-West explanation. (Platonism is hardly a uniquely Western virus.) While rejecting any univocal identification of the sign and thing signified or the consubstantiality of the sign with the thing signified in the earthly elements, Calvin and the Reformed confessions developed a highly eschatological and pneumatological account of the union of sign and reality.

What does the believer receive in Holy Communion? So far is Calvin from reducing salvation to a merely legal and individual as opposed to relational and corporate affair that he writes that God has provided both baptism and the Lord's Supper as a good Father:

> For as in baptism, God, regenerating us, engrafts us into the society of his church and makes us his own by adoption, so we have said, that he discharges the function of a provident householder in continually supplying to us the food to sustain and preserve us in that life into which he has begotten us by his Word. . . .
>
> We are therefore bidden to take and eat the body which was once for all offered for our salvation.[3]

---

[3]John Calvin, *Institutes of the Christian Religion,* ed. John T. McNeill, trans. Ford Lewis Battles (Philadelphia: Westminster, 1960), 4.17.1., 1360–61.

He adds:

> Once for all, therefore, he gave his body to be made bread when he yielded himself to be crucified for the redemption of the world; daily he gives it when by the word of the gospel he offers it for us to partake, inasmuch as it was crucified, when he seals such giving of himself by the sacred mystery of the Supper, and when he inwardly fulfills what he outwardly designates.[4]

Here Calvin openly rejects Zwingli's view, which separates the sign from the reality. By the mysterious working of the Holy Spirit, who is able to unite us to Christ's body in heaven, believers receive nothing less than the crucified body and shed blood of the Redeemer. While Zwingli rationalizes the mystery, Calvin exclaims, "Therefore, nothing remains but to break forth in wonder at this mystery, which plainly neither the mind is able to conceive nor the tongue to express."[5]

The Belgic Confession reflects the same awe in Article 35:

> Now it is certain that Jesus Christ did not prescribe his sacraments for us in vain, since he works in us all that he represents by these holy signs, although the manner in which he does it goes beyond our understanding and is incomprehensible to us, just as the operation of God's Spirit is hidden and incomprehensible to us. Yet we do not go wrong when we say that what is eaten is Christ's own natural body and what is drunk is his own blood— but the manner in which we eat is not by the mouth but by the Spirit, through faith.

Thus, Article 35 goes on, "the sacraments and the thing signified are joined together." Regardless of whether one agrees, Calvin and his successors argued their case from the logic of Chalcedon and the reality of the distinct integrity and full hypostatic union of the two natures.

For Calvin and the Reformed, the consecration of the bread and wine and the *sursum corda* ("Lift up your hearts") become the liturgical moment in which believers are drawn by the signs to the reality united with them in the sacrament, as they partake of Christ in heaven by faith through the Holy Spirit. Veteran

---

[4]Ibid., 4.17.5., 1364.
[5]Ibid., 4.17.7., 1367.

Calvin scholar B. A. Gerrish writes that, although Calvin rejected the Zwinglian view as "profane," evangelicals typically reject the Genevan Reformer's understanding as "mystical" and "too realistic." Gerrish makes this observation:

> It has even become commonplace to make a sharp distinction between "evangelical" and "sacramental" piety. The distinction, as such, could hardly find support in Calvin, for whom the sacrament of the Lord's Supper attested a communion with Christ's body and blood that is given precisely by the gospel—by the proclaimed, as well as the visible, word.[6]

Willem Balke, author of *Calvin and the Anabaptist Radicals*, expresses Calvin's view: "The corporate element in appropriating salvation and the sacraments is significant in itself. It is also a means to avoid the confusion of Anabaptist thinking."[7]

Calvin's view, which became that of the Reformed and Presbyterian confessions, was what many have called "instrumentalism." In other words, the Reformed hold that the sacraments are not merely occasions for subjective faith and piety to act but were principally means of grace. The Westminster Larger Catechism calls them "effectual means of salvation" (Q. 161). In the Supper believers "feed upon his body and blood to their spiritual nourishment and growth in grace" and "have their union and communion with him confirmed" (Q. 168). They feed on him "truly and really," and through the sacrament receive nothing less than "Christ crucified, and all the benefits of his death" (Q. 170).

Much research in recent decades has confirmed the place of Calvin as a patristic scholar in his own right. It is even recalled that he won a Swiss city to the Reformation when he overwhelmed his learned Roman Catholic opponent by his citation of the church fathers by memory. One can discern this influence not only in his stated concerns to recover the doctrinal and liturgical emphases of the ancient church, but also in his abundant references to the church fathers, both Eastern and Western (as is evident by perusing the author and source index in the Battles edition of the *Institutes*).

---

[6]B. A. Gerrish, "Calvin's Eucharistic Piety," in *Calvin Studies Society Papers, 1995, 1997*, ed. David Foxgrover (Grand Rapids: CRC Product Services), 64.

[7]Willem Balke, *Calvin and the Anabaptist Radicals* (Grand Rapids: Eerdmans, 1981), 57.

But we are compelled by the same authority of Christ that Father Rommen claims for Orthodoxy concerning its holy orders to regard the explicit denial of justification by grace alone through faith alone because of Christ alone as an insurmountable obstacle to unity. This is not because we reduce the entire Christian faith to this article, but because without it there can be no Christian faith. May God the Holy Spirit help us overcome this obstacle by patient conversation rather than by trying to go around or over it. And this is as much a caution to us as evangelical Protestants, who in our own manifold ways seem increasingly to find our way around this rock of offense.

A RESPONSE TO EDWARD ROMMEN

Vladimir Berzonsky

Father Rommen begins with a tentatively conditional, and for that reason sensible, evaluation of the possibility to make *some* evangelical doctrines compatible with Orthodox Church teachings. He even defines compatibility for the reader, lest he or she expect too much. As he proceeds with his essay, he begins with the Bible, discussing the Holy Spirit and the understandings of the third person of the Holy Trinity in each communion. Two images come to mind: first, the famous journey to Emmaus (Luke 24:13–35) on the afternoon of the Lord's resurrection day, and second, the pattern of the Orthodox Church's Divine Liturgy.

Why Emmaus? Because the two are on the way with Jesus, who is walking incognito beside them, patiently step by step taking them through the Bible, pointing out all references to his sacred mission, including the cross, grave, and resurrection. It brings them in touch with their inner selves and presumably with each other. Here is where any possibility of shared belief must begin. Regardless of the differences, it is Christ himself who brings us together in spite of the challenges and obstacles that separate us. He is in our midst on the way to the kingdom of the Father. Here is the start of the journey.

The other metaphor is the Divine Liturgy. Where else to meet, other than in the house of God? Here is another challenge—indeed, an obstacle. Early attempts to reconcile Orthodoxy and Protestantism—for example, the case of the Lutheran divines who had approached the patriarch of Constantinople—appeared not to consider the union of worship in the Orthodox temple something to be desired. Communication, but not communion—letters, but no shared prayers.[1] Political concerns were the real reasons for negotiations between Orthodox and Protestants, from the overture by Lutheran divines to Patriarch Jeremiah II to the Nonjuror Anglicans who parted from their Anglican communion in hopes of having their orders validated and of being accepted by Eastern patriarchs. It was only in the nineteenth century that the doctrine of the church entered into discussions in any ecumenical relations.

Father Rommen offers various possibilities of compatibility, which seems to be a somewhat ambivalent term for describing whatever relationship might take place between the two communions. Compatibility is little more than coexistence, the capacity of existing together in harmony. Presently most Orthodox Christian jurisdictions worldwide are members of the World Council of Churches and (in the U.S.) the National Council of the Churches of Christ in the United States of America—which is an issue of contention and an ongoing matter for discussion among the Orthodox themselves. In this sense, some compatibility with Protestants, although not with evangelicals, already exists. Our justification for remaining in these ecumenical organizations is based on the statement at the WCC in Toledo, 1960, declaring that no member communion by its membership is required to recognize any other member organization as having the essential ingredients to be defined as an authentic church. The Orthodox Church and evangelical communities might consider a bilateral relationship based on something like the existing ecumenical organizations, or at the least consider beginning formal meetings, with the goal to be a similar arrangement.

It appears to me that we simply don't know enough about one another, despite our exploratory outreach here in this book and elsewhere. Our stereotypes of one another are so clear that little insight is permitted, or perhaps even welcomed. Before such serious discussions could transpire, we would require a good-faith commitment to meeting with and seeking ways to begin understanding one another. We who claim to venerate the Sacred Scriptures have not found sufficient reason to explore ways to reach out and welcome one another in fulfillment of the

---

[1]See Carnegie Samuel Calian, *Icon and Pulpit: The Protestant-Orthodox Encounter* (Philadelphia: Westminster, 1968).

prayer of our Lord God and Master, who prayed to the heavenly Father, "I do not pray for these alone, but also for those who will believe in Me through their word; that they all may be one, as You, Father, are in Me, and I in You" (John 17:20–21 NKJV). We, on the other hand, continue our separate ways and somehow justify this lack of charity and understanding.

Any hope of success in mutual understanding can come about only by returning to the sources of common faith—back to the pre-Reformation time, indeed to the apostolic period—and moving forward from there. Evangelical Christians must take into account the period following the era of the apostles, as well as the work of the Holy Spirit in every generation, reexamining what may be a presupposition too easily held, namely, that the Holy Spirit went to sleep and awoke in the sixteenth century with the Reformers. As termed by Georges Florovsky, it calls for an "ecumenism in time" before we reach an "ecumenism in space."[2]

Can an iconoclast feel comfortable and at home in a temple adorned with icons? Not by accident do evangelicals prefer tents, stadiums, or functional meeting places rather than conventional temples erected to glorify God in architecture and art. Can an evangelical Christian say "Blessed is the Kingdom of the Father and of the Son and of the Holy Spirit, now and ever and unto ages of ages" (the first exclamation of the Divine Liturgy) in the space set apart as the attempt to imitate the kingdom of God breaking into the present, creating a sacred space different from secular space? Do we both have an identical understanding of each person of the Holy Trinity—especially the doctrine of the Holy Spirit proceeding from the Father?

The place and role of icons in the Orthodox Church is more than simply adornment, and the veneration of them is a stumbling block to evangelicals. The Orthodox Church may explain the practice by using the same arguments the great saint John Damascene used in discourse with the Muslim sultan: the incarnation of the Son of God blesses and sanctifies nature—not only

---

[2]Cited in Andrew Blane, ed., *Georges Florovsky: Russian Intellectual, Orthodox Churchman* (Crestwood, N.Y.: St. Vladimir's Seminary Press, 1993), 104. Blane contributes a biography of Florovsky to this book, in which he details the deep involvement of Florovsky in the Ecumenical Movement and later in the World Council of Churches. [Ed. note: Blane uses "Ecumenical Movement" (uppercase) to denote Florovsky's role in what we might call the Faith and Order Movement.]

human nature but also creation itself. Western Christians especially, influenced by the blessed Augustine, called such a doctrine into question, but for the Orthodox Church it is not accidental that the triumph of Orthodoxy, at which time all the heresies of antiquity are renounced, is celebrated on the feast of the restoration of icons (the Sunday of Orthodoxy—the first Sunday of Great Lent).

To continue the metaphor, assume we are journeying together into the sunset with Christ invisibly present between us. We are "outdoors"—on neutral territory. Will we find a common hermeneutics? It won't do to dilute the exegesis and meaning of the Sacred Scriptures. Such a harness would soon be thrown off. But when we are able to affirm a common understanding of the Bible, do we continue on toward the next milepost, namely, the apostolic era? Again the Holy Spirit rises as our aid and point of contention. The Holy Spirit either led or did not lead the church of the martyrs and confessors through the second and third centuries to the fourth, when heresies compelled the church to gather and define what it meant by Trinity and the incarnation of the Son of God. Are we still together, or must we wait for sixteenth-century Reformers to clarify theology for posterity?

In the second metaphor of the Divine Liturgy, after the prayers and Scripture readings and homily, the doors are open to the communicants and closed to those outside the faith. We are at the entrance of the Emmaus inn. Who sits at the supper? Our Lord Jesus would keep "going farther" (Luke 24:28) unless we agree to invite him in to be with us at the table. But until we are united in all ways theological and spiritual, this meal is not for us—at least not for the present, not together.

Father Rommen places the Eucharist at the end of his essay, and properly so. The question arises as to the menu and setting: Is this an agape meal? The Last Supper? Can it be a foretaste of the feast in the kingdom of heaven in anticipation? And if the question is not to be deemed offensive, what precisely is on the table? Do we all, as the Orthodox Church does, take literally the words of the Master himself—that this is indeed the body and blood of Christ? Or is this a mere metaphor? What is the effect of this sacred communion on the recipient? Indeed, we have a long and arduous road ahead of us. Only grace and goodwill can bring us together.

It is enlightening to compare the various contributors to this book. Father Rommen is wary of any relationship that transcends some doctrinal compatibility, and even that may or may not occur. He uses the subjunctive mood throughout his essay, because his outreach is tentative. Challenges and obstacles to any mutual experience abound.

More winsome is Dr. Nassif. In his yearning for Christian unity, he struggles to work through the impediments on the way, both past and present. He would, if possible, ignore the reluctant, the reticent, and the obfuscators. He allows for them all, while he cherishes the hope that somehow God's grace will prove mightier than the limits of humankind.

Dr. Hancock-Stefan would bring Dr. Nassif down to earth right quick. For him little is to be admired, much less imitated, within Orthodox Christianity. His passion is to lead their sheep away by persuasion, offering them, as he understands it, something relevant and alive.

Finally, Dr. Horton would allow for an accord between the communions—that is, if only the Orthodox Church would be more like the evangelical Christians—but he cannot fathom how this could happen. His view is sclerotic. He can only confirm those parts that meet his criteria of valid Christian theology, while he has never recognized the Orthodox Church for what it is, because his view is filtered through Roman Catholic theology, and even this is mostly that of the past. All of this he rejects out of hand.

A RESPONSE TO EDWARD ROMMEN

George Hancock-Stefan

As I was reading Father Rommen's essay, two thoughts went through my mind. One was the kindness of the local Orthodox priest during my childhood, who on a cold winter day inquired as to why I was not wearing a hat. The second was the term "irenic." The article was written with such kindness and irenic spirit, which is to be commended in all of our conversations with one another.

Being the evangelical "maybe" contributor and one who is familiar with sixteenth-century Reformation thought—which was appreciative of the tradition of the church—I can fully agree with the three factors that facilitate compatibility:

- Orthodox and evangelicals share the same biblical texts.
- Orthodox and evangelicals are equally committed to the authority of those texts.
- Orthodox and evangelicals, to the extent they allow it, are guided by the same Holy Spirit.

However, I have to disagree with the listed factors that make compatibility unlikely, especially Father Rommen's contentions that the East tends to be more interested in relationships and the West in propositions and that the East emphasizes person and the West nature (page 239). While it is true one can argue for a strong segment of strict propositional theology in evangelical churches, this is not to imply a pushing aside of the personal relationship. One of the persons most associated with propositional theology is Dr. Francis Schaeffer, who in his preaching and prayers exhibited a powerful relationship with

God. (J. I. Packer is another propositionalist, and after reading his masterpiece *Knowing God* no one can accuse him of lacking a relational theology.) The evangelicals have the pietistic-Methodist strain as one of the main ingredients in their makeup. Many of the well-known hymns and much of contemporary Christian music emphasize the presence of God, using often the second person in addressing God.

I read somewhere that novelist F. Scott Fitzgerald once said that the wise man is the person who can defend two contradictory ideas with the same passion. Personal convictions are a defining reality. Each of us has what Father Rommen calls "unassailable convictions." I tremble at the implication of Rommen's next sentence: "Once such an individual position is adopted, learning ceases and is replaced by arrogance and deliberately sustained ignorance" (page 240). Earle E. Cairns, professor emeritus at Wheaton College, used to warn us as historians that people without convictions can say anything, because to them truth and falsehood are the same. Evangelicals and Orthodox—who claim to believe the truth—should be willing to evaluate and reevaluate their positions, because truth will strengthen them and not weaken them. And thus I think that quoting Friedrich Nietzsche may give us in academia a feeling of stratospheric supremacy; however, I would rather side with Nicene Creed convictions than Nietzschean implication.

The difficulty over which the Orthodox and evangelicals struggle is illustrated in Father Rommen's quote from Saint Simeon: "We worship exactly as Christ Himself did and as did the Apostles and the Fathers of the Church" (page 242). The Reformers of the sixteenth century and the evangelicals of the twenty-first century have a high view of Scripture but never place their convictions at the same level with Christ and the apostles, nor can we say that we do things *exactly*. Scripture is infallible and inerrant, but everything else is fallible and errant, and therefore subject to revision and change.

The degree of compatibility is another area in which we have to work together. For many who are familiar with the correspondence between Patriarch Jeremiah II and the Lutheran divines, the conclusion of the dialogue came too quickly. We are also familiar with the Marburg Colloquy, a theological meeting between Luther and Zwingli held in 1529. This meeting could have accomplished so much for Reformation thought. They agreed on so much—9.5 points of agreement—yet Luther excoriated Zwingli over the half point, considered him an enemy, and rejoiced when he died on the battlefield.

The main issue between the Eastern Orthodox Church and active evangelicals in what the Orthodox consider to be the Orthodox lands is over the issue of salvation. Is our misunderstanding strictly a different arrangement of the puzzle, or an emphasis of particulars? Has the Orthodox theology of salvation as the restoration of the whole universe, with which I agree, impacted the Orthodox thinking so they have a superb concept of ecology because this is the universe in the process of salvation? Has the concept of ethnic salvation caused in the minds of the Greeks or the Russians a desire to save other nations, without subjugating them and making them Hellenists or Russophiles?—Cyril and Methodius being the exception to this! I am willing to study and learn about these two aspects, yet I would emphasize the primacy of individual salvation. Without a commitment to this, it is something like Barbra Streisand singing beautiful Christmas carols without believing in the divinity of Christ.

The Jesus people once produced a bumper sticker that read "God has spoken, I have heard it, that settles it." With this, I totally agree. Dr. Rommen adds another one: "The church has decreed, I have heard it, that settles it." This perspective offers a lot of comfort—and from my perspective some danger as well. I am willing to revisit the decrees of the church and to see the reasons behind the decrees, because there is a slight possibility that the church could have erred! I guess that's what makes me an evangelical Protestant.

CONCLUSION

Edward Rommen

I have spent a good part of my life training my mind for an analysis of and systematization of divine self-revelation. Yet, my best efforts, while yielding some understanding, have inevitably left me with inadequate answers and systems that were either incomplete or inconsistent. I suppose that this should not have surprised me, since the mind of a single finite creature, no matter how well trained, is quite simply unable to comprehend the vastness of uncreated thought—incapable of wrapping itself around even one divine truth.

The only alternative to the exasperating ineffectiveness of rational self-sufficiency is what has been called the mind of the church—the conceptual context created by cumulative insights of the Fathers. Under the guidance of the Holy Spirit, the Fathers formulated the fundamental, unchanging teachings of the church. It is within the doctrinal safety of this framework that contemporary theologians may seek to better understand, rearticulate, and apply these doctrines to the ever-changing context of human culture.

Far from being a mindless acquiescence to external authority, participation in the mind of the church is an expression of the believer's faith in the work of the Holy Spirit. It does not inhibit the mind but rather provides a context that frees the individual mind to explore without fear of abiding error or truncation and enhances the individual's ability to comprehend. This does not imply that we uncritically accept everything and anything ever written by a teacher of the church. Nor does it imply that we cannot advance our understanding, for example, by learning from recent exegetical investigations. Certainly, there is to be a development of doctrine and practice, "but it must truly be development of the Faith, not alteration of the Faith."[1]

Whatever advance is achieved is not one of dogmatic recreation but rather doctrinal maturation—in the same way that a child, possessing every organ and limb, matures to its adult form. Far from being an offensive rigorist, the modern Orthodox thinker, supported by the mind of the church, is able to dialogue with other Christian groups, making great progress toward mutual understanding, yet without compromise. Orthodox have indeed discussed the Eucharist with Lutherans and Catholics but have not abandoned the basic doctrinal framework of the church by inviting them to the chalice. While it may be true that we must do more to show what it means to participate in the mind of the church, the necessary point of departure remains faith in and submission to the work of God's Spirit in the church. This is the only way to free the individual mind from the constraints and dangers of its own empty arrogance.

In his quest for logical consistency, Michael Horton may well have overestimated mankind's rational capabilities. Surely we cannot believe that our finite minds are in a position to adequately grasp the vast expanse of divine thought. Must we not, at some point, accept our own limitations and admit that we cannot make complete logical sense out of every aspect of divine existence, practice, and revelation? Yet, it is this insistence on a careful and reasoned response that, in my opinion, opens the door to genuine dialogue, i.e., to a real opportunity for mutual instruction and learning.

What encourages me is Dr. Horton's repeated use of the phrase "it does not appear to *necessarily* follow . . ." (e.g., page 255, emphasis added). As I see it, the use of this turn of phrase attributes some degree of legitimacy to the position I articulated. For if a doctrinal position is reasonable, then its implications might also be reasonably allowed, even if our particular frame of reference does not (yet) allow for them. Obviously, every doctrine, truth, or proposition can be viewed from a number of different perspectives.

Early in my own journey to Orthodoxy I faced many teachings and practices that seemed to be utterly incompatible with

---

[1]Saint Vincent of Lerins, "The Development of Doctrine," in Father David Kidd and Mother Gabriella Ursache, eds., *Synaxarion of the Lenten Triodion and Pentecostarion* (Rives Junction, Mich.: Holy Dormition Monastery Press, 1999), 66.

my evangelical Protestant mind-set. Yet I discovered that if I would simply allow for the possibility of approaching a thing in a different way, whole worlds of new and rich spiritual possibilities were opened. Thus, while it may not necessarily follow that, because there is apostolic teaching not recorded in the New Testament, a knowledge of this teaching is necessary for the health of the church, the fact remains that it just might be very useful. Even if ninth-century Byzantine worship is not isomorphic with that of the earliest believers, the claim of historical continuity might still be legitimately allowed.[2] Even if one can (and must) argue that the icon of divinity presented in the incarnate Christ is unique, this does not necessarily preclude the use of other more limited iconographic depictions of the divine, nor does it require us to conclude that the Christology, soteriology, or ecclesiology of those who venerate such symbolic reality is underdeveloped.[3] If, according to the Westminster Larger Catechism, the elements of Holy Communion are effectual means of *salvation* (page 264), it may not be logically valid to conclude that our discussion of salvation should be reduced to one statement concerning one of its subsets, namely, justification.[4] And if the doctrines rejected by the Fathers of the Jerusalem Synod (1672) are not Calvin's,[5] then it does not necessarily follow that we are at an impasse; we may be, rather, at the juncture of opportunity.

Vladimir Berzonsky's insistence on the centrality of Christ holds the key to whatever advances we may hope for in Orthodox-evangelical dialogue. For certainly we are not interested in

---

[2]As Saint Vincent of Lerins argued, "In ancient times our ancestors sowed the good seed in the harvest field of the Church. It would be very wrong and unfitting if we, their descendants, were to reap, not the genuine wheat of truth but the intrusive growth of error. On the contrary, what is right and fitting is this: there should be no inconsistency between first and last, but we should reap true doctrine from the growth of true teaching, so that when in the course of time, those first sowings yield an increase it may flourish and be tended in our day also" (Saint Vincent of Lerins, "The Development of Doctrine," 67–68).

[3]See Alexander Schmemann, *For the Life of the World* (Crestwood, N.Y.: St. Vladimir's Seminary Press, 1973), 135–51.

[4]It is somewhat discouraging to be accused of explicitly denying the absolute necessity of divine grace and personal faith for salvation after having repeatedly affirmed the same.

[5]Of course, it won't do to claim that the doctrine of predestination was taught both in the East and the West and then list exclusively Western sources. Where are the Fathers, recognized as such by the Eastern church, whose teaching on predestination was accepted by the church?

coexistence—a simple acknowledgment of the other's existence—but rather fellowship focused on the risen Lord. It is precisely because we are all committed to Christ that we reject any form of organizational union that issues from a context of diluted or truncated Christian teaching. It is because we honestly seek to remain faithful to Christ that we so tenaciously defend what we believe to be the fundamentals of the faith. Why else should it be so difficult for evangelicals to see the validity of the Orthodox doctrine of salvation? And what other explanation can be given for the Orthodox insistence on closed communion?

No one of us would pretend that this has been or will be a light and easy journey. Still, it is Christ himself who may yet open our minds, guide our thoughts, and grant us unity. It is the example of his love that facilitates ongoing discussion without rancor or sarcasm,[6] without impatience or despair. It is the real presence of the risen Lord that energizes continued effort, no matter how challenging it might be.

Of the four responses to my essay, Dr. Hancock-Stefan's is the most puzzling. The author states that he has to "disagree with the listed factors that make compatibility unlikely" (page 271). But what does that mean? Is he suggesting that these factors *do* facilitate compatibility? Or does he believe there are other factors that are more likely to impede dialogue? Whatever his intention may have been, the way in which he uses my categories to promote his own agenda illustrates the very point I was trying to make.

He rejects the idea that the fundamental differences between the two very distinct conceptual frameworks (East and West) limit compatibility—in particular, the way in which each side weights the propositional and the relational aspects of theology—by pointing out that evangelical Protestants also emphasize a personal

---

[6]We have, of course, had our share of this kind of thing. Consider the boorish tone taken by one writer who does not understand even the most fundamental aspects of Orthodox doctrine: "Eastern Orthodoxy shows no concern for conforming any aspect of its worship to the requisites of the Lord. They rejoice in imitating the inferior worship of the Old Covenant temple and shallowly overturn the ancient prohibition on venerating images." "Since deification is grounded in the incarnation rather than the atonement, Christ's cross becomes, in principle, non-essential, a quaint sideshow in deification" (Douglas Jones, "Eastern Heterodoxy" *Credenda/Agenda* 6, no. 5 [September-October 1993]; can be viewed on the Web at www.credenda.org/old/issues/vol6/them6-5.htm.

relationship with God. No one is suggesting they do not. I am gratefully aware of the deep and personal spiritual commitment of many an evangelical friend. All I was suggesting is a difference in emphasis, not the absolute absence of one or the other. This author's unnecessary defensiveness seems to underscore the stated difference and pursuant difficulties.

Dr. Hancock-Stefan trembles at the notion that there are individuals engaged in Orthodox-evangelical dialogue who hinder the discussion, not because they have convictions, but because they view those convictions as unassailable and as a result refuse to learn from or even acknowledge truth in other positions (page 272). As an Orthodox Christian, I can only rejoice at Hancock-Stefan's willingness to commit himself to the convictions of the Nicene Creed. This, I suggest, is a great place to begin our dialogue. As for Friedrich Nietzsche, I quoted him not to achieve some academic effect but because (at least in this case) he spoke the truth.

He latches on to one word in a quote taken from Saint Simeon's *Book on the Church* and seems to reject the idea that the Orthodox worship *exactly* as did the apostles and the fathers of the church. He does this by pointing out that only the Holy Scriptures can claim infallibility (page 272). Why this? No one is claiming infallibility for the Fathers, their statements, or their form of worship. What I did suggest is that because the Orthodox are driven by a desire to faithfully preserve the teachings of Scripture and the apostolic tradition, their form of worship most closely expresses what Christ intended. In other words, the validity of worship forms is measured in terms of the degree to which they conform to the teaching of Christ and the apostles.

Finally, Dr. Hancock-Stefan seems to reject Orthodox soteriology as though it were an expression of a particular ethnic context, seeming to imply we teach that one has to become Russian or Greek in order to be saved. To his credit he does acknowledge the contextualized efforts of Saints Cyril and Methodius. But are they the only examples of this in Orthodox missions history? What of Saint Steven of Perm, Saint Innocent, Saint Herman of Alaska? What of the efforts of the North American Orthodox community today?

To take out of context, twist, and redirect the words of one's partner in dialogue is not only unfair; it is poor scholarship. Nietzsche, it would seem, was right after all.

EPILOGUE

James J. Stamoolis

Is there a final answer to the question of compatibility? You, the reader, must ultimately decide which of the arguments are convincing.

It has been demonstrated that there is substantial agreement on some essentials of creedal orthodoxy: the person of Christ, the nature of the Trinity, and the necessity of redemption. But there are still differences in theology, as well as in governance, worship, and tradition.

Obviously, much of the debate hinges on whether the oral tradition referred to in the New Testament has all been recorded in Scripture. Moreover, did the church authenticate the Bible, or is the Bible self-authenticating? Should Tradition be observed and given the same authority as Scripture? The answers to these fundamental questions determine how much authority one gives to the pronouncements of church leadership over the centuries.

This assumes, of course, that there is only one expression of the church that is allowed or sanctioned by God. We do have the prayer of our Lord Jesus in which he pleads for his followers to all be one (John 17:21). This oneness is a sign to the world, so that the world may believe that the Father has sent the Son. Does this oneness dictate organic unity? If so, most of us will not see it in our lifetime—as these essays suggest. In fact, Christian disunity over doctrinal and practical issues is greater now than it has been in recent memory. Among evangelicals the role of women in ministry is a disputed issue. While some evangelical denominations accept women as senior pastors, others would maintain that this role is reserved for men. Both sides claim support from the Scriptures.[1]

If there is to be a legitimate diversity of expression, then questions still arise as to what is essential and whether there can be spiritual unity with diversity of practice. The New Testament gives us the example of the Jewish church and the Gentile church. The leadership of the Jerusalem church told Paul, "You see, brother, how many thousands of Jews have believed, and all of them are zealous for the law" (Acts 21:20). Paul has just returned from ministering in Gentile churches, some of which were no doubt mixed congregations that had Jewish believers in Jesus among their number. Paul did not subject his converts to keeping the law; this is clear from his writings, notably his letter to the Galatians. Yet the two traditions could exist, side by side as it were, as authentic examples of believers in Jesus as the Messiah.[2] Problems arose later on, especially after the destruction of Jerusalem.[3] But the point remains: there were legitimate differing expressions of Christianity in the first century and perhaps longer.

What differences are permitted, and can new churches be recognized as true churches? Every day churches that speak the vernacular and work in the culture of their surroundings are started around the world. Whether these churches are formed among the upper classes in South America, the native groups of

---

[1]The acceptance of women's ordination by the Anglican Church is the reason Michael Harper gives for leaving and converting to Eastern Orthodoxy. See his *A Faith Fulfilled: Why Are Christians Across Great Britain Embracing Orthodoxy?* (Ben Lomond, Calif.: Conciliar Press, 1998).

[2]See Oskar Skarsaune, *In the Shadow of the Temple: Jewish Influences on Early Christianity* (Downers Grove, Ill.: InterVarsity Press, 2002) for an understanding of the Jewish influence on the early church.

[3]The Caspari Center for Biblical and Jewish Studies in Jerusalem has embarked on a multivolume history of Jewish believers in Jesus, starting from the first century. Information on the project can be found at the Caspari website: www.caspari.com. The following is taken from the web page (www.caspari.com/jbj/) describing the project: "*They just don't fit very neatly; they never did.* The Jewish scholar Burton L. Visotzky wrote this in an essay on Jewish believers in Jesus, and it is very true. The Church of Gentile believers has never been quite able to accommodate the Jewish believers in its midst. Jewish believers who formed their own communities outside the Great Church were often branded as heretics; within the Jewish community they were regarded as apostates. They still are."

Papua New Guinea, or the ethnic minorities in North America, they function as churches with basic Christian doctrine. While respecting historical precedence, does the fullness of the sense of church require adherence to the ancient traditions? Without taking a minimalist approach to Christian history or doctrine, the confession of Jesus as Savior and Lord and belief in his incarnation have been used as the foundation for interchurch cooperation. Certainly agreement on the doctrines covered in *The Fundamentals* forms a basis for mutual recognition and possible cooperation (page 16).

WHY DO PEOPLE CONVERT?

Leaving aside conversions resulting from marriage, the reasons for people converting are complex and varied. Complicating matters is that these factors can be similar but perceived differently. As an exchange I had with Father Rommen demonstrated, the same arguments can be advanced from both sides.[4] Rommen felt he needed to leave evangelicalism because of poor sermons, uninspiring worship, and the sense that the church was more of a social club than a living fellowship. In my response to him, I used the same reasons for my departure from the Orthodox Church. Now it is conceivable that both of us had an unrepresentative experience of the tradition we were leaving. Or since my conversion took place at a younger age, it may have more to do with my spiritual immaturity than with actual Orthodox practice. But I rather think that the quest for authentic spiritual nurture drove both of us.

At the risk of simplifying the reasons for conversion between Orthodoxy and evangelicalism, I would advance the following categories. These categories aren't meant to be exhaustive or even mutually exclusive. Many people list more than one reason for their conversion. The categories overlap, but in an effort to discern what is really happening, I've separated them for the sake of clarity.

---

[4]Edward Rommen, "Reflections on Becoming Orthodox" (can be viewed on the Web at www.missiology.org/EMS/bulletins/rommen.htm); James Stamoolis, "Reflections on Becoming Evangelical" (www.missiology.org/EMS/bulletins/stamoolis.htm). Both articles appeared originally in the *Occasional Bulletin of the Evangelical Missiological Society* (Spring 1999).

Seeking Truth

The first is a quest for truth.[5] In an age of uncertainty, there is a strong desire to convert to a sure system in which the issues are worked out and there are few, if any, ambiguities.[6] This quality of certainty is characteristic of the Eastern Orthodox, but it is also true of evangelical churches and organizations. Many converts to evangelicalism have done so because of the clarity of the presentation of the Christian message. Even in a relativistic age, the human heart wants to know the truth. Evangelical churches and the Eastern Orthodox Church both provide answers to theological and societal concerns. For converts the conviction that the church they have chosen has the correct interpretation of the Bible (and in the case of the Orthodox, Tradition) is a powerful draw.

Seeking the Original

The second category would be an attraction to the earliest form of Christianity. There is a human desire to return to what may be termed the primitive form of Christianity. Many Protestant denominations were founded on the conviction that their form of worship was, in fact, a return to the original, simple, unadorned pattern of worship in the early church. This quest is behind many reformist movements in the history of Christianity and is best seen in certain Baptist denominations. It was part of the motivation of churches that insisted on only singing psalms or refused to use any instruments in corporate worship. It is also a motive behind Gentiles crowding into contemporary Messianic congregations with a view to recreating the earliest church. The appeal to tradition depends on what one believes is the most ancient form.

---

[5]Frank Schaeffer converted to Eastern Orthodoxy because he was searching for truth (see Frank Schaeffer, *Dancing Alone: The Quest for Orthodox Faith in the Age of False Religion* [Boston: Holy Cross Orthodox Press, 1994]).

[6]See Colleen Carroll, *The New Faithful: Why Young Adults Are Embracing Christian Orthodoxy* (Chicago: Loyola Press, 2002). Orthodoxy here does not mean the Eastern Orthodox Church, but the traditional formulation of the Christian faith. Carroll includes in that category evangelical churches and movements, Eastern Orthodox churches, and Roman Catholic churches. She argues that the younger generation seeks a return to the values and beliefs that were rejected by their parents and professors.

The Eastern Orthodox can appeal to the concept of unchanging tradition. There is something to be said for a liturgy that goes back unchanged for thirteen hundred years. The basis of the liturgy is perhaps as early as the fifth century. Some Orthodox would maintain that it is the most primitive of all liturgies; and while no doubt the form comes from the synagogue service, the rite can be seen to have developed over the centuries.[7] Nevertheless, it remains a monument to an older form of worship and as such draws some seekers.

Seeking Meaningful Worship

A third reason is worship styles. For some there is tremendous comfort and strength in the Eastern Orthodox liturgy. For them, it models the changelessness of God. This liturgical movement is not limited to Eastern Orthodoxy. Other liturgical churches throughout Christendom have also attracted those seeking a meaningful worship experience.[8] Other Christians are drawn to the freedom of expression in some Protestant traditions and the newness and creativity of contemporary worship.

Seeking Worship That Appeals to the Senses

A fourth reason given by some converts to Orthodoxy is the aesthetic appeal of the worship services. This refers not just to the rhythm of the liturgy but to the smell of incense and the iconography that address the senses as well.[9] And yet it is also true that converts choose worship in an evangelical church because it is uncluttered by what they consider to be distractions.

---

[7]See Alexander Schmemann, *Introduction to Liturgical Theology* (London: Faith Press, 1966); Benjamin D. Williams and Harold B. Anstall, *Orthodox Worship: A Living Continuity with the Temple, the Synagogue and the Early Church* (Minneapolis: Light & Life, 1990).

[8]See Thomas Howard, *Evangelical Is Not Enough: Worship of God in Liturgy and Sacrament* (Fort Collins, Colo.: Ignatius Press, 1988). Howard was raised Plymouth Brethren, which has a very nonliturgical and simple worship style.

[9]This was true in the case of an earlier migration. See Robert E. Webber, *Evangelicals on the Canterbury Trail: Why Evangelicals Are Attracted to the Liturgical Church* (Waco, Tex.: Word, 1985).

CONCLUSION

Will the postmodern world find the Christian faith it needs in the various forms of evangelicalism, or will the Eastern Orthodox Church fill a spiritual void for postmoderns? Some observers believe that postmoderns are interested in a return to ancient tradition.[10] On the other hand, many postmoderns have found spiritual homes in charismatic churches and community-based evangelical churches.

In either case, it is hoped that the essays and responses in this volume foster a greater understanding of Eastern Orthodox and evangelicals alike. Both bear witness to the Lord Jesus Christ, who is the King of kings and Lord of lords. Both share the deep conviction that true believers will worship the triune God when the Lord Jesus Christ returns in power and glory.

---

[10]Robert E. Webber, *The Younger Evangelicals: Facing the Challenges of the New World* (Grand Rapids: Baker, 2002).

ABOUT THE CONTRIBUTORS

Bradley Nassif (Ph.D. Fordham University) is professor of biblical and theological studies at North Park University (Chicago) and lecturer in Eastern Orthodoxy theology at the Antiochian House of Studies (Balamand University, Lebanon/U.S.A.). He has been an adjunct professor of Eastern Orthodoxy at several evangelical seminaries and is the founder of the Society for the Study of Eastern Orthodoxy and Evangelicalism. He is an enthusiastic promoter of Orthodox-evangelical dialogue around the world. As a representative of the Standing Conference of Canonical Orthodox Bishops of North America, he serves on the Orthodox-Lutheran Bi-Lateral Dialogue of North America. He has been a commentator for the documentary series "Christianity: The First Thousand Years" and "The Jesus Experience: Jesus Among the Slavs." He is the general editor of *New Perspectives on Historical Theology: Essays in Memory of John Meyendorff* and the author of the forthcoming *Westminster Handbook to Eastern Orthodox Theology*. He and his wife, Barb, reside in Rancho Santa Margarita, California. They are the parents of one daughter.

Michael Horton (Ph.D., Wycliffe Hall, Oxford, and University of Coventry) is professor of theology and apologetics at Westminster Seminary California, president of the Alliance of Confessing Evangelicals, and editor-in-chief of *Modern Reformation* magazine. He is the author of numerous books, including *In the Face of God; A Better Way: Rediscovering the Drama of God-Centered Worship; Covenant and Eschatology;* and *Lord and Servant*. A minister in the United Reformed Churches in North America (URCNA), he resides with his wife, Lisa, and their four children in Escondido, California.

Vladimir Berzonsky (D.Min., Ashland Theological Seminary) is pastor of Holy Trinity Orthodox Church in Parma, Ohio, and the author of *The Gift of Love* and several other Orthodox publications. He and his wife, Margarita, reside in Seven Hills, Ohio, and are the parents of three sons.

George Hancock-Stefan (Ph.D., Trinity International University) is the pastor of Central Baptist Church, Atlantic Highlands,

New Jersey, and an adjunct professor of church history, missions, and Baptist history and polity at Eastern Baptist Theological Seminary, New Brunswick Theological Seminary, Princeton Theological Seminary, and New York Evangelical Divinity School. He and his wife, Ginny, reside in Atlantic Highlands, New Jersey, with their four daughters.

Edward Rommen (D.Theol., University of Munich; D.Miss., Trinity Evangelical Divinity School) is an Orthodox priest and pastor of Holy Transfiguration Orthodox Mission in Raleigh, North Carolina. An evangelical missionary church planter and professor in Europe for fifteen years, he taught missions and theology at Trinity Evangelical Divinity School and Columbia International University. After his conversion to Eastern Orthodoxy he became a priest and returned to pastoral ministry. He has a special interest in prayer and spirituality. He is the author (or coauthor) and editor of many books in German and in English, including *Contextualization: Meanings, Methods, and Models* and *Christianity and the Religions: A Biblical Theology of Modern Religions.* He and his wife, Ainee, live in Dunn, North Carolina. They have two daughters.

James J. Stamoolis (D.Theol., University of Stellenbosch) is a consultant to educational and missionary organizations. A convert from Greek Orthodoxy to evangelical Protestantism, he was a missionary in South Africa, a theological secretary for the International Fellowship of Evangelical Students, graduate dean of Wheaton College, and chief executive officer of a mission agency. He is adjunct faculty at Wheaton College, Northern Baptist Theological Seminary, and Columbia International University. He is the author of *Eastern Orthodox Mission Theology Today* and numerous journal and encyclopedia articles. He and his wife, Evy, reside in Wheaton, Illinois, and are the parents of three grown sons.

Stanley N. Gundry (S.T.D., Lutheran School of Theology at Chicago) is senior vice president and editor-in-chief at Zondervan. He graduated summa cum laude from both the Los Angeles Baptist College and Talbot Theological Seminary before receiving his M.S.T. degree from Union College, University of British Columbia, and his S.T.D. degree from Lutheran School of Theology at Chicago. With more than thirty-five years of teaching, pastoring, and publishing experience, he is the author of *Love Them In: The Proclamation Theology of D. L. Moody* and coauthor of *The NIV Harmony of the Gospels.*

SCRIPTURE INDEX

SUBJECT INDEX